A SELECTION FROM THE PUBLIC AND PRIVATE CORRESPONDENCE OF VICE-ADMIRAL LORD COLLINGWOOD; INTERSPERSED WITH MEMOIRS OF HIS LIFE (VOLUME 2)

Collingwood, Cuthbert Collingwood, Baron, 1748-1810 and newnham Collingwood, G. L. (George Lewes), 1783-1838

www.General-Books.net

Publication Data:

Title: A Selection From the Public and Private Correspondence of Vice-Admiral Lord Collingwood; Interspersed With Memoirs of His Life
Volume: 2
Author: Collingwood, Cuthbert Collingwood, Baron, 1748-1810 and newnham Collingwood, G. L. (George Lewes), 1783-1838
Reprinted: 2010, General Books, Memphis, Tennessee, USA
Publisher: London : J. Ridgway
Publication date: 1828
Subjects: Great Britain – History, Naval

1

A SELECTION FROM THE PUBLIC AND PRIVATE CORRESPONDENCE OF VICE-ADMIRAL...

A Selection From the Public and Private Correspondence of Vice-Admiral Lord Collingwood; 1
Interspersed With Memoirs of His Life (Volume 2). Collingwood, Cuthbert Collingwood, Baron,
1748-1810 and newnham Collingwood, G. L. (George Lewes), 1783-1838

CORRESPONDENCE AND MEMOIR
LORD COLLINGWOOU.
TO CAPTAIN CLAVELL.
Ocean, January 14, 1807.

I AM much obliged to you, my dear Clavell, for your letter of the 1st October, and give you many thanks for your good wishes. The Adriatic, I hope, will prove a good station for you, until something better can come; and whenever I have it in my power to promote your interest in any way, you may trust me that I will not forget your zeal and activity for the public service, 1 sent you where you are, because I had confidence in your diligence, and thought it probable that much would be done there by so active and intelligent a man as Captain Campbell. Cultivate his esteem: he has a great deal of enterprise, vol. II. B and can step out of the beaten path to do a good thing. You will gain experience, and that will fit you to fill the superior stations to which I hope you will speedily arrive. Cherish your men, and take care of your stores, and then your ship will be serviceable. They are articles very difficult to recruit. There never was an idea of my leaving this station for any other: there seems indeed so much to be done here, that I do not desire it; and I hope my Adriatic squadron will have a great share in it. I am your sincere friend and servant.

TO LADY COLLINGWOOD.
Ocean, off Cadiz, January 22, 1807.

I was expecting to hear of

Mr. 's death. He is happily released from a life that has been of little comfort to him for some time; nor does the prospect before us promise much for any body: but I was sorry to find that he made so unkind a return for his brother's affection. This is a queer world we live in, or rather that you live in; for I reckon that I have been out of it for some time past, except the mere ceremony of shaking off mortality, which we do with great facility here. The only thing

LOD COr. ljNCJWOOD.

we have in common witli you, are our assemblies, concerts, and plays. We have an exceedingly good company of comedians, some dancers that might exhibit at an opera, and probably have done so at Sadler's Wells, and a band consisting of twelve very fine performers. Every Thursday is a play night, and they act as well as your Newcastle company. A Moorish officer, who was sent to me by Hadgi Abdrahman Ash Ash, the Governor of the province of Tetuan, was carried to the play. The astonishment which this man expressed at the assembly of people, and their order, was itself a comedy. When the music began, he was enchanted; but during the acting, he was so transported with delight, that he could not keep his seat. His admiration of the ladies was quite ridiculous; and he is gone to his Prince fully convinced that we carry players to sea for the entertainment of the sailors: for though he could not find the ladies after the entertainment, he is not convinced that they are not put up in some snug place till the next play night. Thank God! 1 have no complaints, except sometimes a little cold in my head; for I have not seen a fire these two years.

THE RIGHT HON. THOMAS GRENVILLE.

Ocean, January 31, 1807.

Whenever the Adelphi brig arrives with the rockets, I will forward them, and the officers skilled in the management of them, to Sir Thomas Louis. As I have never seen these instruments, I can say nothing on their probable effect; but I shall recommend to Sir Thomas Louis that they may be used upon the principle you have stated, and which perfectly corresponds with my own sentiments, that the violence of war should be as little levelled at the civil inhabitants of the enemy's country as circumstances will admit. From the defenceless state in which Sir Thomas Louis represents the Turkish ships to be, I should be sanguine in the expectation, that if demanded at a proper period, and with a stern countenance in the disposition of the ships, they may be surrendered, rather than that the town should be subject to the devastation with which it would be threatened. To this the instructions particularly point.

On all occasions I have ordered that the strictest regard be paid to the flag of neutral nations, and only directed the Ragusans to be stopped when the French possessed their country, and they could not be considered as neutral. The general feeling which I have endeavoured to impress on the minds of officers has ever been, that it is better to err by lenity in such a case, than to strain a right. The flags of Etruria and of the Pope have always been respected upon the sea. It is upon the shore, at their forts, where the French colours are displayed on the same flagstaff with theirs, that English ships are fired at on their approach.

I am perfectly possessed of the great importance of seizing Alexandria, and have taken every preparatory step I could devise towards the accomplishment of that part of my orders, and have given the most minute instructions on the subject to one of the most zealous and experienced officers in the service; and I am confident Captain

Hal-lowell will spare no pains, that in this business of the transports there may be no delay.

Ocean, off Cadiz, February 3, 1807.

The poor King and Queen of Prussia in an apothecary's shop! How reduced! And unable to get their breakfast until the bed is made! What a fall for greatness! This, however, is but the humiliation of the body, subject to chances and changes, as a condition of its being; " subject to the " skiey influences that do it hourly afflict." But if his mind be still upon his throne, he may, even in an apothecary's shop, devise the means of rescuing his distressed kingdom from its present thraldom. Gustavus Vasa planned the emancipation of his country among the iron mines of Dalecarlia. Charles XII. did not feel himself less the Monarch when a stone kitchen was his palace, and cooks and grooms of his council. If the King possesses mind and talents, and by justice, and a strict regard to their happiness, has gained the affections of his people, his case is not hopeless. Wherever Buonaparte reigns, there is the domination of power, which is felt or dreaded by all. His rule is repugnant to the interests and welfare of the people; and whenever his tide of greatness be at the full, his ebb will be more rapid than his rise. I cannot help thinking that epoch is not distant. In that event, the world may hope for peace for a few years, until ease and wealth make them licentious and insolent, and then our grandchildren may begin the battle again. What I am most anxious about, is the plantation of oak in the country. We shall never cease to be a great people while we have ships, which we cannot have without timber; and that is not planted, because people are unable to play at cards next year with the produce of it. I plant an oak whenever I have a place to put it in, and have some very nice plantations coming on; and not only that, but I have a nursery in my garden, from which I give trees to any gentleman who will plant them, and instruction how to top them at a certain age, to make them spread to knee timber.

Captain Waldegrave is gone upon a little expedition, from which I do not expect his return immediately; but when he comes, 1 am confident he will have executed his commission well, and hope the route he has taken may be advantageous to him, for he deserves success. I should be sorry that he were out of the way when any thing seriousi mean any thing great were to happen here; for although I do not admire boasters, I detest a miserable croaker; and I must say, I feel myself, as Lord Castlereagh observed, " upon " a bed of roses," and able to contend with any thing that can come to me from any quarter. My ships are complete in every thing; they never go into port more than one at a time: for myself, I have not let go an anchor for fifteen months; and on the first day of the year had not a sick list in the shipnot one man. The doctors are the only people who are in danger of scurvy, if want of employment be a cause of it.

THE RIGHT HON. THOMAS GRENVILLE.

Ocean, off Cadiz, February 27, 1807.

Our affairs here are become very interesting. The French Admiral Rossily has orders to sail whenever he can, and his ships are moved down the harbour. You may depend, Sir, on my best exertions for a happy issue. In so extensive a coast, where there are so many objects of great importance to engage the enemy's attention, with the little information I am able to get here, any judgment of his intention must rest upon a very narrow basis, and much remain of doubt. My first object has been to keep my force complete to meet every exigency wherever it may arise. By Mr. Marsden's letter I am told their Lordships are very anxious that the Port of Toulon should be blockaded; and could it be done without reducing the force which is absolutely necessary in other quarters, it would be very desirable. I have hitherto considered Sicily, the Adriatic, and Egypt, to be more securely covered and protected from the Navy of the enemy, by a well-appointed squadron on the coast of Sicily, than if that squadron were off Toulon. Seldom a fortnight will pass without an opportunity offering for them to escape even the most vigilant watch, particularly in the winter. Experience has shewn that they have always done it; and, if I remember rightly the letter which Admiral Richery wrote to the Directory, he assigns, as the reason for his not having sailed, the doubt which he had of the position of the English fleet; but he adds, " they have now come " in view: I have seen from the hills the

CORRESPONDENCE AND MEMOIR OF

"direction in which they are, and will sail " to night."

I suspect that Egypt is their object; for, however the Russian and Turkish affairs may be ultimately settled, an equal argument will remain to the French for seizing on Alexandria. If the negociation terminate in peace, they will seize it in hostility to Turkey: if otherwise, they will think it necessary to garrison it, to prevent its occupation by Russia. On this subject I hope every thing very soon will be decided: but the argument I assign to the French appears to be applicable to ourselves, if the Turks could be brought to consent to it; for the French will never lose sight of possessing that country, however the difficulty they would have in preserving a communication with Europe at this time may induce them to delay the attempt.

TO CAPTAIN CLAVELL.

Ocea7i, March 23, 1807.

I had hoped that your long cruise in the Adriatic would have turned out more profitable to you than it has done; but I trust you will always look upon that as quite a secondary consideration. You have done much good in intercepting the supplies in Dahnatia, and making the people of that country feel the horrors and misery which attend upon French friendship. I hope you have had nothing to do with the Imperial or Papal vessels, except such as came clearly under His Majesty's Order in Council, being bound from one enemy's port to another. There is nothing that requires more moderation and forbearance than those changes of politics which make neutral States assume for a time the appearance of hostility towards us. They are often compelled to take such a part, however contrary it may be to their policy or wishes; and officers, whose duty it is to act under the orders of their Government, should not be too hasty in determining of themselves what the Government might think proper to do in such new and varying circumstances. We must take care that those nations whose hearts are really with us, and who on the first happy change would be openly on our side, may not, by any intemperate acts of ours, be thrown into the hands of the enemy, and led to regard us as even more violent and offensive than Buonaparte himself Great tenderness should be shewn to peaceful merchants, if they are not supplying military stores, or violating a blockade, which they know is forbidden.

TO SIR ALEXANDER BALL.

Ocean, March 23, 1S07.

In all the enemy's ports they are ready for a push out; and on the 27th ult. they sailed from Rochefort and Brest almost at the same hour; but, finding it impossible to elude the squadron oif Brest, went back again. You know their coast signals are not more than half an hour communicating from one port to another. The people at Cadiz are perfectly ready, but still have the appearance of waiting for some reinforcement. My idea of their intention is, that the northern squadrons will come here in force enough to drive us off, and being joined from Cadiz, will proceed rapidly up the Mediterranean, where they will gather as they go. In this reckoning they may be disappointed. They cannot come more than seventeen. I shall have twelve; and were double their numbers to come, I have no doubt I should stop their career until their pursuers arrive; for I reckon always upon some honest men being at their heels.

We are identifying ourselves at Constan- tinople with the Russians; an excess of friendship that I do not think they are disposed to shew to us. If they have beaten or effectually resisted the French armies, as it is said they have, Buonaparte will cajole the Emperor Alexander, and make peace with him upon any terms that relate to the Continent; for anarchy and impotence are sufficiently established there for all his purposes. They will then dispose of Turkey as they please, and the Russian squadron may find a welcome reception in Brest before the year have expired. I may be thought to hold the Russian friendship light; indeed I do not, but I believe that if Buonaparte can convince Russia that her interest goes another way than ours, her friendship will soon follow.

Thornborough is here with the poopless Royal Sovereign. What ingenious con- trivances they have in England to spoil the ships! but were those great artists to fight a ship themselves, they would be glad of a poop.

March 29, 1807.

I am almost worn to death with the fatigue of writing, but cannot let a ship go without telling you that 1 am well, and that although my head aches my heart does not, for I look forward with hope and expectation that the French will be here before long; then, my love, you may depend upon it your husband will not disgrace you.

All the Turkish business has been managed so much to my satisfaction, that I am feeling very much pleased. Duckworth passed the Dardanelles on the 19th, before the Turks could suspect that we knew what was doing. We have run even before our own Ministers, and Alexandria I expect is at this moment in our possession. I hope every thing will go on well, for there never was a business done with such rapidity. For aught I know, Constantinople may by this time be burnt, and all the sweet little Sultanas on board the English fleet for protection.

Ocean, of Cadiz, April 5, 1807. I have received Sir J. Duckworth's letter of the 15th February, informing me of the unfortunate fate of the Ajax, and most sincerely condole vith you on so great a misfortune befalling you, at a moment when our Country would have derived essential benefit from the services of that ship. This event is made more calamitous, if possible, to me by the sensations it has awakened in you at the delay in holding the court martial. 1 beg. Sir, you will believe that nothing is more repugnant to me than giving uneasiness or cause of remonstrance to any person; and I am sorry that, in your address to the Court of Inquiry, which Sir J. Duckworth ordered, you had occasion to make any complaint. I believe I ought not to have required courts martial to be held here; and that, as you have explained at large to the Board of Inquiry, in your address, the act of parliament requires that there should be as little delay as possible. It was my error, to which I was really led by a desire to establish officers and men, who had been unfortunate, in ships where there were vacancies for them. It did not occur to me at the time that it was either, contravening the law, (which I have ever revered), or likely to be attended with those disadvantages which, I am sorry to find, have given you cause of complaint. I have now sent an order to Sir J. Duckworth, or the officer who shall remain in the command of the squadron, to hold courts martial; and I hope the delay which has occurred will not be attended with any other consequence than that of keeping a mournful subject longer on your mind than I wish it to be.

THE RIGHT HON. THOMAS GRENVILLE.

., April 27, 1807.

I have transmitted to the Admiralty an extract of Sir J. Duckworth's letter, giving an account of the misfortune which befell the Ajax. This event, in all its circumstances, has given me much concern and uneasiness. The national loss of men and of the ship is calamity enough to excite extreme pain; but that an act of mine should be considered to increase the misfortune of the survivors, adds to it very much. I have explained to the Admiralty the motives which induced me to require the investigation of ships lost to be held here. I considered that it offered an accommodation to the sufferers, and enabled me to bring some sooner into service again; and those to whom I was not empowered to give employment in the squadron were still so far on their way home. I do not mean to contend that it would not have been better to have left the subject of ships lost to have taken their course with other matters of trial, but I was not aware that such restriction could be construed to be a violation of the law. I have too much reverence for the law to violate it intentionally. I have ever, to the best of my understanding, made it my guide, and the temperate administration of it my study. So far from distorting it, to aggrieve any person, I have constantly sought the means of softening its rigour, when it could be done in justice to the service; and if I have in this instance exceeded the power prescribed by it, I am anxious to establish in your mind, Sir, that my motive was rather lenient than harsh.

The two frigates and sloop of war which were taken at-Alexandria are said to be good

VOL. II. c ships. Captain Hallowell, in his letter, of which I have sent a copy to the Admiralty, states the good conduct and long service of the First Lieutenant of the Tigre, and recommends him to their Lordships for promotion. Should their Lordships direct them to be taken into the King's service, I beg, Sir, you will allow me also to recommend to you Captain Clavell of the Weazle to be appointed to one of them. He has served with me many years, and I have full experience of his ability as a good officer. He was severely wounded last year, but is now quite well; and if you are pleased to promote this gentleman, I shall esteem it a very great favour.

Lord Collingwood's desire to mitigate, as much as possible, the miseries of war, was so generally known among the Spaniards, that applications were frequently made to him for passports for the removal of sick and wounded persons from one part of Spain to

Lord Collingwood could never procure an Admiralty appointment for this officer; but he was, after some time, enabled to make him a Post Captain by a death vacancy.

another, and for various other acts of humanity and courtesy. The following letter from a Spanish lady, respecting a little boy who was on board a captured ship from South America, appears to have given Lord Collingwood considerable pleasure, as he was particularly fond of children in general, and as it brought his own family to his mind, although, indeed, they were seldom absent from his thoughts.

Madrid, March 30, 1807.

With sentiments of the warmest gratitude, I address your Lordship, to return you thanks both for your polite letter of the 7th of February, and for the release of my favourite Anselmo, who, as I am informed, has already arrived at Algeziras. The motives which I have for being attached to that boy are of a nature not to be easily forgotten. He was born of one of our slaves on the very day that I myself gave birth to my last child. On that day my husband freed Anselmo's father and mother, together with their babe. It was a day of joy celebrated by us every year, till cruel Fate snatched away my little girl, who was the being to whom I bore the greatest affection in this world, and whose loss I shall never cease to deplore. Anselmo was brought up as the plaything of my darling: she loved him excessively: and I have the weakness to see in that boy a kind of shadow of my lost angel. By this you may conceive, my Lord, the present which you have made me, and how greatly I value the humane sentiments contained in your kind letter. I shall conclude by requesting that you will remember that my husband is Lord Chief Justice of the kingdom of Guatemala, and that in him you will always find a person ready to receive and obey your Lordship's orders.

Praying God to grant you, my Lord, a long and prosperous life, I have the honour to remain.

Your Lordship's humble and most grateful servant.

The expedition to Constantinople had failed, and the English squadron had already retired from the Dardanelles, when the Russian fleet arrived at Tenedos. Sir John Duckworth, who had expected to have been assisted in his meditated attack by a Russian detachment, received several applications from Admiral Siniavin, who desired that five or six sail of English line-of-battle ships and two frigates might be placed under his command, with which he proposed to renew the attempt to burn Constantinople, and destroy the fleet. He stated his own force to consist of eight sail of the line, with 2000 soldiers on board; but Sir John Duckworth declared, that he considered it as an indispensable duty to reject a proposal which could only tend to the unavoidable sacrifice of both squadrons; and stated to Lord Collingwood that the whole object of the Russian Commander was to justify himself for desisting from an enterprise, which, as he had confessed, he knew to be impracticable, and which, as Sir J. Duckworth was well convinced, he had never designed to attempt.

TO LORD RADSTOCK.

Ocean, April 13, 1807.

I have had a great deal lately to try my patience. The misfortunes and miscarriages which we have had weigh heavily on my mind. The capture of the, with all the despatches, is one of the most foolish things that ever came within my knowledge. Her Commander, I understand, aspires to the silly character of a fire-eater, and could not believe that the gun-vessels would presume to attack him; and although he was told he could not pass the Straits without the greatest caution, and a gun-brig was sent to escort him, I have heard from Gibraltar, that he was hardly under weigh before he stood in to draw the fire of Cabreta Point. The next they saw of him was his trying to cut off a gun-boat from Tariffa. He sailed fast enough to leave his escort behind him; and on the wind coming foul, instead of returning to Gibraltar, anchored on the coast of Barbary, where he lay twenty-four hours. The gunboats came; and when he saw them, he did not get out of their way, intending, I suppose, to snap them up, and carry them in triumph to Gibraltar. They took him, and killed several of his men, in five minutes, not leaving him time to throw his despatches overboard, and they all went to Madrid. It is not the fashion for young men to be seamen now: they are more attentive to the outward furniture of the head, than to any thing within it; and they all dress a la Bonaparte, as if a great hat and tassels constituted a hero. I could laugh at their nonsense, if the public interest were not too much affected by it.

The attempt at Constantinople has not succeeded at all; and yet, as far as depended on me, we were well prepared. Sir John Duckworth, you will have heard, passed the Dardanelles, and burned the ships which lay above them. The squadron stopped at Prince's Island, the winds, the currents, and every thing being unfavourable for their getting up to the town. The ten days they were there were spent in an attempt, by negociation, to prevent the war, and detach the Turks from the French. On our part, it was faithful: on theirs, it was an expedient to gain time, until their defences were completed, and their fleet secured in the Bosphorus. When they had fully accomplished this, they dropped all further intercourse, and the squadron returned. Constantinople appears to be more difficult to attack than has generally been thought: the strong current from the Black Sea prevents access to it with a light wind; and then between it and Scutari, both sides of which are well fortified, it is like going into Portsmouth harbour. The French have established their interest completely; or rather, the Russians did that for them, by their premature attack on the Turkish territory. How they are to profit by it, I am not politician enough to discover; but we have increased the number of our enemies most unfortunately. I say so, because I believe the Turks esteem the English nation as much as they detest the Russ. I am afraid I have tired you with this long history of miseries; but I shall never lose sight of the hope some day to make you amends, by the relation of exploits more gratifying to you.

TO GENERAL SIR HEW DALRYMPLE.

Mai 23, 1807.

The Admiralty Court at Gibraltar appears to me to be very oddly constituted, and certainly wants regulation. Any body may be judge there; for legal knowledge does not seem to be a necessary quahfication. One day, a merchant is trying causes in which perhaps he himself is a party: the next day, a military officer is discussing and explaining knotty points of civil law, and deciding important questions of property, which he is not qualified to do, either by the course of his studies or the habits of his life. I suppose you have heard from General Fox that the Court of Sicily is exceedingly impatient to undertake the conquest of Naples. The General, who is wary, and looks at every circumstance with the eye of an experienced soldier, does not approve it, and will not move the troops: in consequence of which, they have made a request for

English transports to carry their Sicilian troops to the Continent, where they are to conquer Naples, and destroy the French without our help.

TO LADY COLLINGWOOD.

Ocean, May 17, 1807.

I am pretty well in health, but exceedingly out of spirits at the failure of our Turkish business. It ought to have succeeded: there was nothing in the state of the enemy to prevent it: but the day is completely gone by; for the defences which were neglected and nought, are now impregnable. I often think of getting home, if I knew but how: but the time is not far off; for although I am not sick, my body weakens; and I know enough of the structure of the human animal to understand, that when the body weakens by age, the mind also loses its activity. If nothing should happen this summer at sea to rouse me and give me spirits, I shall think seriously of my return.

Do not let our girls be made fine ladies; but give them a knowledge of the world which they have to live in, that they may take care of themselves, when you and I are in heaven. They must do every thing for themselves, and never read novels, but history, travels, essays, and Shakspeare's plays, as often as they please. What they call books for young persons, are nonsense. They should frequently read aloud, and endeavour to preserve the natural tone of voice, as if they were speaking on the subject themselves without a book. Nothing can be more absurd than altering the voice to a disagreeable and monotonous drawl, because what they say is taken from a book. The memory should be strengthened by getting by heart such speeches and noble sentiments from Skakspeare, or Roman History, as deserve to be imprinted on the mind. Give them my blessing, and charge them to be diligent.

Ocean, June 14, 1807.

It is a great satisfaction to me that my daughters will probably be educated well, and taught to depend upon themselves for their happiness in this world: for if their hearts be good, they have both of them heads wise enough to distinguish between right and wrong. While they have resolution to follow what their hearts dictate, they may be uneasy under the adventitious misfortunes which may happen to them, but never unhappy; for they will still have the consolation of a virtuous mind to resort to. I am most afraid of outward adornment being made a principal study, and the furniture within being rubbish. What they call fashionable accomplishment, is but too often teaching poor misses to look bold and forward, in spite of a natural disposition to gentleness and virtue.

Our miscarriages at Constantinople, and misfortunes at Alexandria, have worn me to a thread. I am so so in health not ill. My labour is unceasing, and my vexations many; but I cannot help them. My eyes are weak, my body swollen, and my legs shrunk to tapers; but they serve my turn, for I have not much walking. Mr. has written to me about a young gentleman who wishes to enter into the Navy; but at nineteen years of age it is far too late. I will, however, do what I can for him, if he comes; but people are mistaken if they think it is a good thing to be with me. I hardly ever see the face of an officer, except when they dine with me, and am seldom on deck above an hour in the day, when I go in the twilight to breathe the fresh air.

TO LORD RADSTOCK.

Ocean, June 23, 1807.

I have just heard from Alexandria, where they find now that they are abundantly supplied with every thing by the Arabs. What a misfortune that they should have lost so many men in an attack from which no advantage could have been derived, without making the experiment of what was to be done without it! Sir A. Paget is going to try if he can effect any thing with the Turks. If he be a very ingenious man, perhaps something may be done; but it appears to me very doubtful. I am going to do all the good I can: my days and nights are occupied in devising what is best. If I am unsuccessful, I lay my account to be censured, criticised, and sneered at; but if otherwise, and we accomplish every thing, it is only what it is very easy to talk about. How little do the people in general know of war, and of the anxious midnight hours which we experience! while they rest as happily in their nests as a full stomach will allow.

FROM THE BEY OF TUNIS.

Most honoured and most excellent Lord, It was with the greatest pleasure that I found myself favoured, a few days ago, with a gracious letter from your Excellency, written at sea; and it is also very lately that I had the satisfaction of explaining fully my pacific and friendly sentiments to the illustrious Signior Alexander Ball. As doubtless that most worthy Governor has informed your Excellency of my reply, I will confine myself here to repeating, what I have many times declared and proved to Signior Ball, and to your illustrious predecessors in the chief command of the British Navy in this sea, my

Lords Keith and Nelson, that my chief care and greatest ambition have ever been to maintain the alliance which happily subsists between me and the King your august Sovereign, of whom I am, and ever wish to be, the friend. I think it right to lay before your Excellency's knowledge and judgment the following extracts from the letters which you wrote to me, and from my answer, as they contain all the reasons which guide my conduct towards every nation which is at peace with me, and particularly towards England.

Your Excellency most wisely observed, " that there ought to exist a law in our " hearts superior to the written stipulations " of treaties, but founded on the general " maxim that acts of kindness should ever " manifest the existence of a real friend-" ship;" to which I observed, on my part, " that nothing but a reciprocal kindness and " equality of good offices can maintain " friendship between the Governors of " States."

In fact, looking to the continued proofs which I have not ceased to give to the different authorities of your Excellency's Country of my desire to assist them in all questions and matters of dispute, and looking also to the proofs which I have received in matters admitted to be contrary to twenty of our treaties, what reciprocity, what equality, have I obtained from the admitted justice of His Britannic Majesty as to the claims made to him in my name by my Embassador Mahomet Koggia, whom I isent to London in 1796, notwithstanding the promise made to him by the Ministers that justice should be done for the losses of my poor subjects? What effect have I derived from all my complaints to the Court of Vice-Admiralty at Malta, where, in truth, they have confiscated ships undoubtedly Tunisian, without the shadow of a just suspicion? Because I am particularly attached to the English nation, shall I, or shall my subjects, be exposed to loss and injury, which we have never experienced from any State, great or small, which was in friendship with the Regency of Tunis? No. I will not believe it. The justice of the King, and the valuable mediation of your Excellency, assure me of the contrary; and will soon, I hope, put an end to every thing which could render doubtful my friendship to your powerful Sovereign.

Praying from Heaven the most complete and unbounded happiness on your head, I finish by declaring myself, with high respect, most excellent Lord,

Your sincere Friend, HAMUDA PACHA, BEY OF TUNIS.

Ocean, at Sea, June 30, 1807.

To the most illustrious His Highness the Bey of Tunis, the English Admiral wishes health and peace.

I cannot but regret, most illustrious Pacha, that there should exist any cause of remonstrance from your Highness, or that any event should occur which could raise a doubt in your breast of the equitable spirit in which the rights of your subjects are maintained in our courts. It is the desire of my King that justice should be administered with the utmost purity to all people; for which purpose, he selects from the wisest and most learned of his subjects the Judges who are to administer his law.

I had not before this time any knowledge of the capture of the vessels whose cargoes your Highness states to have been the property of your subjects. Our enemies I. OKl) COLLINC; WOOD. S3 are artful, and have always been in the practice of veiling their property under the mask of a neutral country, which is in amity with us. They have two reasons for this: the hope to save their property; or, if they fail in that, to create contention between friends. It is only great experience in those subtilties that can enable the officers of justice to distinguish such false claims from those which are just and right; but when the right appears, a judge would ill conform to that spirit of justice which dwells with our King, if he withheld what was due to his friend. Without professing to know on what particular grounds those cargoes were condemned, I cannot doubt that it had been discovered that the property belonged in fact to the enemy, and that to ensure it from capture, they endeavoured to convey it to its port under the protection of a Tunisian name. When I go to Malta I will not fail to inquire into those circumstances; and, although I have no control over the courts, or the administration of the law, my best offices shall always be exercised in favour of the subjects of your Highness; and in doing them every kindness in my power, I shall only obey the will of my Sovereign.

VOL. II. D I beg to assure your Highness of my highest respect, and pray God to preserve you in health many years, that your state may be great and your people happy.

I have the honour to be, most illustrious Pacha, your most sincere friend and humble servant.

TO LORD CASTLEREAGH.

Ocean, at Sea, July 4, 1807.

I have received a letter from the Bey of Tunis, which is in reply to one I had written him on the subject of the claims made by the Consul for the restitution of vessels captured by his corsairs. I had seconded those claims generally, and not specifically for each individual vessel. My reason was, that I was at a loss for any argument on which they could be well established; and with all the consideration I can give the subject, I cannot find a better now.

Passports had been granted to vessels of countries at war with Tunis, which vessels continued to navigate under their national colours: their crews were the same, and they had their ordinary cargoes. The Tunisians take them; and when the passport is produced, they refer to the treaty which is their maritime code. They cannot understand how that instrument, which was intended to give security to British subjects and property, can extend to our allies, who are at war with them; and finding the vessels not to come within the direct stipulations of the treaty, they consider them enemies, as if such passports had never existed.

Those States of Barbary, whatever might have been their former condition as to their knowledge of treaties, or their regard for them, at present shew no deficiency in either way, and their respect for a treaty can only be maintained by a scrupulous adherence to it on our part. Until I received the Pacha of Tunis' letter, I had no knowledge of the claims which he had made, on his part, of vessels captured so long since as the year 1796, as well as during this war, which your liordship will find annexed to this letter; and they would probably have rested in his chancery if our claims had not called them forth.

Lord Collingwood received instructions from the Admiralty that his presence at the Dardanelles, to conduct the naval service in that quarter, woukl be attended with much advantage to His Majesty's service, and he was accordingly required to proceed to that part of his station, to consult with Sir Arthur Paget, and use his best endeavours for the accomplishment of the object of his mission.

LIEUT.-GENERAL SIR JOHN MOORE.

Ocean, at Malta, Juli 19, 1807.

On my arrival here I had the honour to receive your letter to me, enclosing one to General Eraser, and a copy of it for my information that orders were received from England for the evacuation of Alexandria. I have also received orders of the same purport from the Admiralty; but as it is obvious that they were given at a time when our affairs there bore a most unfavourable aspect, and the perfect and secure establishment in which the army now is could not well be expected, I have great satisfaction that General Fox and yourself have resolved to delay the execution a little. This cannot possibly be attended with any evil, while precipitancy might have the most fatal effects upon the proposed negociations of Sir Arthur Paget. Every hour since the return of the army to Alexandria their con- dition has been improving; and we are now the only respectable power in Egypt, the Pacha fearing us, the Beys courting us, and the Arabs manifesting their attachment most unequivocally. To shrink from it at this moment would be ruinous to the negociation.

TO THE MOST ILLUSTRIOUS THE CAPITAN PACHA.

Ocean, off the Dardanelles, August 15, 1807.

I cannot permit the Officer who bears the letter of His Majesty's Embassador to the Ottoman Minister to depart without offering to your Excellency an expression of my esteem; for although circumstances have arisen which at present interrupt the friendly intercourse of our nations, they have not lessened those feelings of regard which Englishmen have ever entertained towards the ancient ally of their Sovereign.

I beg your Excellency to accept the assurance of my high regard for your illustrious person, and that I am your Excellency's most humble, obedient servant.

8 COllileSroNDENCK AND MEMOIH OF

FROM THE CAPITAN PACHA.

To his Excellency the most high, honoured, and enlightened Admiral, our ancient Friend.

After offering you our compliments, and inquiring in a suitable manner about the state of your health, we now most amicably acquaint you, that we have received the letter which you sent us yesterday, and have understood its meaning. The letters which you sent for the Government were immediately forwarded by a Tartar. It is to inform you of this that we write this present letter. If it please God that you receive it, we hope and ask in the spirit of friendship that you will not forget us.

SEID ALI THE ALGERINE,

CAPTAIN OF THE SEA.

TO LORD MULGRAVE.

Ocean, off' the Dardanelles, August 19, 1807.

I have considered Sir Arthur Paget's mission to establish peace between Turkey and the allied Powers as an object of the first importance, which is indeed increased by the little prospect there is of our giving annoyance to the Turks as their enemy. It was hoped that by a rigorous blockade the capital would be reduced to such a state of want, as would urge them to a speedy treaty; but, by the best information which I can get here, the supply of Constantinople depends very little on the navigation of the Dardanelles; and, indeed, it would appear that it ought not to do so even in times of profound peace, as the strong N. E. winds which prevail during the summer months, and strong current which runs out, as effectually prevent vessels from entering as any blockade. The supplies are said to go by caravans to Galipoli, or other shipping places on the Sea of Marmora, and it is the Greek islanders who suffer most from the interruption of trade. Those islands drew most of their supplies of corn from the Continent; so that there appears little reason to expect that an insurrection in the Capital from scarcity will urge them to treat; and there is not the smallest attempt made by vessels of any kind to enter the Straits. The Turks in their correspondence with us profess a friendly disposition, and a desire to restore the peace and good understanding which have been interrupted; but 1 am told their communications with the Russian Minister are not in the same tone of conciliation, which creates a suspicion with me that, however desirous they may be to terminate their difference with us, they will never even enter on the necessary discussion of it in concert with the Russians.

The Greeks of the Islands, whose trade was for the most part foreign, carrying wax and corn to Spain and Portugal, which they received either from the Continent, or (as those of Ipsera) from the large islands of Scio and Miteline, which, from their nearness to the Continent, may be reckoned as a part of it, have laid up their ships; and none are to be seen at sea, except a few to whom the Russians have given commissions, and whose employment is to commit depredation upon all who cannot resist them.

The Turkish fleet, which on my arrival here was lying near the outer castles of the Dardanelles, where they had been since the action with the Russian squadron, have since taken every opportunity to move farther up, by warping when it was calm, and sailing when they had a favourable wind for an hour or so. They have heard at Constantinople, that it is intended that our army should abandon Egypt, and probably delay the acceptance of the Embassador's proposals until they learn from thence that the troops are gone. This information they must have received before our arrival, and before it could be known at Alexandria. The coming up of Sir John Duckworth was current at Constantinople before Sir Thomas Louis knew it; and hence your Lordship will perceive how little is to be depended on from any measure of secrecy. The French engineers arrived at Constantinople the same day that squadron did, and were probably sent to prepare for it.

The accounts I have received from Captain Hallowell state the improved condition of our affairs. He considers the security of the garrison at Alexandria as perfect, their supplies abundant, every article of provisions cheap; and notwithstanding the doubts which were entertained of the capricious friendship of the Arabs, that port is become the mart of a considerable trade. The divisions amongst the Beys, the dissatisfaction of the Albanians in the Turkish army, and the consequently diminished power of Ali Pacha, give a high importance to our forces at Alexandria. Many of the Beys have avowedly identified their cause with ours. I enclose to your Lordship the copies of three letters from them, which shew the depend-ance and expectation they have from us. Their circumstances seem to require that some security should be stipulated for them in any treaty that should be made here, because, if left to their fate, they will certainly ever after give themselves up to the direction of France. When the Turks landed at Tenedos, they put to death all the Greek inhabitants who had not embarked in the Russian fleet, or gone into the castle with the Russian garrison. When they retired from the island, the remaining Greeks quitted it, knowing what their fate would be when the Russians should abandon it. The place being thus left desolate. Admiral Siniavin ordered the fort to be blown up, the town burnt, and every thing to be destroyed. That populous and fertile island is now a waste.

I shall be glad to be able to inform your Lordship that a negociation is begun with this Court, because they appear to feel no effect of the war beyond the suspension of their commerce, which perhaps is more detrimental to us than to them.

Ocean, off the JDardanelles, August 20, 1807.

My business here is of the most important nature, and I am exerting all my powers to derive good from it. My mind is upon the full stretch; for my body, I do not know much about it, more than that it is very feeble. We precipitated ourselves into this war without due consideration. We had no quarrel with the Turks, and a temperate conduct would have carried all our points. This is now seen, when it is too late; and I am afraid the measures we are taking to restore peace are not calculated to accomplish it. The Turks are kind, and take every opportunity of expressing their respect and friendship for the English nation; but while we make common cause with the Russians, their inveterate enemies, I am afraid they will not listen either to them or us.

On the 9th I arrived at Tenedos, where I found the Russians employed in desolating the country. The island was inhabited by Greeks; and in an attempt which the Turks made to retake it from the Russians, they had put all the Greeks to death, who, de-siring to be neutral, had not gone into the castle. On the Turks being repulsed, and quitting the island, the remaining Greeks, who had been in the castle and the ships, abandoned their country, leaving their houses, their estates, vineyards laden with the fruits of their labour, and corn-fields with the abundant harvest ready for the sickle, to seek a habitation amongst strangers, as rich as they were on the day of their birth, and having nothing to take with them but their miseries. That the Turks may not at any future period profit by what they left, the Russians have burnt every thing, making a complete ruin.

Having made my arrangement with the Russian Admiral, the two squadrons sailed; but our friends were not in sight when on the 13th we stood close in with the castles of the Dardanelles. It was not possible for us to get in, though the Turks thought we meant to attempt it. When we were very near, they put out flags of truce from all quarters, and a Capagi Bashi, (a sort of Lord Chamberlain of the Seraglio), came off to me with letters to the Embassador of a pacific import; and had we only ourselves to treat for, I believe there would be few impedi- ments, but as it is, I am not sanguine. I gave him coffee, sherbet, and smoked a pipe with him. The day after, the answer was sent to them by the Dragoman. The ship that carried it anchored in the port, and the Captain was invited to dine with the Capitan Pacha, who is the Lord High Admiral. There were only five at table; the Capitan Pacha, the Pacha of the Dardanelles, my friend the Capagi Bashi, with beards down to their girdles, Captain Henry, and the Dragoman. There were neither plates nor knives and forks, but each had a tortoise-shell spoon. In the middle of the table was a rich embroidered cushion, on which was a large gold salver, and every dish, to the number of about forty, was brought in singly, and placed upon the salver, when the company helped themselves with their fingers, or if it was fricassee, with their spoon. One of the dishes was a roasted lamb, stuffed with a pudding of rice: the Capitan Pacha took it by the limbs, and tore it to pieces to help his guests; so that you see the art of carving has not arrived at any great perfection in Turkey. The coffee cups were of beautiful china, which, instead of saucers, were inserted in gold stands like egg-cups, set round with diamonds, rubies, and emeralds. They drank only water, and were waited on by the Vice and Rear Admirals, and some of the Captains of the fleet. They spoke lightly of the Russians when they mentioned them at all, and seemed to consider themselves as quite a match for them, if the English were out of the way. When our gentlemen left them, the Pacha of the Dardanelles presented them each with a shawl, which is considered as a token of friendship. I think a specimen of manners so unlike those of Europeans will amuse you. I live here poorly enough, getting nothing but bad sheep and a few chickens; but that does not offend me. I have written to Mrs., to charge her not to make our girls fine ladies, which are as troublesome animals as any in the creation, but to give them knowledge and industry, and teach them how to take care of themselves when there is none left in this world to take care of them; for I think, my dear, you and I cannot last much longer. How glad I should be, could I receive a letter from you, to hear how all my friends are! for I think the more distant they are, the more dear they become to me. We never estimate the true value of any thing until we feel the want of it, and I am sure I have had time enough to estimate the value of my friends. The more I see of the world, the less I like it. You may depend on it that old Scott is a much happier man than if he had been born a statesman, and has done more good in his day than most of them. Robes and furred gowns veil passions, vanities, and sordid interests, that Scott never knew.

I am much afraid we shall never do any good in concert with the Russians; they hate the Turks, and the Turks detest them, which neither party is at any trouble to conceal. The Turks like us, and I am afraid the Russians are a little jealous of us. Conceive, then, how difficult a part I have to act amongst them; and what mortifies me is, that I see little hope of good from all my cares. To give you an idea of the Turkish style of letters to the Russians, the Capitan Pacha begins one to the Admiral Siniavin, by telling him, "After proper inquiries for " your health, we must observe to you, in " a friendly way, what yourself must know, " that to lie is forbidden by all religions. " Your friend should not receive a false-" hood from you, nor can he be a friend

"who would offer one." In a sort of battle they have had, the Turks accused the Russians of something contrary to the received law of nations, which the Russian denied to be the case; and the Turk tells him, that his religion forbids him to lie. I am much disappointed in the appearance of these Greek islands; they are, for the most part, thinly inhabited, and but a small portion of the land is cultivated. It always blows strong, and there is sunshine in abundance. Cattle are not plentiful, but money is still more scarce; and we buy a bullock for less than SI. when they are to be got, and exchange the hide for three sheep. A sheep, when fat, weighs about 20lb. Of all climates and countries under the sun to live in comfort, there is none like England.

August 30. The Russians have made a separate peace with France, who is nego-ciating their affairs with the Porte. An armistice is proposed by them here, and they have withdrawn themselves from co-operation with us. Admiral Siniavin gave me official notice of this in a civil letter, and separated his squadron from ours. I see no prospect of peace with the Turks. We turned them over to the French, and they have skill enough to keep them. I have seen enough now to be well convinced they cannot and will not treat with us but under the direction of Buonaparte. The Embassador has been paying friendly visits to the Pachas, who were extremely civil to him, and accepted the valuable presents from him with as much cordiality as if we really were on our way to friendship; but I have not an idea of such a thing.

TO LORD MULGRAVE.

Ocean, off the Dardanelles, August 28, 1808.

I have to-day received the honour of your Lordship's letter of the 16th June, enjoining me to promote, by every possible means, the good understanding and harmony with the Russian squadron and our allies at Corfu. I assure your Lordship it has always been an object of my first consideration, and I have given the most positive orders that all our communications with them should bear the stamp of cordiality and kindness. Nothing can be more satisfactory than the friendship that has existed here, and which the Russian officers seem as desirous to cultivate as we can be. I removed, on my arrival here, all

VOL. II. E the stiffness which strangers feel in making an acquaintance, by going to Admiral Si-niavin, and entering upon the subject of our affairs with the freedom and openness with which a friend would be consulted; and I endeavoured to give to the proposals which I had to make to him the appearance of their being the result of his advice.

The squadron has remained at this anchorage for the purpose of convenience and communication with the Turkish Government, in which, I am sorry to say, I observe a tardiness in coming to any decision on the proposed negociation, which has raised in my mind a suspicion that, in what relates to it, they will be much influenced by the councils of the French. With much fair language, and professing a desire of peace, they still hold off, and do not advance to the principal point; viz. that of receiving the Embassador, and appointing a person to treat with him. Their ships continue to move farther up the Hellespont, with every opportunity when they can warp: the Capitan Pacha is now near the Dardanelles' upper castles.

In the event of not succeeding in establishing peace, I do not conceive, my Lord, that a squadron of large ships can be of the smallest utility whatever here. To keep the sea is not possible among the islands, and to find a port where they can be secure is not easy. Almost every island has a port for polaccas and small vessels, which navigate here in summer; but there are very few places where ships can be in safety in the winter. The port at Skiro is a fine inlet of the sea, but has very deep water, from thirty-five to above fifty fathom, and the ground foul and uncertain. Paros has a small and good port; but with the prevailing north wind it is impossible to get out of it. I have sent the Sea-Horse to examine other places, but have found only Paros that can give a safe anchorage. My opinion is, that when the season is so advanced as to make it improbable that their fleet will move, a cruiser being stationed between Cape Matapan and the west end of Candia, and another between Rhodes and the east end of Candia, would more effectually blockade the ports in the Archipelago than any number of ships which might be amongst the islands, where they could not keep the sea. Last winter two vessels were lost. Nautilus and Moucheron; for in thick weather it is not a sea navigable for more than the passage through it.

Those reasons I hope your Lordship will think sufficient for adopting the stations which I have proposed. Whatever produce the Turks have in the country, on either side the Dardanelles, appears to be conveyed to the capital without entering this passage by sea: whatever may come from Egypt, or the traders of foreign nations, will be more effectually stopped by those stations than by any other.

TO THE MOST ILLUSTRIOUS ALI, CAPITAN PACHA. MOST ILLUSTRIOUS PACHA, It is now near a month since I arrived in these" seas with a squadron of His Britannic Majesty's ships. Your Excellency knows that it is the duty of British fleets to present themselves to the enemies of their Country: but I had entertained the hope, that God would have inspired the Sultan of the Turks with the same holy desire, which has ever animated the breast of my King, that peace may be established among all nations; and that in the Turkish fleet I should have found not enemies, but that friendship renewed, which has most unhappily been suspended for a time by the convulsions that have shaken the Governments of Europe.

His Majesty, with this impression of friendship for the Sublime Porte, had sent his Embassador to propose a renewal of that harmony and friendly intercourse that he wished to maintain with a nation, whose interests and preservation from the intrigues of ambition have ever been a subject of his solicitude, and which a few years since called forth the exercise of his arms. The Sublime Porte, professing a desire that this friendship which we offer should be established, have not yet proceeded one step towards it; and this irresolution calls on me, most illustrious Pacha, to propose to the Sublime Porte the following questions, which, as the Turkish Ministers are already fully informed on the subject, I expect they will reply to promptly, and with that ingenuousness and truth with which they are proposed.

Will the Sublime Porte accept the friendship offered by England, with a renewal of all the relations of peace and amity, the particular terms of which may be settled by the Plenipotentiaries?

Or do they reject the proposal, and, influenced by malign councils, determine on a state of war?

If the Sublime Porte accepts the proposal to establish friendship, in what place shall His Majesty's Embassador meet the Plenipotentiary whom the Sultan may appoint to conclude the treaty which is necessary to declare the renewal of former engagements, and seal the bond of friendship between our nation?

I have said before, most illustrious Pacha, that the subject is not new to the Ministers of the Porte. They have already, doubtless, determined in their minds the conduct to be pursued; and I expect in their reply that ingenuousness and truth with which God inspires the hearts of honest men, and that they give it immediately. If, in a short period, I have not an answer, I shall conclude that they intend to take such a part, or are under such influence, as they cannot without regret reveal. I cannot omit this opportunity of assuring your Excellency of my high respect for your person, that I am, most illustrious Paclia, your most humble servant, and that I desire to be your friend.

FROM THE CAPITAN PACHA.

To our Friend, Admiral Lord Collingwood.

The friendly letter which you have done me the favour to write to me has been received, and I have perfectly understood its contents. The letters which had been previously transmitted to us were, by me in conjunction with Ismail Pacha, forwarded to our Ministers at Constantinople, accompanied by our strongest recommendations. No answer has yet been received. You are of course aware, that in business relating to Governments, eight or ten days are requisite before it can pass through the regular forms; but be assured, that the moment an answer is received, it shall be communicated to you. Be satisfied that I love only the real truth, and of this I take God to witness. You are, doubtless, anxious for an answer, and it is your duty to your Government to be so; but in this anxiety of yours Ismail Pacha shares with me. Be then thoroughly persuaded that there will be no delay on our part in the immediate communication of the expected answer. You are perfectly aware of Government formalities, and we must all conform to what is proper. I hope to God that every thing will succeed for the advantage of both nations; and in order to convince you of what I have said, this has been written.

TO J. E. BLACKETT, ESQ.

Ocean, off the Dardanelles, September 5, 1807,

Sarah ought not to wish to hear from me often, for I have nothing to recount to her but the history of my miseries. I think I never was in a situation of more anxiety, one more hopeless of any good, or more vexatious in all its circumstances. Poison is sometimes sweet, but this is poison with all its bitterness. An Embassador came here to negociate a peace, and endeavour to renew a friendship which had too hastily been given up. In all the attempts to open a negociation, they have professed a friendship for the English, but without approaching the point of negociation one jot. We appear languid about it, and without having accomplished any thing, seem to be content, and my patience is worn out with the nothingness of our progress. The fleet is wanted every where, and the ships with me are, in fact, doing-nothing. The indignity that we seem to be suffering has long been the cause of much uneasiness to me; but when I received the accounts of the new possessions which the French are to have in the Adriatic, the disposal of Sicily, and many other arrangements, all of which require the fleet, I lost all patience, and wrote a letter to the Capitan Pacha, proposing certain questions to him, which I hope will draw from the Porte a declaration of what they have resolved to do. The Embassador did not like this: I suppose he thought it was interfering with his treaty, which it was not. I know too well the absolute necessity of each branch of His Majesty's service confining itself to its own proper and peculiar province, ever to intermeddle with the duties of another; but it was an effort on my part, as the Commander here, to have him accepted as Plenipotentiary, or to make them declare that they would not receive him. I could no longer bear patiently to see the important service of our Country totally at a stand, and not attempt to set it in motion. I scarce know how this will be received in England, neither do I care. I considered it well, and shall always be satisfied with it in my own mind; and if any displeasure be expressed on the occasion, J shall desire to come home. God knows how truly I have served, how unremittingly I have studied my Country's interest, and how I have exerted myself to promote it. What judgment I have I will use, or have nothing to do with it; and whenever that day comes when I can retire from the labours of public service, it will be a happy one indeed. In bodily strength I am worn out; and whoever enters so entirely into the state of our Country as I do, and have done, cannot be much otherwise. My astonishment is to find that in England this does not seem to enter into the minds of people, or at least not to interrupt their gaieties. England, on the verge of ruin, requires the care of all; but when that all is divided and contending for power, then it is that the foundation shakes. Alas! poor England! Heaven knows but we may yet live to mourn over its grave. I pray God to bless you all. Tell Sarah that 1 hope she will have a comfortable house for me when I come home.

The farther it is from the sea shore, the less we shall be annoyed.

Alexandria, which had been captured under one administration, was immediately abandoned by that which succeeded it, although the apprehension of a scarcity of provisions, which had led to the disastrous attack on Rosette, had been dispelled. Captain Hallowell, in whom Lord Colling-wood reposed the most implicit confidence, represented in the strongest terms the despair of the inhabitants of Alexandria at the prospect of being left without defence to the fury of the Albanians, and urged the necessity of making an arrangement for retaining the town till a Turkish garrison could be sent from Constantinople. " On " this station," observes that gallant officer, in a letter which Lord Collingwood read with great satisfaction, because it was written in a spirit that corresponded with his own, " it is impossible for me to derive any " advantage, except that of serving my " Country and meeting your approbation; " but I would willingly remain here the " whole war, without any chance of dis-" tinction or emolument, rather than suffer "the English name and character to be " disgraced by deserting those poor wretches " who have thrown themselves on our pro- tection."

TO THE HON. W. W. POLE.

Ocean, off Imbro, September 5, 1807.

I have received a letter, with its enclosures, from Captain Hallowell, at Alexandria, representing the extreme distress of the inhabitants of that town, at the preparation which they had observed to be making for the departure of the British troops. They know how little mercy they have to expect from the Albanians, who are alike the dread of Turks and Egyptians, and consider the departure of the British forces as determining their fate. I forward copies of the letter and its enclosure, which will fully inform their Lordships of the unhappy state of those poor people: in addition to which, Captain Fellowes acquaints me that they were to be seen in crowds upon their knees in the streets imploring protection. Sir A. Paget has requested the Turkish Government to send an officer of rank to command in Alexandria, whose authority might check the ferocity of the Albanians; but, considering the character of that people, I doubt whether this expedient would be of much avail.

Instruction giveyi by Lord Colling wood to all the Flag Officers and Captains-Ocean, September 19, 1807. In the event of an action with the enemy, in which it shall happen that any of their ships shall be in extreme distress by taking fire or otherwise, and the brigs, tenders, or boats which are attached to their fleet, shall be employed in saving the lives of the crews of such distressed ship, they shall not be fired on, or interrupted in such duty. But as long as battle shall continue, His Majesty's ships are not to give up the pursuit of such as have not surrendered, to attend to any other occasion, except it be to give their aid to His Majesty's ships which may want it.

TO SIR ALEXANDER BALL.

Ocean, off Matapan, September 22, 1807.

Our affairs here are become, by the Russian peace, so complicated and so critical, that they require the utmost circumspection and activity. I left Tenedos the corre-spondence: and memoir of igth. Admiral Martin and the Kent stay there until the Embassador is satisfied that he can do nothing. I thought it necessary to send down a well appointed ship to aid Hallowell, who has had a most laborious time since he went there. The Turks have continued to profess for us the greatest esteem, and desire of being our friends; but at the same time, it is very obvious that they have submitted themselves entirely to the direction of the Government of France, and in all their intercourse with us have avoided any engagement to treat.

The Russians, I understand, have agreed to give their ships in the Mediterranean to France, and they will be employed immediately in the transport of troops. I hope this will not be undertaken under the Russian flag, or by the Russian people, because that would be identifying themselves with the enemy. In the uncertainty of affairs, and of what is about to be done, I think I cannot do better than to get as near the enemy as possible, and am now with four good ships making the best of my way towards Corfu, where I shall expect to meet some of our cruisers to give me information. The moment I heard the French were to have Corfu and the ships, I sent orders to Campbell to drop down the Adriatic, doing what good he could in his way, and to take a station between

Corfu and Cape St. Mary. I think I shall be able to ruin them before they reach Sicily, without bringing them to a general action.

O, my dear Ball, how this Turkish war has embarrassed all our affairs, without a possibility of its having one good consequence from the beginning! It was undertaken in defence of Russian injustice; and behold how we are rewarded for it. The blockade of the Dardanelles appears to me to have been represented to our Ministers of much more importance than it really is. Since the month of April no vessel of any kind is known to have gone into that channel, and yet there does not appear to be the least want of any kind at the capital. The constant N. E. winds during the summer months are a complete bar to regular trade.

TO LORD MULGRAVE.

Ocean, off Syracuse, October 16, 1807.

I received the honour of your Lordship's letter, informing me of the in- telligence which His Majesty's Government had received of the nature of certain stipulations in the treaty of Tilsit, which were hostile to the interest of our country, and threatening to the Ottomans.

Since the conclusion of that treaty, where so much ground was left for conjecture as to what part the Russians were to take, I have paid a strict regard to their movements, with as little appearance of attending to them as possible. The language they held in their ships was, that they were destined to the Baltic, and Admiral Siniavin, with a great part of his fleet, sailed down the Mediterranean on the 6th instant. Admiral Greig, with about eight ships, I believe, is still in the Adriatic; but of these, five or six are so bad as to be unfit to go into the ocean at this season. Should the Turkish Government accede to the proposals of the Embassador, and conclude a treaty of peace, I shall be ready to give every protection to their country that is in my power; but the Turks, I believe, feel themselves in a predicament which makes them slow to determine. Anxious for a peace with England, they still fear to avow it; because a treaty with us would bring on them the vengeance of France, arid our fleet can give them no aid against the armies of the enemy. To this consideration alone I, attribute the tardiness with which the nego-ciation with Sir Arthur Paget got forward. Our correspondence with the Russian Officers, to the last hour of their being with us, was perfectly friendly: they lamented the misfortune that had befallen their Country with an air of having nothing to conceal; and when they left us, I believe that they had no suspicion of any hostile intention of their Court towards us.

TO VICE-ADMIRAL THORNBOROUGH.

Ocean, ojf Sijracuse, October 18, 1807.

The practice of detaching boats on a distant service out of the protection of the ship, is a cruel thing to gallant young officers, who do not like to return, even when their judgment dictates to them that they ought. They are enterprises highly injurious to the public service, because they disable the ship from performing her real duty; and they are discouraging to the men, because they shew, even to those of the least observation, that they are schemes not directed by judgment. The Hydra performed lately

VOL. II. F

CORRESPONDENCE AND MEMOIR OF a very gallant thing against a great force. Three privateers, well armed, and a battery of four 24-pounders, were taken with the loss of one man; but the ship and boats acted in concert, and in every part the skill and conduct of Captain Mundy was as conspicuous as the gallantry of his officers and men.

In the returns of the, I observe a supernumerary received from an American frigate. I hope he was given up in an amicable way, because the present situation of our affairs demands that we should not enter into discussions with any neutral Power, which, without being of great importance in themselves, would be likely to create animosities. The affair in America I consider as exceedingly improvident and unfortunate, as in the issue it may involve us in a contest which it would be wisdom to avoid. When English seamen can be recovered in a quiet way, it is well; but when demanded as a national right, which must be enforced, we should be prepared to do reciprocal justice. In the return I have from only a part of the ships, there are 217 Americans. Would it be judicious to expose ourselves to a call for them? I see, in the journal of the, that when cruising they spoke an American

LORD Ct)IXINGWOOD. ()?

from Leghorn, bound to Salem, and tlie only remark about her is, that they pressed a man out of her. What should we say if the Russians were to man themselves out of Englisli ships?

FROM THE QUEEN OF NAPLES.

Le 23 Octobre, 1807.

La confiance que j'ai dans votre digne personne me fait vous envoyer copie exacte de deux relations re9ues ce matin, desquelles probablement vous serez deja in-forme. Selon les demarches de I'escadre Russe, il paroit qu'elle a voulu s'assurer si Siracuse Auguste etoit accessible, et I'ayant vu defendue, elle a passe Messine pour aller a sa destination, que ne peut que nous etre tres suspecte, apres la paix, ou, a I'article 14, la Russie reconnoit Joseph comme Roi de Naples, et par la lettre de Joseph, qui est dans nos mains, ou il parle a Napoleon des troupes Francoises, qu'a la paix il croit neces-saire pour garder la Sicile. Preuve pleine que meme cet asile on a accorde a Joseph, encore avant de I'avoir conquis. Voila done I'escadre Russe, naviguant a pleines voiles, soit pour Naples, ou pour s'unir aux 12,000 hommes, unis aux 16,000 autres, dont les premiers sent prets a Genes et les autres a Toulon, pour fondre probablement sur nous. Tout cela, avec le depart dans ce moment des troupes Angloises, est bien triste; mais je fie en Dieu, protecteur du juste. Au moins, si nous serons entierement perdus, le serons nous avec honneur, sans la moindre lachete ni foiblesse; et cela nous fera souffrir nos malheurs et ceux de notre famille. Je compte toujours sur votre grande genereuse nation; et croyez moi, pour la vie, avec la plus sincere estime,

Votre bien affectionnee,

CHARLOTTE.

TO J. E. BLACKETT, ESQ.

Ocean, off the Coast of Sicily, October 24, 1807.

The tour which you made on your return must have been very pleasing, and would have done me infinite good, could I have been of the party. I am sure that I want something like amusement to relax my mind, which is like a bow for ever bent. I fear the tone of some of my letters may have made you think that it is bent somewhat awry. I cannot help it. My natural temper is anxious, and the critical affairs I have on hand wear me; nor am I less IOlid COr. l. ING'WOOD. GO

Anxious for tliose whom I have left at home.

I was ordered to proceed from Cadiz to the Dardanelles, where the Russian fleet was, not so much to carry on an active war against the Turks, as to conciliate them, and give the Embassadors of Russia and England an opportunity of making a peace which ought never to have been broken. I found they had made no progress, but soon managed to introduce a friendly correspondence on our part. To the Russians they would have little to say, as they always bear them a most inveterate hatred. To us it was the very reverse: all their correspondence bore the marks of kindness; but we had unadvisedly thrown them into the hands of France, and it was not possible to extricate them. They do not hesitate to say now, that the fear of France alone prevents their making peace with us; and when or how that fear is to cease, I do not know. I have no doubt on my mind, that at this moment the line of division is drawn through Turkey, to mark what is to be in future French, and what Russian. By the good management of our officers in Egypt, the peace of that country was pretty well restored before we left it, the prisoners all released, and terms made for the inhabitants who remained. The Pacha made presents to the officers; but those intended for my friend Captain Hallowell were refused, because he felt the impropriety of receiving any token of friendship from an enemy, against whom he would act an hour after the truce was withdrawn. 1 followed the Russians down; and being doubtful of the part they were to take, thought it necessary to keep near them: however, they have all sailed, and they said were destined for the Baltic. Admiral Siniavin and I were great friends: he seemed to like me, and I had a kind of regard for him, because he professed to hate the French. All the Turks liked me because I talked to them as if we were old friends, and smoked with them. Nothing but the fear of the French could have prevented our peace with them. I have got my friend, Sir Alexander Ball, who is Governor of Malta, to hoist his flag there, and conduct the business of the port: at sea, I shall do as well as I can. This island of Sicily is in a deplorable state of government. I am afraid its inhabitants will do little towards its preservation: they are poor, oppressed, and wretched, and cannot be worse off. They once hoped that the English would rescue them from their miseries; but now look on us as the supporters of their Governors, and we are become obnoxious to them.

I hope Sarah is settled comfortably at Chirton, and that her house is warm. I shall be happy when I am there, and never before; for this life, though it is a necessary one, is totally devoid of comfort. It is the ladder, the precarious and unsteady ladder, by which I have mounted to rank and fortune, but happiness lies quite another way.

I am going now in search of the French. If I have the good fortune to find them, and Heaven blesses my endeavours, I shall immediately after desire to go to England, and in my family's affection receive the reward I wish for.

TO VISCOUNT CASTLEREAGH.

Ocean, at Syracuse, December 9, 1807.

I have the honour to enclose to your Lordship a despatch from the Reis Effendi, addressed to Sir Arthur Paget. He sent it to the Vizier Ali Pacha of Joannina to be forwarded, who found means to put it on board one of His Majesty's ships cruising on the coast of Albania; and as the letter 72 correspondp: nce and memoih of of the Pacha which accompanied it was iii the language of conciliation and friendship, I conclude the Reis Effendi's letter may be a proposal for the renewal of peace with the Porte, and lose no time in forwarding it to your Lordship. As a considerable time must now elapse before His Majesty's Ministers can reply to this subject, I shall inform the Vizier of that circumstance, and endeavour as much as I can to confirm that disposition which seems to be indicated in his letter. In the conference which Captain Leake had with the Pacha, he did not conceal his apprehensions at the French being put in possession of the Ionian Islands, and his desire to have St. Maura reduced for him; but in the present state of the land forces here any enterprise which would take them from the defence of Sicily seems to be out of question. A few days since I returned from a short cruise off Toulon, where the French squadron of five ships of the line made the usual appearance of being perfectly ready for sea. In all the ports, both French and Spanish, they constantly make this shew; but as for two years past they have' not moved to any great distance, it is not from this appearance that their intention can be discovered. I consider it as rather practised to keep us constantly at sea, wearing out our ships, while every exertion is made to increase the number of theirs.

Your Lordship will observe, that notwithstanding the most friendly footing on which the Consul is with the Government of Tripoli, while the Pacha is complying with all his requests, he still is desirous that a line-of-battle ship should appear there. It is too frequently the case, that instead of maintaining the esteem of those people by an equitable and temperate conduct towards them, the idea of coercion, and of acting upon them by fear, is so predominant, that it pre sents itself when there is really no occasion which calls for it.

TO ALT PACHA OF JOANNINA.

H. B. M. S. Ocean, at Sicilij, Dec. 9, 1807-MOST ILLUSTRIOUS PACHA, I have received the two letters brought by your messenger, but as it is now more than two months since the Embassador who had made proposals to the Porte returned to England, I shall take the earliest opportunity of transmitting those letters to the British Ministers in England, and I shall lose no time in forwarding any communication which your Highness may have to make, either on the part of the Sublime Porte or yourself.

I am glad of this opportunity of stating to your Highness the great satisfaction I have had in the friendly attachment to our Sovereign and the British nation, which is expressed in your letter; and although the arts and intrigues of our enemy, whose unbounded ambition has made him the enemy of all mankind, have interrupted that amicable intercourse which England ever wished to maintain with her ancient ally, the Porte and her dependencies, I hope the time is not distant when all the relations of friendship will be restored. To a prince of your penetration and knowledge of the political intrigues by which France has ever sought to aggrandize herself, I need not point out the dangers which threaten the Ottoman empire by the late treaty concluded between France and Russia, and how imperiously all the energies of your Government are required to repel, on every occasion, so dangerous a foe, and to resist, in every step of its operation, a plan which has the total overthrow of Turkey and its dependencies for its object.

Albania, where your Highness governs, is a powerful country; your people, loyal and warlike, and under the direction of a prince skilful and valorous, would, perhaps, be amongst the last assailed; but you will doubtless look forward to your condition when you may be surrounded by a not less powerful people, who, practising upon the minds of men, more by their arts than by their arms, have subdued so many nations. I have given strict injunctions to the officers who are blockading Corfu and the Islands, to prevent as much as possible all intercourse by the French with that island; and while it is so blockaded, I think your Albanians would possess themselves of it in a few days. The British army is at present so engaged, that troops cannot be sent; but if your Highness expects success, you must find pretexts for stopping the supply of provisions from your country, and for sending off those Frenchmen who surround and watch your motions. At present, while the British squadron is cutting them off from all supplies by the way of Italy, your Country, which is much more interested in their extirpation from Corfu, is affording them tlieir only means of subsistence. I take this oppor- tunity of expressing to your Highness my high respect for your illustrious person, and my desire that happier times will soon allow me to style myself your Highness's friend.

TO THE EARL OF MULGRAVE.

Ocean, Sracuse, December 11, 1807.

When I was on my way to the station off Toulon, I received intelligence that the Russian squadron under Admirals Siniavin and Greig had passed the Straits of Gibraltar, and finding the French vessels lying in the same state in which they have long been, I returned to this port to refit and caulk the ships, which have been much strained by the hard gales.

Off Toulon I found that two frigates and a corvette had escaped, and their route was not known until I came here, and found they were at Corfu. There was no want of vigilance in the vessel which was watching the port. It is what may frequently happen at Toulon. As the direction in which the blockading ships are can be seen from the hills, they can always be avoided.

With respect to this island I have nothing to communicate to your Lordship. I 'have already mentioned my opinion, that whenever it is assailed, its defence will en' tirely depend on the British forces. In a country which might he abundant, nothing can exceed the misery and poverty of its populace. The body of the people have nothing to defend, and little assistance in repelling an enemy can be expected from them. I now send the Tigre to England, in obedience to their Lordships' orders, and shall miss Captain Hallowell very much, for he is one of the most zealous and skilful officers in His Majesty's service. Of the frigates I wrote to you before; in addition to those I then mentioned, the Endymion is complaining very much, owing to her enormous masts, which are more than can be secured. On this subject I must observe to your liordship, that the wall-sided ships, and those heavy masted, are a continual burden upon the docks and arsenals; while the ships of the old establishment, as the Terrible, Saturn, Zealous, Queen, and such whose sides fall in, are most to be depended on in winter for service.

I have lately been informed, that a practice prevails amongst the prize agents at Malta of compounding with the claimants of detained neutral vessels, by which they agree to drop the suit against them in the Admiralty Court, in consideration of a sum of money. This practice I apprehend to be totally unauthorized, in its consequences attended with many evils, and probably the origin of those complaints which have been made by foreign courts. The property must either be enemy's or not. In the one case they compound with the enemy; in the other a neutral is laid under contribution. The merchant would, perhaps, rather pay a certain sum than risk the expenses and loss of a long and tedious suit; but when he goes home, he states to his court that he has been seized by a British ship, and laid under contribution at Malta.

With the total want of intelligence, your Lordship will know how difficult it is to form a conjecture of what the enemy is likely to undertake, whether against this island, the Morea, or Egypt. I shall keep the best watch I can upon them all, and whenever they make a movement be ready to oppose them.

FROM THE MARQUESS DI CIRCELLO,
MINISTER OF STATE TO THE KING OF NAPLES.
Palermo, December 22, 1807.

I have the honour to introduce to your Excellency the bearer of this letter, the Chevalier Micheroux, a Colonel and Capitaine de Vaisseau in His Majesty's navy. The particular object of his mission is to welcome your Excellency, on the part of the King, my master, on your arrival at Syracuse. His Majesty, at the same time, has charged me to convey to your Excellency the sincere satisfaction which he has felt on receiving the intelligence of your appearing before one of his ports, and to add, that His Majesty has been always most desirous to be personally acquainted with your Excellency, and that on this occasion His Majesty has a pleasing prospect of seeing this wish realized.

I feel very happy in communicating to your Excellency these sentiments from my royal master, and I indulge a sanguine hope that, together with the honour of making your acquaintance, I shall have the advantage of expressing my admiration and the homage of my highest consideration.

TO HIS CHILDREN.
Ocean, on the Sea, December 26, 1807. MY DEAREST CHILDREN,

A few days ago I received your joint letter, and it gave me much pleasure to hear that you were well, and I hope improving in your education. It is exactly at your age that much pains should be taken; for whatever knowledge you acquire now will last you all your lives. The impression which is made on young minds is so strong that it never wears out; whereas, every body knows how difficult it is to make an old snuff-taking lady comprehend any thing beyond Pam or Spadille. Such persons hang very heavy on society; but you, my darlings, I hope will qualify yourselves to adorn it, to be respected for your good sense, and admired for your gentle manners. Remember that gentle manners are the first grace which a lady can possess. Whether she differ in her opinion from others, or be of the same sentiment, her expressions should be equally mild. A positive contradiction is vulgar and ill-bred; but I shall never suspect you of being uncivil to any person. I received

Mrs. 's letter, and am much obliged to her for it. She takes a lively interest that you should be wise and good. Do not let her be disappointed. For me, my girls, my happiness depends upon it; for should I return to England, and find you less amiable than my mind pictures you, or than I have reason to expect, my heart would sink with sorrow. Your application must be to useful knowledge. Sarah, I hope, applies to geometry, and Mary makes good progress in arithmetic. Independently of their use in every situation in life, they are sciences so curious in their nature, and so many things that cannot be comprehended without them are made easy, that were it only to gratify a curiosity which all women have, and to be let into secrets that cannot be learned without that knowledge, it would be a sufficient inducement to acquire them. Then do, my sweet girls, study to be wise.

I am now at sea, looking for some Frenchmen whom I have heard of; but I was lately at Syracuse, in Sicily. It was once a place of great note, where all the magnificence and arts known in the world flourished: but it was governed by tyrants, and a city which was twenty-two miles in circumference is now inconsiderable. Its inhabitants have great natural civility; I never was treated with so much in my life. The Nobility, who live far from the Court, are not contaminated by its vices: they are more truly polite, with less ostentation and show. On my arrival there, the Nobility and Senate waited

VOL. IL G on me in my ship. Another day came all the military: the next, the Vicar-General, for the Bishop was absent, and all the clergy. I had a levee of thirty priestsall fat, portly-looking gentlemen. In short, nothing was wanting to shew their great respect and regard for the English. The nobles gave me and the officers of the fleet a ball and supper, the most elegant thing I ever saw, and the best conducted. The ladies were as attentive to us as their lords, and there were two or three little Marquisinas who were most delightful creatures. I have heard men talk of the (lienor de la danse, but no goddesses ever moved with the grace that distinguished the sisters of the Baron Bono. God bless you! my dear girls.

TO VISCOUNT CASTLEREAGH.

Ocean, at Sea, December 27, 1807.

I transmit to your Lordship a packet of papers, which, having been thrown overboard from a Russian light transport, when she was spoken with by a ship of our squadron, on her passage from Ancona to Corfu, was taken out of the sea by Captain Lord Cochrane. Some of those papers appear to me of considerable importance. They shew the Value which the French attach to Corfu, and their impatience to provision it. In this they have hitherto met with great disappointments, as above 500 of the troops, and most of the provisions going over to them, have been captured, and the vessels sunk. The correspondence of the Consul Bessiere with Ali Pacha contains the arguments used to attach that Pacha to the French, and to reconcile him to the French General Berthier, who had held a menacing language towards him. It does not appear in any of them what was the proposal of Ali Pacha to the French Government, as the condition of his alliance; but it is probable that the Pacha's farther discovery of their hostile plans has caused him to relinquish his views in such connexion.

In the letter of M. Bessiere to Ali, your Lordship will find, that the letter which the Pacha had ordered to be written to General Villette, at Malta, was obtained by a French agent there, from the person in whose hands it was when General Villette had left the island, and was sent to the French Consul, by way of Leghorn. I have written to Sir Alexander Ball, to endeavour to discover who is the agent employed by the French at Malta, for the purpose of communicating intelligence; and have only to observe to your Lordship, that ve contend on very unequal terms, vshen the most important secrets of our Government, and those who would be our allies, are thus to be obtained by the enemy; while, on the part of the French, the most trifling operation of intrigue or war is kept profoundly secret, until it is unfolded in the cxecution.

Our frigates, cruising before Corfu and in the Adriatic, have been such an impediment to their establishing themselves in Corfu, that I apprehend they have found it necessary, for that purpose, to send from Toulon the squadron which was discovered at Tunis on the 17th. Admiral Thorn borough, vsith six sail, left Palermo on the 19th. On the 22d, a fleet wsls seen from Malta, which was doubtless the French. On the S3d, I sailed from Syracuse, to proceed towards Corfu; and at this time have every reason to believe that the enemy's fleet are somewhere between this squadron and Vice-Admiral Thornborough's. I hope for every good.

Ocean, off Cephalonia, January 1, 1808.

I beg to offer you my congratulations on this your birth-day, that you may see many returns of it in uninterrupted health and tranquillity; then may long life be borne patiently. All it can give of happiness I wish you, and that my dear Sarah may be a comfort to you through many succeeding years. My children have written me many letters, and it is very delightful to me that they appear to be happy and contented where they are. I hope they will acquire a knowledge of such things as will enable them to go through the world creditably. Poor things, they have a long time to live, and a thorny path to make their way through: I hope they will be as little torn as possible by the rude briars that may stretch across their way, and have spirits firm enough not to mind a little scratch. I had delightful letters from them lately, in which they tell me that they are labouring to gain wisdom.

In October and November I was off Toulon, where my ships suffered much from the severity of the weather. On the 6th of December I came to Syracuse to refit them: it is a good port, and all the people there were particularly kind and polite in their attentions to us. The Sicilian Nobility of that district gave us a ball and supper, which was one of the most magnificent things ever seen. Notwithstanding all this, there are reflections which press upon the mind irresistibly in viewing the ruins and tracing the extent of this once famous city, which was twenty-two miles in circumference, and is scarcely half a mile long. Where the palace of Dionysius was, there are now a little mill and a pig-sty. The foundations remain of the amphitheatre, where formerly 100,000 people assembled to view the public spectacles. The cavern called Dionysius's ear is perfect and curious. Sound is so reverberated and increased from its sides, that the least whisper is made as loud as a trumpet; and a little pistol with a thimbleful of gunpowder roars like thunder. In this cavern Dionysius is said to have kept his state prisoners, and by means of a hole in the side and near the top to have discovered all their secrets and plans. Within the ancient wall there are farms, and vineyards, and pastures, as, in the course of time, there may be corn-fields and hop-grounds in St. James's Street or the Royal Exchange.

I was too busy to see much of it, for it is long since I had any leisure. An express from the Sicilian Minister, to inform me that the French were at sea, caused me to sail very suddenly; and as, from the route in which they were discovered, and the great preparations making in the Adriatic, (to direct which Buonaparte is at Venice,) I had every reason to believe they were coming to this point, I have endeavoured to intercept them in their way, and to sustain the squadron of frigates which I have off Corfu. Hitherto I have been disappointed. I am, however, not yet without hope: but should they escape me, it will grieve me to the very heart. I have left nothing undone to defeat their purpose: if they succeed, I shall be very unfortunate. God help me!

TO THE RIGHT HON. W. DRUMMOND.

Ocean, Syracuse, January 9, 1808.

I arrived here yesterday with the squadron from off Cephalonia, and have received the honour of your Excellency's letter. Our situation with the Russians and Austrians (for except that Austria is not a maritime power, our political relation is much the same) is at this period very critical. I have no doubt that both have entered fully into the measures of France; and the Russian, in the novelty of his situation, would recommend himself to his new ally by a violent and presumptuous demeanour to his former friend; but such intemperance should not sway us from a conduct which is due to our Country's honour and its interest.

The information from Mr. Adair, that Lord Granville Leveson Gower had been ordered to quit Petersburgh, made measures of precaution necessary, that we should be prepared to repel any hostility; but it is for His Majesty alone to determine when war shall be commenced.

The Russian ship at Palermo is under peculiar circumstances: if Admiral Thornborough stop her in port, it is an interference with the civil government of Sicily; if, after her departure, he detain her at sea, it is an absolute commencement of war. This is the highest prerogative of the crown, which no officer can invade under any circumstances; still less can he presume to decide, with the present scanty information, as to what are to be the future relations between the two kingdoms. I should therefore recommend that an application be made to the Sicilian Court for an embargo to be laid on all Russian ships in the ports of Sicily, which, as her defensive ally, we may justly enforce with our power. We shall thus shew respect to Sicily, by not infringing her rights, and in the meanwhile prevent one who may soon become our acknowledged enemy from doing harm.

TO THE EARL OF MULGRAVE.

Oceai, at Syracuse, January 11, 1808.

On a report of the French squadron having put to sea, I sailed from hence with a view to intercept them in their way to the Adriatic, whither I had no doubt they were going. The information was founded in a mistake; and on my return I was relieved from much anxiety by the receipt of their Lordships' order to act against the Russians. Mr. Adair, at Vienna, had prepared me for such an event; but a subject of such importance required that the necessity of acting hostilely should be most clearly ascertained. The Russian ships sailed from Corfu on the 26th last, when they were probably informed of the war: yet they passed our squadron without shewing the least disposition to annoy them, though there was only the Standard with two frigates. I now propose to proceed into the Adriatic; and if I find them in any situation where they may be assailed, I shall be glad of it. Your Lordship may trust I will spare no pains to get to them.

The state of Sicily is becoming exceedingly critical. The French are marching a large body of forces into the south of Calabria, which have already approached so near to Scylla as to skirmish with the Massi, quartered near it. I think it probable that a great effort will be made against this island, when I believe the principal, perhaps the only resistance, will be by the British forces. The want of frigates on the coast, to bring and convey intelligence to all quarters, is very great; and I entreat your Lordship to reinforce me with ships of that class. I should be glad that Captain Hoste, of the Amphion, should come, for he is active, vigilant, and knows the coast; and more depends upon the man than the ship. In general, the ships are overmasted for the constant sea service which they have. For a summer's passage they might do very well, but some ships here are from port sixteen or twenty months; and those with preposterous masts, as the Endymion, Canopus, and some others, are soon to pieces by the weight of them, while ships masted as the Ocean is do not suffer. It is past doubt that the light-masted sail best.

The Turks have sent a letter, which I forwarded to Lord Castlereagh by the Tigre, which I believe to contain some proposal for an accommodation with us; and I have directed Captain Stewart, who is an intelligent officer, stationed off the Dardanelles, to endeavour to open a correspondence with the Capitan Pacha, for the ostensible purpose of recovering some Englishmen who have been wrecked in a prize on the island of Cyprus, but really to give that Government an opportunity of sending any proposal which they have to make to His Majesty's Ministers.

TO THE SENATE OF SYRACUSE.

Ocean, at Siracuse, January 13, 1808.

I have received the honour of your letter, in which, adverting to the proposed dismemberment and division of the bishoprick of Syracuse, and representing the former happy state of the diocese through many ages, its declension, from events over which the inhabitants had no control, and your apprehensions of the consequences of the proposed measure, you request my intercession with His Majesty the King of the Two Sicilies, that he will be graciously pleased to continue the present establishment of the Cathedral, the dismemberment of which you conceive would be injurious to the interests of religion, to the cultivation of learning and science in the seminaries, and to the general happiness of the people.

I am a stranger. Gentlemen, who in the service of my King am come to your coasts to aid in the defence of the states of his friend and ally: I have found at Syracuse a people generous, hospitable, and warm with attachment to their Sovereign, and am already inspired with a sincere interest in whatever relates to them, and nothing shall be wanting in which I can contribute to their happiness. I am a stranger also to your Sovereign, for I have not yet had an opportunity of shewing my true devotion to the honour of his crown and the welfare of his people. You will feel with me all the weighty motives which must restrain me from any interposition which may be deemed improper and unauthorized; but from my strong impression of the justice and wise policy of abstaining from all doubtful innovations, as well as from the respect and esteem which I bear to you, I will presume to approach His Majesty with my humble request that he will be graciously pleased to give a favourable ear to the petition of his loyal Syracusans, and defer the intended division of the diocese until the Clergy and Senate shall have submitted to him a representation of the probable consequences of that measure.

THE RIGHT HON. WM. DRUMMOND.

Ocean, at Sijracuse, Ja)iuari 13, 1808.

Syracuse is so particularly situated, and so much may depend on the exertion of its people, that I should conceive that a policy the reverse of diminishing its power, a policy to aggrandize it, to increase its population, and to attach them strongly, and by every means, to the true interests of their Country, would, in the course of events, be found highly beneficial. They have an admirable port, but no trade; a beautiful country, but the badness of the roads makes it a desert.

As the port is at this time a station of great importance to the safety of the state, it is a misfortune that any innovation should be made, which may lessen the ability of its inhabitants to render good service to their Country, or diminish tiieir number. I have written to the Marquess di Circello on this subject, and I entreat your Excellency's good offices to prevent a measure which will be so injurious to Syracuse.

TO THE MARQUESS DI CIRCELLO.

Ocean, off Calabria, January 15, 1808.

I have not until this day received the honour of your Lordship's letter, which was brought to Syracuse by the Chevalier Micheraux; for having proceeded to sea before the arrival of that officer, the letter was sent after me. I am exceedingly flattered by the honourable attention which His Majesty has been graciously pleased to shew me in his desire that I should be presented to him at Palermo. No circumstance would be more gratifying to me than to be enabled to pay my personal respects to His

Majesty and the Queen. I hope their Majesties already know me to be zealously employed in their service; and whenever the urgency of it will permit me to repair to their court, I will not fail personally to assure them of my anxious desire to render to their states every benefit which is in my power. To do it most effectually is to seek the enemy before he approaches them, which is the reason that I am so little in the ports of Sicily, or in any port.

TO VISCOUNT CASTLEREAGH.

Ocean, at Sea, January 26, 1808.

I do not know that your Lordship has given the Consul at Tripoli instructions as to exciting the Pacha to hostility against the French. I should rather think not; because a state so insignificant in its marine could give little aid to our operations here, and their neutrality secures to them a communication with Malta, more free than it would be in a state of war, which is of the first importance to us. All their losses would be considered as the consequence of their attachment to us; and there would be continual demands for indemnification for them. This would probably give rise to discussions unfavourable to the harmony which we would preserve with them; and considering how versatile and capricious a people they are, whenever the French bid higher for their friendship, they would be sure to have it.

TO SIR ALEXANDER BALL.

Ocean, off Syracuse, January 27, 1808.

When I arrived at Corfu, finding the Russians were gone quite up the Adriatic, by all accounts in no condition for any service, but sent from Corfu because the means of subsisting them was difficult, I did not see the necessity of my going up with the large ships; I therefore victualled the Standard, and am returned to know here what the French are doing in Calabria. The Emperor Alexander has acted unwisely; without gaining a friend in the world, he has drawn on himself the contempt, and perhaps the hatred of his subjects. He should have known that Buonaparte has no passion but ambition, no friend but such as can be made subservient to his aggrandizement. Having gained his object, he no longer cares for him, and is by this time ready to go to war with him upon the smallest difference.

The plea of the Russian Bishops for not renouncing the anathema against Buonaparte, speaks their disgust at his conduct, and at the servile debasement of their Prince. Infallibility I have understood is not a tenet of the Greek Church, and was one of those on which they differed with the Church of Rome when they separated: but the wisdom of their argument is not weakened by that. You read the letter from the Consul at Tripoli, and would observe that he also is panting for a political intrigue, a little snug war of his own making. It is very extraordinary that Consuls, peaceful ministers, sent abroad to promote friendship and maintain harmony amongst nations, never think that they have done half their business until they can stir up a little mischief.

TO THE RIGHT HON. W. DRUMMOND.

Ocean, at Syracuse, February 6, 1808.

As the French are making approaches to this Island, having taken Reg-gio, and, with the heavy cannon obtained from the captured Sicilian gun-boat, being prepared for the attack of Scylla, I could not but with surprise and concern observe the perfect indifference among the Sicilians

VOL. 11. II at those events. I wrote a letter to the Governor of this place to inform him of what had happened, and to inquire of him what Sicilian force he had under his orders, and within the limits of his government, to oppose an enemy which might appear. His reply must be painful to every one who takes an interest in the defence of Sicily, and would preserve its Monarch from the humiliation which must be the consequence of its conquest. He states, that of all sorts of men on the military roll there are above TOO, including artillery, invalids, and militia; but that they are merely upon the roll, for they are unarmed, undisciplined, and without any kind of pay. In answer to my request to know what the establishment of Officers was, by whom those men were to be directed in battle, he tells me that the only officers are two Ensigns, without experience in military affairs, and who, I suppose, know as little of their corps as the men do of them. This I understand to be the general state of places on the coast, and that no where is the population of the country organized, or prepared to take that part in its defence which may be expected from a loyal people. To repair those defects, I would propose a mode to be immediately adopted, which will prepare the minds of the people for the part they are to take, give them enough of military knowledge for them to act with effect, be attended with little expense, and, above all, inspire the nobility and people of Sicily with that pride which men feel when they possess the confidence of their Prince.

The language of the Court to the people should be this: " Our friends the English " will assist us; but it is from Sicilians, from the energies of a brave and loyal people, in " the defence of their Country, that we look " for the preservation of our honour, and for " deliverance from our enemies." I would propose that four Sicilian officers of experience should be appointed to this district, not nominal, but effective men, who could drill, exercise, and instruct the people in the use of arms. To them should be added such young men of the noble and most attached families as can be assembled, the more of them the better, who, by some little attention of the Court, might be made to receive their appointments as a high honour, and serve without pay. A large quantity of arms came to Sicily from England; and every day one-third of his militia, artillery, c. should march off from the Governor's house and exercise. An emulation would thus be created among the three divisions for superiority and skill; and the people in general, nobility and peasantry, would begin to think- their individual well-being connected with the defence of their Country.

TO THE EARL OF MULGRAVE.

Ocean, Sicily, February 10, 1808. ' I have received a letter from the sister of Mr. William Chalmers, who was Master of the Royal Sovereign, and slain in the battle with the combined fleet off Cape Trafalgar. His death reduced to great distress a family, whose dependance for comfort, and almost support, appears to have been on the aid which he gave to an aged, infirm, and kind parent. He was himself a man of most respectable character, and a faithful servant of his Country. His family has received the allowance that Government has appointed for them in such cases, and are yet in distress. What can I do for them but submit their misfortunes to the humane consideration of your Lordship? and express my belief, that if any little pension could be given to this now unprotected family, it would be most worthily bestowed.

The fickle policy of the Sicilian Court had now veered round to the Russians, whose invasion they had so lately dreaded; and this change was attributed by Lord Couingwood to a not unreasonable apprehension on the part of the Queen, that the few English troops in that island, though they might draw down upon it the vengeance of Napoleon, were insufficient for its defence. After the declaration of war by Russia, the most marked attention was paid to the Minister of that Country at Palermo, and all the remonstrances which were made against the continuance of the Russian frigate in the port were unavailing. In the meantime, the French were occupying Calabria; and the heavy artillery of which they were in want for the siege of Scylla, was supplied by the surrender, without resistance, of some Sicilian gun-boats.

Ocean, Syracuse, February 14, 1808.

Ever since the reduction of the English forces in this island, the Queen has been most active in bringing forward her plans; and her party, which is composed of numerous French, with M. St. Clair at their head, are now very powerful. Their views and intentions open, without reserve, as the French army advanced, which is in complete possession of every place on the Continent, except Scylla, and that, it is supposed, cannot long be maintained, I do not know whether troops are coming from England to reinforce the army here; but unless they arrive soon, I think they will be too late: for they will not only have to repulse the French, but to maintain that consideration and influence in the Country which every day is growing less. I have ordered the communication between Sicily and Calabria to be stopped, and all boats passing without passports from the commanding officers to be seized as conspirators against the Government of Sicily, and carrying on correspondence with the enemy.

Ocean, at Sicili, Februan 20, 1808. MOST EXCELLENT PACHA,

Although I fully expected that the engagement which your Excellency made to the British officers, when they left Egypt, for restoring the prisoners then in the country, would have been religiously complied with, I am willing to believe that no want of good faith on your part is the cause of their detention, but that the persons whom your Excellency employed in recovering them have been less diligent than they ought to have been in the execution of your commands. I trust that no time will be lost in performing what you solemnly engaged to do. Ten men only were returned, and I have now sent a ship to receive the others. I am glad to hear that the differences and discontents which existed among the Beys are all composed, and that Egypt, which has the happiness of being under your protection and government, is enjoying those blessings which must ever be the effect of a temperate and wise dispensation of the laws. Although we are unhappily, through the intrigues of France, in a state of war with the Sublime Porte, yet

Englishmen never lose that regard which they naturally feel for an ancient friend; and I look forward to the day, when God will open the eyes of the Sultan to his true interests, and put him on his guard against the arts of those who, feigning friendship, have only the subversion of the Ottoman Empire in their view. It behoves you, at this time, to be much upon your guard, and to put Alexandria in the best state of defence you can, to repel any enemy that may come there. I would recommend you to close your harbour, so that large ships may not enter it. Alexandria is a city well situated for a great commerce. Ports to hold your merchant vessels are all that are necessary to you; for larger ships only endanger your peace. That the French, who, as your Excellency well knows, are the enemies of all Governments, have the design of establishing themselves in your Country, can be little doubted; and they are at this time busied in preparing the minds of the people to receive them favourably. A small French vessel was lately taken by one of my cruisers from Marseilles, bound to Candia, Cyprus, and the coast of Syria. She was full of books, printed in the Turkish language, which were to have been distributed amongst the subjects of the Porte, for the purpose of persuading them that resistance to the French was folly, and that it was their interest to betray their Country, and attach themselves to France. This single circumstance, when your Excellency considers that they have subdued nations more by the practice of their insidious arts than by their arms, should put you on your guard against their emissaries who may come to Cairo or Alexandria. I wish your Excellency much happiness, and that God may please to give us peace, that I may indeed be your friend.

TO VISCOUNT CASTLEREAGH.

Ocean, off Maritimo, March 2, 1808.

The Pacha of Albania having requested that a vessel which he had at Constantinople, on his own personal service, might be allowed to return to him at Prevesa, I considered that advantages may arise from keeping those States in a friendly temper, and in the hope that he may be induced thereby to interest himself for the liberation of some seamen who have unhappily fallen into the power of the Turks, I have granted him this indulgence, of which I trust your Lordship will not disapprove.

The Minister of His Sardinian Majesty has repeated his request that more naval force may be sent to the coasts of that island. There are at present a frigate and a sloop; and I would comply with his wish, if there were ships which could be disengaged from other services which appear to be more urgent; but no immediate danger to that island is stated to be impending, nor more troops in Corsica than are usually kept there. It therefore appears to me, that the observance of an honest and impartial neutrality by that kingdom, would more effectually preserve it from insult from France, than the protection which many more ships of war could give them, although they would tend to excite against them the animosity of the French.

FROM THE MARQUESS DI CIRCELLO.

Palermo, March 9, 1808.

I feel extremely gratified in fulfilling the duty imposed upon me by my Royal Master, of conveying to your Excellency the sentiments which His Majesty has expressed on receiving the assurances which you have been pleased to give, of your determination to defend this island against any attempt of our common foe. His Majesty, impressed with a due sense of gratitude, desires your Excellency to receive his sincere acknowledgments, and the assurance of his unbounded reliance on the zeal of an officer so justly reckoned among the first supporters of the Empire of his august Ally. The King has heard with much pleasure that the British squadrons have safely joined under your Excellency's command, and anticipates, as we all do, the happiest results, if so brave a Commander should succeed in drawing the enemy out of their holds.

I cannot close this letter without mentioning again His Majesty's earnest hope, that your Excellency will some day or other appear before his Capital, whenever your zeal for the service will allow you to give way to a little repose; and in stating thus much, in the King's name, I anticipate the gratification of my own particular wish, to become personally acquainted with your Excellency, and convince you of the high esteem, respect, and admiration with which your conduct has impressed me.

l. OS CORRESPONDENCE AND MEMOIR OF

TO LADY COLLINGWOOD.

Ocean, March 9, 808.

I am just now cruising with mjr fleet off Maritimo, and intend continuing here until I get information to lead me to the French, which I expect very soon, and then hope that God will bless me. Our Country requires that great exertions should be made to maintain its independence and its glory. You know, when I am earnest on any subject, how truly I devote myself to it; and the first object of my life, and what my heart is most bent on, (I hope you will excuse me,) is the glory of my Country. To stand a barrier between the ambition of France and the independence of England, is the first wish of my life; and in my death, I would rather that my body, if it were possible should be added to the rampart, than trailed in useless pomp through an idle throng.

I suppose at Newcastle every thing is in its usual style of mirth and festivity; so that you would know nothing of the war, were it not for a newspaper. I seldom read newspapers, having quite enough of war without them. I have now as large a fleet as was ever employed from England, consisting of thirty sail of the line, and eighty ships of war of different sorts. You may easily conceive, that in the common occurrences of such a fleet, I have not much time to amuse myself. I have been rather unfortunate lately in not catching a small squadron of the enemy; but it was chance. I went to Corfu in January: the hard gales disabled my ships, and I found that, by continuing there, I should have no fleet when better weather came. A month after I left them, the enemy appeared there. Where they came from, is not well ascertained; but I hope, before it is long, we shall know a great deal more about them. I have had many misfortunes lately in my fleet, and dread more: they have made me sad. I believe I told you Clavell was a Post-Captain, at which I rejoice; and yet it is a great drawback on our gratification at the success of friends, that it has its origin in the misfortunes of others. God bless you, and make you completely happy!

TO VISCOUNT CASTLEREAGH.

. Ocean, of Naples, March 13, 1808.

When the Saracen went to cruise off" the coast of Egypt, I directed the

Commander to take an opportunity of communicating with Alexandria, and endeavour, through the means of Mr. Petrucci, the Swedish Consul, to obtain the liberation of the soldiers who were taken at Rosetta, and are still prisoners. They are become the property of individuals; and the Pacha pleads in excuse for not performing his engagement, that he is unable to raise the money for their purchase, which is 200 dollars each.

The intelligence which has been received from Smyrna, that the Turks have engaged to join their squadron to that of France and Russia, is of high importance; and the only thing that makes me doubt it is, that the most perfect secrecy is observed by the French of their real intentions, while it is a common practice to circulate rumours of measures which either are not meant to be undertaken, or are very remote. Sicily is the point to which their force seems now to be directed, and every report which might remove my force to a distance from it is likely to be circulated. I am endeavouring now to get intelligence where the Toulon ships are, and whether they have been joined by those from Rochefort, or any others: but as there is no communication with the Continent (the embargo having completely closed the little there was), nor a ship of any nation to be met with on the sea, your Lordship will conceive how difficult it is to obtain any information. I am come here for the purpose, and afraid at the same time of being too distant from Sicily. It is exceedingly distressing to be so entirely without any knowledge of them, either where they are or what their force is.

TO LORD RADSTOCK.

Oceauj off Sicily, April 4, 1808.

I am much obliged by your Lordship's kind letter of the 7th December, which I received when I was last in port, and have since been so completely occupied, and my mind so entirely engaged with those Frenchmen, that I have really thought of nothing else. I have great satisfaction in telling you that I think I have a fair prospect of having a battle with them soon. The Rochefort squadron came into the Mediterranean on the night of the 26th January. I never heard of them until the 22d of February, nor had any certain account where they were till yesterday. They joined, it seems, the Toulon ships, and with them sailed to Corfu. I do not understand this movement to have had any object but that of drawing our fleet up thither. I had sought them at Naples, and sent frigates every where to discover them; but no intelligence is now to be depended on except that which is obtained by our own ships meeting them. I expected to have found them at Tarentum, with an armament to proceed against Sicily; but when I went thither, not a ship was there. After refitting at Corfu, before I was certain they were there, they sailed, and three days since were seen going down the Mediterranean; I apprehend to Minorca, to join the Spaniards. From all quarters I hear that their object is the reduction of this island, and have, therefore, little doubt that I shall before long find them, and find them confident of their own strength, and therefore in no haste to go off. Sir Richard Strachan, having pursued them to this station, makes the fleet strong enough for any thing, but Sicily itself is as weak as can be. It is a kingdom which has nothing in it which constitutes the strength of a country, but divided councils, a King who ought to rule, and a Queen who will, no army for its defence, its military works ruinous, without revenue, except just enough to support their gaieties, a nobility without attachment to a Court where foreigners find a preference, and a people who, having nothing beyond their daily earnings, are indifferent as to who rules them, and look to a change for an amelioration of their condition. Every cause of weakness in a country is to be found here; factions alone are abundant. Our army is increasing on the east side, and will do all that such an army is capable of; yet I think that beating their fleet alone will save it. You will suppose that this is a very anxious time for me, but I study day and night what is best to be done, and I trust in God that the event will be happy for our Country. From Turkey I hear they are making preparations of defence every where, doubtless against the French. They have strengthened the passage of the Dardanelles very much, and have a boom across it, which is ingenious, and perhaps the only kind of boom that could be used in so wide a passage. Several rafts of old masts and large timber, chained together, are moored across the strait, at the distance of a hundred yards, so that a passage

VOL. II.

for vessels is left between them. Those rafts, on any alarm, are connected by a chain from one to the other, quite across, and the whole is flanked by three hundred guns.

My health is pretty good, as well as I ought to expect, considering the cares upon my mind; but they have worn me very very much. I hope Captain Waldegrave is well, and has got such a ship as he likes: he knows how much I esteem him. He is an officer who will do justice to his Country whenever he is employed.

TO THE EARL OF MULGRAVE.

Ocean, at Sea, April 2, 1808.

It is certain your Lordship cannot know many of those gentlemen who are recommended by their friends: one of them is turned off the quarter-deck for some un-officer-like behaviour. I think your Lordship will approve of his reforming before he is promoted.

I some time since recommended, that as ships came out, they should bring 80 or 100 boys of fourteen or sixteen years of age. Such boys soon become good seamen: landsmen very rarely do, for they are confirmed in other habits. One hundred Irish boys came out two years since, and are now the topmen in the fleet. I am very much distressed that no intelligence can be obtained of the enemy: finding they had not joined the Spaniards, I suspected they might have come round the islands to Sicily. Nothing can be more distressing than our present situation. The Amphion is gone to Toulon, and to search the ports of Italy.

TO THE REIS EFFENDI.

Ocean, at Sea, April 24, 1808.

Captain Stewart, the Commander of His Majesty's ship the Seahorse, has communicated to me a letter which he had received from your Excellency; which letter afforded me much satisfaction, as it contained expressions of regard towards my Sovereign and the British nation, and of the desire of the Sublime Porte that peace should be restored between two nations, whose esteem and amicable relations to each other had been strengthened by a friendly intercourse through a long series of years, but have been suspended by circumstances resulting from that political convulsion which has shaken so many States in Europe, and continues to threaten more.

I am sorry that while the Sublime Porte entertains sentiments which promise benefits of such importance to both our States, there is not any person in the Mediterranean authorized by the King to confer with the Turkish Plenipotentiary on the terms on which hostilities may cease, and friendship be renewed. As I understood from His Highness the Pacha of Joannina that the letter of your Excellency which he forwarded to me in December contained a desire that peace should be restored, I lost no time in forwarding it to His Majesty's Ministers in London, and doubt not that a reply is now on the way hither, and probably a Minister, for the purpose of negociating. Until such powers shall arrive, there is no person authorized to suspend hostilities; but it is my sincere hope that this delay may not be of long continuance.

TO LADY COLLINGWOOD.

Ocean, of Toulon, May 15, 1808.

I hope you are very well, and more at your ease than I am, for I have had labour and anxiety enough to wear any creature to a thread. Since the 23d of February, when I first heard of the French coming into the Mediterranean, I have been in constant pursuit of them, with little intelligence, and what came to me was often very contradictory, sometimes, I believe, fabricated for the purpose of deception, so that in all my pursuits I have arrived at places only to learn that they were gone from thence. The only satisfaction that I have is, that they have done nothing; for when they found that there was a probability of being overtaken, they quitted the place immediately. At sea there is no getting intelligence, as there used to be on former occasions, for now there is not a trading ship upon the seas nothing but ourselves. It is lamentable to see what a desert the waters are become. It has made me almost crazy; and if I had not a very good constitution, would have worn me quite out, for I know tliat in England success is the only criterion by which people judge, and to want that is always reckoned a great crime. But I have felt the service in my heart, and have left nothing undone that my anxious mind suggested. I never despair of meeting them, and making a happy day for old England.

Young has returned to me, but I have little hope of his being a sailor. He does not take notice of any thing, nor any active part in his business; and yet I suppose when he has dawdled in a ship six years he will think himself very ill used if he be not made a Lieutenant. Offices in the Navy are now made the provision for all sorts of idle people.

I was sorry to hear any shyness should exist between; but politics and parties are great drawbacks on friendship. I shall always be of old England's party, and of that alone.

The Turks are now holding out both their hands for peace. I have managed to keep up a sort of correspondence with the Porte, and the Pachas of Albania and Egypt, in order to have an opening for any proposal which they might choose to make; and I lately had a letter from the Reis Effendi, which expressed, in the strongest terms, their desire of peace. I have transmitted it to the Ministers, and hope they will send somebody to treat with them. It would relieve a part of our force, and open an advantageous trade, which we seem now to want.

I have been long at sea, have little to eat, and scarcely a clean shirt; and often do I say, Happy lowly clown. Yet, with all this sea work, never getting fresh beef nor a vegetable, I have not one sick man in my ship. Tell that to Doctor.

The attention which Lord Collingwood paid to the health of his men has been already mentioned; but it may be added here, that in the latter years of his life he had carried his system of arrangement and care to such a degree of perfection, that perhaps no society in the world, of equal extent, was so healthy as the crew of his flag-ship. She had usually 800 men; was, on one occasion, more than one year and a half without going into port, and during the whole of that time never had more than six, and generally only four on her sick list. This result was occasioned by his attention to dryness, (for he rarely permitted washing between decks,) to the frequent ventilation of the hammocks and clothes on the booms, to the creating as much circulation of air below as possible, to the diet and amusement of the men, but, above all, by the contented spirits of the sailors, who loved their commander as their protector and friend, well assured that at his hands they would ever receive justice and

kindness, and that of their comforts he was more jealous than of his own.

FROM

H. R. H. THE DUKE OF CLARENCE.

Bushy House, May 21, 1808. MY DEAR LORD,

A few days ago I received your Lordship's letter of the 30th March, which has given me great satisfaction. I am most warmly interested in all your operations, and must be allowed to be a sincere friend and wellwisher to the Navy; for though I have lost one son on board the Blenheim, I have just started another with my old friend and shipmate Keats, and I have another breeding up for the quarter-deck. From the secrecy of those Frenchmen, and their power on the Continent, which are equally known to your Lordship and myself, the affairs of war are more intricate than ever; but in your Lordship's hands the interests of our Country are safe. The great object of the enemy must be Sicily, for your Lordship observes with as much truth as wisdom, that we cannot maintain ourselves in the Mediterranean without that island. I sincerely trust that the next time the French venture out, your

Lordship will fall in with them. The event will speak for itselfanother Trafalgar. All I ask is, that the life of the gallant Admiral may be spared to his grateful Country.

Your Lordship mentions my approbation and friendship. Had not circumstances, which it is unnecessary to dwell upon, prevented my following our profession, I should have been proud to have seen the word approbation in your Lordship's letter; but situated as I am, I must to your Lordship confess that I merit not that epithet: but every individual that does his duty well is sure of my friendship. I need not say more to Lord Collingwood, the bosom friend of my ever to be lamented Nelson.

I took my second son to Deal, which gave me an opportunity of visiting the different ships there. I was very much pleased with what I saw, and found the Navy infinitely improved. This Country cannot pay too much attention to her naval concerns. We are the only barrier to the omnipotence of France; and it is to our Navy alone that we owe this superiority.

Though I have not yet the advantage of being personally known to your Lordship, I trust I may be occasionally permitted to take up my pen, and that as events may arise your Lordship will favour me with a few lines. I know your time is valuable. For the present, adieu. Believe me most sincerely interested in your Lordship's welfare, and in the success of those valuable officers and men under your Lordship's command.

I remain ever, my dear Lord,

Yours unalterably,

WILLIAM.

GENERAL ORDER.

March 23, 1808.

From every account received of the enemy, it is expected they may very soon be met

This General Order should, according to its date, have been printed somewhat earlier. In the battle of Trafalgar Lord Collingwood's ship broke the enemy's line, without having sustained much damage during her approach; but Lord Nelson's ship, and many others in both squadrons, while running down, were greatly injured by the raking fire of the combined fleet. The Order is inserted here, to shew how Lord Collingwood proposed to guard against this, by making his ships, as they should draw near the enemy, keep a line as nearly parallel to the hostile fleet as they could, and by preserving, at the same time, that celerity of attack which the order of sailing in two columns presents.

with, in their way from Corfu and Tarentum, and success depends on a prompt and immediate attack on them. In order to which it will be necessary, that the greatest care be taken to keep the closest order in the respective columns during the night, which the state of the weather will allow, and that the columns be kept at such a sufficient distance apart, as will leave room for tacking or other movements; so that, in the event of calm or shift of wind, no embarrassment may be caused.

Should the enemy be found formed in order of battle with his whole force, I shall, notwithstanding, probably not make the signal to form the line of battle; but, keeping the closest order, with the van squadron attack the van of the enemy, while the Commander of the lee division takes the proper measures, and makes to the ships of his division the necessary signals for commencing the action with the enemy's rear, as nearly as possible at the same time that the van begins: of his signals, therefore, the Captains of that division will be particularly watchful.

If the squadron has to run to leeward to close with the enemy, the signal will be made to alter the course together; the van division keeping a point or two more away than the lee, the latter carrying less sail; and when the fleet draws near the enemy, both columns are to preserve a line as nearly parallel to the hostile fleet as they can.

In standing up to the enemy from the leeward upon a contrary tack, the lee line is to press sail, so that the leading ship of that line may be two or three points before the beam of the leading ship of the weather line, which will bring them to action nearly at the same period.

The leading ship of the weather column will endeavour to pass through the enemy's line, should the weather be such as to make that practicable, at one-fourth from the van, whatever number of ships their line may be composed of The lee division will pass through at a ship or two astern of their centre; and whenever a ship has weathered the enemy, it will be found necessary to shorten sail as much as possible, for her second astern to close with her, and to keep away, steering in a line parallel to the enemy's, and engaging them on their weather side.

A movement of this kind may be necessary; but, considering the difficulty of altering the position of the fleet during the time of combat, every endeavour will be made to commence battle with the enemy on the same tack they are; and I have only to recommend and direct, that they be fought with at the nearest distance possible, in which getting on board of them may be avoided, which is always disadvantageous to us, except when they are flying.

The enemy will probably have a convoy of ships carrying troops, which must be disabled by the frigates, or whatever ships are not engaged, or whose signals may be made to attack the convoy, by cutting their masts away, and rendering them incapable of escaping during the contest with their fleet.

In fine weather the watch are to bring their hammocks on deck with them in the night, which are to be stowed in the nettings; so that on any sudden discovery of the enemy, they will have only to attend to the duty on deck, while the watch below clear the ship for action.

If any ship be observed by her second ahead to drop astern during the night to a greater distance than her station is, she is to notify it to her by shewing two lights, one over the other, lowered down the stern, so that it may not be seen by ships ahead; and should a ship not be able to keep her station, those astern of her are to pass her and occupy the place she should have been in.

FROM

MAHOMED ALI, PACHA OF EGYPT.

Cairo, May 24, 1808.

To the Excellent among the Chiefs of the Christian Powers, the Moderator of the Princes of the Religion of Jesus, the Possessor of sage counsel and luminous and abundant talent, the Expounder of the truth, the Model of courtesy and politeness, our true and real Friend, ColLinGwood, Admiral of the English Fleet. May his end be happy, and his course marked with brilliant and great events!

After many compliments to your Excellency, we inform you, most illustrious friend, that we have received your kind letters translated into Arabic, and have read them, and understood your advice (as beautifully expressed as it is wise), respecting the management and defence of our ports. Your assurances that you preserve a regard for an old and sincere friend, and your sage counsels, have given us infinite content and joy. For what concerns your soldiers who remained in Egypt, you observe that, according to our treaty, all ought to be restored but those who have embraced the Mahometan religion, but that only ten had reached you: and you express your opinion, that this has arisen from the fault of those whom we had charged to collect them. We have not neglected these stipulations, but have ordered the soldiers to be collected; and all that have been found (except those who had become Turks) have been sent away by Mr. Petrucci, and their number is specified in letters addressed to your Excellency, beyond the ten of whom you speak. We desire and long for the strengthening of our friendship, by the making of peace and the renewal of our amicable intercourse; and we will employ all our efforts to deliver all the soldiers who remain. You express also your hope that God would grant us peace, that you might in truth be our friend: that is what we ardently desire and pray for. You shall ever have proofs of our abundant friendship and of our respectful affection; and we implore God to give effect tliereto, and to preserve you ever in respect and esteem.

MOHAMMED ALI PACHA.

The French fleet, under Admiral Gan-teaume, unfortunately escaped into Toulon about the middle of April, returning along the coast of Africa, while Lord Collingwood continued to watch the island of Sicily, which he ever believed to have been the real object of the expedition, and for the safety of which, as will have been seen in the preceding letters, he had such reasonable causes of apprehension. The disappointment of his hopes preyed upon his health, and greatly contributed, with the toil to which he continued to be exposed, to shorten his days.

In the meanwhile. His Sicilian Majesty's brother. King Charles the Fourth of Spain, had reduced his dominions to the brink of ruin. From the year 1806, Ferdinand, then Prince of the Asturias, had engaged in secret plots against his father and his favourite, Godoy; and, to procure the concurrence of Napoleon, had solicited, in October 1807, that a lady of the Buonaparte family might be granted to him in marriage; but in October he was arrested, and charged by the King, in a proclamation, with having attempted parricide. On the 18th March a tumult broke out at Aranjuez: on the 19th, Charles the Fourth abdicated his throne in favour of his son, Ferdinand the Seventh; and on the 21st delivered to Murat a protestation, in which he declared that his abdication had been extorted by force, and reclaimed his rights. In April, the royal competitors proceeded to Bayonne, to plead their respective causes before Napoleon. On the 5th May, Napoleon and Charles, animated, as they declared, " by an equal desire to put an " end to the anarchy to which Spain was a " prey, and to place her in the single position " in which she could maintain her integrity," concluded a treaty, by which Charles ceded Spain and the Indies, an empire within whose limits, as it was said, the sun never sets, in return for the chateau of Cham-bord, with the parks and farms which belonged to it. Ferdinand, on the 10th of the same month, acknowledged his father's renunciation, and ceded all his own rights

VOL. II. K for an annual salary and the palace and parks of Navarre. They were both, in the result, deprived by Napoleon of the indemnity for which they had stipulated, the father being sent first to Compiegne, and afterwards to Marseilles; and the son being detained in the custody of Prince Talleyrand, at his chateau of Valen9ay. The Spanish people, however, resolved to maintain by arms the independence of their country; and communications were made by Castanos and the other generals to the English authorities at Gibraltar, in which they declared their determination, in case Napoleon should seize the persons of the remaining members of the Royal Family, to solicit the aid of the Archduke Charles of Austria, and to bestow upon him the provisional, or, if it should be ultimately needful, the permanent power.

When this intelligence was communicated to Lord Collingwood, he foresaw the difficulty which would occur in establishing any general government in the divided state of Spain; and being convinced that great advantage would be derived in the approaching contest from the direction of the power of that country being confided to a person of such authority and military talent as the Archduke Charles, he lost no time in despatching a letter to that Prince.

ARCHDUKE CHARLES OF AUSTRIA.

Ocean, May 29, 1808.

By a letter which I have received from the Governor of Gibraltar, and which encloses certain communications made to him from Spain, I am informed that, in consequence of the recent unhappy events that have happened to that kingdom and its Monarch, it is probable that the time may soon arrive when it will be desirable that your Imperial Highness should have the means of a speedy and safe conveyance to that country. As I do not doubt that, in providing your Imperial Highness with a proper ship for that purpose, my conduct will be approved of by His Majesty, I have sent one of the best appointed frigates to Trieste, to wait your Imperial Highness's commands; and should your Imperial Highness embark in her, her Captain is ordered to proceed to whatever port in Spain you shall please to direct.

I have the honour to be, with the most profound respect, c.

HON. WILLIAM WELLESLEY POLE.

Ocean, of Toulon, May 29, 1808.

Having learned the intention of the Spanish Government, in the event of their Princes all falling into the hands of the enemy, and considering the great distance which the Archduke Charles of Austria is from them, I have sent the Amphion to Trieste, with a letter addressed to that Prince, of vhich I enclose you a copy. If the Archduke should in this crisis be called to Spain, His Majesty's ship is ready to receive his Highness; should it be otherwise, Captain Hoste will be employed in the public service, where the enemy is very numerous. I hope their Lordships will approve of this step, which I have been induced to take immediately, lest, from the length of voyages at this season, the moment when that Prince could serve the Spanish nation might be past before he could appear there.

The enemy have now at Toulon twelve sail of the line; viz. ten French and two Russians, beside frigates. I do not think it is possible to maintain constantly a squadron before the port sufficient to blockade them, considering the great distance to which the ships must go for supplies of provisions and water. At the Magdalene Islands water cannot be got in summer, nor at any place nearer than Pula Bay; the consequence of which may be, that whenever the French sail, the squadron which is off that port may be few in number, and not sufficiently provided to follow to a great distance.

The practice of blockading the port where the enemy is lying, has been so long established, that I feel great diffidence when I offer my opinion to their Lordships, that it never will at this place answer the intended purpose. I would propose instead of it, that the place of rendezvous should be off Cag-liari, where the ships can be supplied in a short time from Sicily or Malta, and be always kept complete in water from Pula; while the look-out frigates should watch Toulon, and on the French sailing, communicate the intelligence to a ship off Toro, I am convinced the ships cannot be supplied where they now are; and shall direct Vice-Admiral Thornborough, before they get low, to adopt what I have described, because it appears to me to be the only practicable means of keeping the fleet connected and effective.

Austria was now preparing for war by a general reform and augmentation of her armies; but as farther time was necessary for the completion of her projects, Count Metternich made repeated protestations to Napoleon of the pacific intentions of the Cabinet of Vienna, and, as one proof of them, communicated to him the letter which had been received from Lord Collingwood. The

Mr. Schoell, in his elaborate and valuable work, "Histoire des Traites de Paix," tome ix., mentions the receipt of this letter as an historical fact which had not been sufficiently explained, and which it was important to record, " as the veil which covered it might some day " be removed." It will be seen that the letter did not, as Mr. Schoell seems to have supposed, pretend to offer the Spanish throne to the Archduke Charles, neither had the English Government " at that time formally acknow-" ledged Ferdinand the Seventh;" for the letter was written in May 1808, whereas the King's first order for the cessation of hostilities with Spain was dated 4th July, 1808; and it was not till January 1809 that the treaty acknowledging Ferdinand the Seventh was signed between the two countries.

Emperor Francis also, in a letter written in September, assured Napoleon of his unalterable attachment, and spoke of the entire confidence which subsisted between them, in which nothing could be wanting to their mutual satisfaction; and so far was Napoleon deceived by these declarations, that in October he directed the disbanding of the troops of the Confederation of the Rhine. At the same time, he informed the Emperor Francis in reply, that he had the power, but not the inclination, to dismember the Austrian Monarchy; that such as it was, it subsisted by his pleasure; and that the only useful policy in these days was simplicity and truth. He was then holding his Court at Erfurth, whither the Emperor of Russia and the German Monarchs had thronged to meet him; and there Alexander, in return for the permission to seize Moldavia and Wallachia from the Turks, engaged that he would not interrupt the designs of Napoleon upon Spain. At this congress also, it appears that a formal partition of Turkey between France, Russia, and Austria, was proposed to the latter Power; but in the meanwhile her preparations were completed, and in April 1809 she began the war which led to the capture of

Vienna, and was terminated by the battle of Wagram.

TO THE RIGHT HON. WM. DRUMMOND.

Ocea? i, off Toulon, May 29, 1808.

By a despatch which I have just received, I am informed that the affairs of Spain are become exceedingly critical; and as I understand that the French troops in Italy have been much reduced, and see that their squadron here are not preparing in a way which indicates an intention to leave the port soon, I consider Sicily as relieved for the present from the danger which seemed to impend over her when the enemy's squadron approached. I intend, therefore, to proceed to Gibraltar, leaving Admiral Thorn-borough with the command of this part of my squadron.

I regret very much that things have happened to prevent my having the pleasure of seeing you, and paying my respects to His Majesty; but my mind was more occupied in the security of his Kingdom than in the personal gratification which I should have had in presenting myself at the Court of Palermo. I shall never lose the hope of having that pleasure.

Although the efforts of the French appear for the present to be directed to another object, Sicily will ever be in their view; and I hope that the interval of time which these events have gained for that Country will be turned to good advantage, by the establishment of a national defence, which will secure it against any sudden assault. The ruin of Spain has been caused by the administration of a minion; and I hope the King will profit by the example, and dismiss from his States those people whose characters are not merely suspicious, but whose influence is certain ruin.

FROM ALI PACHA OF JOANNINA.

June 2, 1808.

I am persuaded that it will be most agreeable to my Government at Constantinople to renew the good old friendship that subsisted with the English, and I feel extremely happy in being placed in a situation where I may render any service to two nations who were once the strictest friends and allies. I hope that, with your Excellency's concurrence, I shall ere long effect the wish of my heart, in the restoration of friendship with the illustrious British nation, and that the union of the two kingdoms will be confirmed for ever. If the machinations of the French be as bad as your Excellency represents them to be, the event must still depend upon the Divine will. In God's mercy are all our hopes, and frequent are the examples which we have of it; for he has many times left our enemies deluded with shame. I hope, however, that I shall soon have the pleasure to hear of the triumphs of the British arms, and that the enemy will be destroyed in the midst of his evil projects. As for myself, I shall be ever the same, at all times and in all circumstances. I spoke to Mr. Leake of what I thought most necessary at present, and I hope he has mentioned it to your Excellency. I anxiously wish that it may be put in execution as soon as possible, until we can stop the supplies of troops and provisions from entering the islands. The French Embassador endeavours, by the most flattering words, to lessen the vigilance and attention of my Government; but all this will have no effect on the attachment which we bear to the English nation. I beg of your Excellency to favour me with any news you have; and I should be glad if you would write to me in future either in Italian,

French, or Greek, as I have not a good interpreter for the English language. In the name of God, I wish you health, happiness, and the accomplishment of all your desires. Your sincere and true Friend,

THE VIZIER ALI PACHA.

TO DON THOMAS DE MORLA,

CAPTAIN-GENEEAL OF ANDALUSIA.

H. M. S. Ocean, of Cadiz, June 12, 1808.

Rear-Admiral Purvis has forwarded to me the copy of the summons which your Excellency, induced by that humanity which distinguishes the Spanish character, had sent to the Admiral commanding the French squadron. It may be true that Admiral Rosily feels no hostility towards the Spanish nation; but when his Government are taking the most active measures to subjugate your Country, and have led your Princes captive to their capital, there needs no more to prove the violation of every friendly connexion and alliance. The proposal which the Admiral makes to your Excellency's second summons appears to me to be merely an expedient to gain time, as he has no reason to believe that his squadron can pass the English without being assailed.

Ocean, off Cadiz, Sunday, June 12, 1808.

I have received the letter of the 11th June, which your Excellency addressed to Admiral Purvis, in which your Excellency is pleased to ask the concurrence of the English commanders in the measures you propose to take against the French squadron. The line of conduct to be pursued is obvious. The French Government is engaged in overturning the constitution of your Country, and subjugating it to the will of their leader. A squadron of their ships is in your power. As the resistance which the French Commander has already made, and the proposals which he has offered to your Excellency, must fully justify him to his Country as having used every means that ingenuity could suggest to save his fleet, I should hope that, seeing how unavailing his efforts must be, he may spare his people from the consequences of farther resistance, and surrender; but if he determines to engage in the farther contest, your Excellency's humanity, in having endeavoured to spare a useless effusion of blood, will not be the less manifest.

THE HON. WM. WELLESLEY POLE.

Ocean, of Cadiz, June 12, 1808.

Their Lordships will be informed by Admiral Purvis's letter (which accompanies this) of the proceedings of the Spaniards against the French squadron, which lie up in the channel of the Carraccas, since which the French Admiral has offered terms of capitulation, proposing to dismantle his ships; but all conditions short of surrender are rejected by the Spaniards. I understand, indeed, that the irritation of the populace against the French is such, that the experiment of admitting them to any thing but unconditional submission is not likely to be attempted by the Governor. I learn that the higher orders do not shew that ardour in the cause which animates the people, but that they are borne along by an enthusiasm which they dare not resist. From this information, and from the unsettled state of their present establishment of Government, I conceive that all our intercourse with them requires much circumspection.

H. M. S. Ocean, off Cadiz, June 14, II I lose no time in returning you my sincere thanks for your kind congratulations on my arrival near Cadiz, where I shall be glad to render my best assistance to a nation which I have ever held in the highest estimation. It is from the energies of the Spanish people, and from the example of what a great country can do when unanimous, that the Continent of Europe is to learn the means of repelling that usurpation which has bound so many States in a degrading dependence. It has always been the policy of France to cause divisions before she resorted to arms. The attempt has been made in Spain, it has failed, and the nation is more firmly united, from a sense of the danger from which it has escaped. Allow me to offer your Excellency my congratulations on the surrender of the French squadron; and I hope it will soon be known, that the success of your army has not been less advantageous. I shall be glad to hear that the irritation of the Spanish people towards the French seamen has ceased, and I believe them to be too generous to insult or offend an enemy who has submitted.

TO LADY COLLINGWOOD.

Ocean, off Cadiz, June 15, 1808.

I left a station which had almost worn me out with care, to be upon the spot where a great revolution was taking place in Spain, and to give my aid to it. Every body here was very glad to see me, both English and Spanish, The French at Toulon had heard, I believe, what was going on before we did; for suddenly they seemed to give up their preparations for sea, and moved several of their ships into an inner harbour. I left Admiral Thornborough to look after them, and came to see what good I could do here. The Spaniards seem determined to expel the French from their Country, and are carrying on their operations without those horrible scenes which disfigured and disgraced France in her revolution. They have declared themselves at peace with England; and four Commissioners are going to London, for the purpose of settling the relations of our Country and their's. We are doing every thing for them that we can. Yesterday we supplied them with gunpowder for their army; and their cause and ours are now the same. The French army under Dupont has advanced near to Seville, where the Spanish headquarters are. An army is marching from Grenada, to possess the Sierra Morena, which is a strong pass between Andalusia and Madrid; so that the French are likely to be surrounded on all sides, in a country where they cannot be supported. Their squadron, which had moved up to that part of the harbour where they hope they could be sustained by their army, after having been bombarded two days by the Spaniards, surrendered, and are now in their possession. They consult with us on every thing, and I do what is in my power for their aid and succour. When our Oibcers land at Cadiz, which they do every day, they are surrounded by multitudes, crying, "Vivan los Ingleses!" " Viva King George!" Every person wears a small red cloth cockade, with F. 7. embroidered on it. They say that Buonaparte has hitherto had only armies to contend with, but that now he has a nation, where every man is a soldier. I sincerely hope it may give a turn to affairs, and an example to other nations which have been oppressed, how, by a vigorous effort, they may recover their independence. Lord Algernon Percy came to see me the day after I arrived here. He is a very fine young man, and Bennet tells me that he makes an excellent sailor. A decision was lately given in my favour in the Court of Admiralty, on the claim of Sir J. Duckworth, Louis, and Cochrane, to share the St. Domingo prizes among themselves, and exclude me. They have appealed from the Judge's decree, which will keep it in law for two or three years more, and cost most of it; but they say the decree must be affirmed at last.

I have the kindest letters from the Duke of Clarence. I do not know him personally; but my brother Wilfred was intimate with his Royal Highness, and I believe he likes me for Wilfred's sake.

I am a poor lack-linen swain, with nothing but a few soldier's shirts, which I got at Gibraltar. All my own were left at Malta and Palermo, and when I shall get them I know not; but such wants give me little disquietude.

VOL. IL

Ocean, off Cadiz, June 17, 1808.

Your Lordship will probably have been informed, by my letters to the Admiralty, that on receiving intelligence from Sir Hew Dairymple, when off Toulon, of the critical state of affairs in Spain, I left the squadron there under the orders of Vice-Admiral Thornborough, on the 1st June, and repaired to this point of my station, where I arrived on the 11th.

Upon the first removal of the Royal Family from Madrid, and when General Castanos and the Spanish leaders were yet doubtful of the temper of the people, and of the means which would be in their power for sustaining their Country, at some of the communications at the lines of Gibraltar, the surrender of the French ships to us was mentioned; but when the people rose, as by a national impulse which they could not resist, they altered their tone, and declined every proposal for bringing either the fleet or the troops to Cadiz. The French Admiral, considering that the only chance of saving his fleet was to remove them far above the town, in hopes that a part of the French army might make its way down to the island of Leon, drew them up in the channel of the Carraccas. On the 8th and 9th they were bombarded; and after a suspension of the attack for four days, on the morning of the 14th they struck their colours by signal from the Admiral, were taken possession of by the Spaniards, and now bear the Spanish flag. The spirit of resistance to the French tyranny, the abhorrence of the acts which have been practised against the Royal Family and the State, and the enthusiastic desire to restore the country to its independence, were perhaps never surpassed. In no country, nor in any cause, was there ever greater unanimity, even in those parts (as near Madrid and Barcelona) where the French are in force. It is not necessary for the Ministers of Government to devise means to raise men, but rather to make regulations for restraining and selecting them.

The French are said to be exceedingly embarrassed by the want of communication with the different parts of their army, for every Frenchman found in the country is slain; and the Spanish peasants who are sent with letters, bring them to the magistrates.

The form of Government is very defective. The Juntas of the different provinces appear to be totally independent of each other; and, in the present condition of the country, correspondence is difficult. From Biscay they have not yet heard what is doing. In this state of things, I considered your Lordship's instructions of the 25th May carefully, and in the spirit of them informed the Spanish Chiefs here that it was His Majesty's command that every aid should be given them to repel the French, and enable them to maintain the independence of their Country; and that there might be no appearance of assuming a control over their measures, I desired them to point out how the British force upon the coast could be most useful to them. The proposal for the troops to land at or in the neighbourhood of Cadiz, had before been rejected; and from the officers who had been much on shore, I understood that there existed a visible suspicion that we had views particular to ourselves, and which had nothing to do with preserving their independence as a nation; and that their jealousy was less disguised as the number of troops off Cadiz increased. Major-General Spencer had been informed of this, and had acceded to a proposal of theirs to go to Ayamonte, to be ready to act as circumstances and his information of the enemy's force might make necessary.

As soon as I received the first account of what was passing here, I opened a communication with Minorca. The Governor-General Vives had at the same time sent from Majorca to request that an officer might go thither, authorised to agree to such measures as the interests of both Countries required; and Captain Staines had been sent by Vice-Admiral Thornborough, with whom I left instructions to suspend hostilities, take every means to preserve the islands from the French, and keep the Spanish fleet in Port Mahon until farther instructions should be received. They had near 12,000 men in those islands; and I hear from Cadiz, that a large portion of them have passed over to Catalonia, to join the army there, under a convention made with Vice-Admiral Thornborough.

The Junta, in all its acts and expressions, describe the British nation as that on which they depend for support against the usurpation with which they are threatened. All the people of this part of Spain are obedient to their Government, and zealous in its cause. But I should inform your Lordship, that, from all the information I get, it is the populace that is the spirit which gives vigour to their measures; and if their Councils can keep this spirit alive, and direct it judiciously, all may be well. I have pointed out to the Government the necessity of an early communication with the provinces abroad, to explain to the people what events have passed in Spain, and what is doing. I was sorry to find them tardy in what appears so necessary, and can only account for it by the difficulty of carrying on correspondence in the country, and of coming to common resolutions in the several Juntas. The subjects nearest home press first upon the consideration of all. The Council at Seville do not consider themselves authorised to give instructions without the concurrence of the whole.

I do not perceive that it will be necessary at present to make use of the authority which your Lordship has given me to draw for money for secret service. They will certainly require great supplies of powder and military stores, and want money for their troops; but it is probable that peace will soon be agreed to. The secret objects for which your Lordship thinks that this money might be applied, would then be no longer of any value; for fleets and individuals will all be involved in the contract which their nation will form, and be bound to co-operate with us. Some of the Juntas have already declared themselves at peace with England, and all have declared against France.

TO DON THOMAS DE MORLA.

Ocean, off Cadiz, Jime 18, 1808.

In reply to the letter which your Excellency has done me the honour to write, I beg to inform you that the vessel which, on her way from England to the West Indies, brought despatches to me, will sail as soon as possible this day. All your despatch-vessels, or a frigate, should the Spanish Government desire to send one with officers to the provinces in America, shall be provided by me with the necessary papers to protect them, and the quicksilver which is wanted for the immediate use of la Vera Cruz; but for the ships of the line, I should be glad if your Excellency would not make any request about them, until some arrangement be entered into by the British Government for establishing peace in all its relations.

Your Excellency's letter to the Marquess de la Rom ana shall be carefully forwarded to England, and I have great expectation that the activity of the British Government will rescue his force from the power of the French.

I beg your Excellency will not apologise for giving me trouble. The more I can do for the Spanish nation in the present crisis, the greater will be my satisfaction.

TO LORD RADSTOCK.

Ocean, Gibraltar Bay, Jinie 18, 1808.

I have received a letter from Captain Waldegrave, and, I must say, it has vexed me to find that he is appointed to command the Thames. I should have been delighted to have had him near me in a ship of durance; but this Thames came here from the West Indies with the copper off her bottom. In other respects, I believe she is an excellent ship, and nobody can sooner make her perfect than my friend. I have had the most fatiguing and the most mortifying cruise that ever any person experienced, in the pursuit of those Frenchmen. It has worn me very much; for I suffered an anxiety, of the pain of which only those can judge who have been in similar situations. My heart was bent on the destruction of that fleet; but I never got intelligence where they really were, until they were out of reach. They went to Corfu, where I still believe they had no intention to go, but were driven from their purpose, upon the coast of Italy, by a storm, and Corfu was their place of refuge. They did nothing there that I can learn. I know that success, or the want of it, is the scale on which all men's merits are measured, and that the French flying from one end of the Mediterranean to the other, will be imputed to great stupidity and want of judgment by those who are not capable of forming a true estimate of circumstances; and as they compose a large majority, the unfortunate, however great their exertion may have been, will suffer in the general opinion. Their escape was by chance; for at one time we were very near them, without knowing it.

TO THE EARL OF MULGRAVE.

Ocean, of Cadiz, June 20, 1808. I have not received any official despatch from Malta; but by the Packet, I hear that the Unite has captured, off Venice, a very fine brig of war, mounting sixteen 32-pounders carronades. As the Lords Commissioners of the Admiralty will probably order this brig, if upon her survey she be found fit, to be taken into the service, I beg to recommend to your Lordship the First Lieutenant of the Unite, Lieutenant J. Wilson, to command her. He is entirely unknown to me, except from character; but Captain Campbell has so often had occasion to mention his skill and experience as an officer, and his devotion to the service, as having so much conduced to the high character which the Unite bears, that I am sure your Lordship will approve of my making his merits known to you.

Ocean, of Cadiz, June 20, 1808. MOST EXCELLENT PACHA, I received the honour of your Highness's letter of April only two days since. My having left that part of my command, to attend to the affairs of Spain, prevented my receiving it sooner. I have already assured your Highness of my sincere desire that peace may soon be established amongst us. You know that my Government took much pains last summer to settle it; but the artful intrigues of the French at Constantinople prevented the Ministers of the Sublime Porte from seeing their true interests. That is past; and I hope the proposal which has now come from your Government will be more successful: for peace with all Powers is what the British nation most desires; and if there were no Frenchmen in the world, I believe there would be no difficulty in it. In the mean time, we wdll endeavour to shew your Highness how much the Turks are esteemed, and how much we desire your friendship. I have given directions to the Captains of the ships stationed on your coast to give their best assistance to any operation which you may undertake against the enemy, and have requested that Sir Alexander Ball would permit your agents to purchase at Malta whatever arms or necessaries of war you may want. Whenever peace is settled between our nations, I will do what is possible for your success in whatever you undertake. I hope it will be soon.

I wish your Highness health, and am, most excellent Pacha, your sincere friend.

TO VISCOUNT CASTLEREAGH.

Ocean, of Cadiz, June 25, 1808.

Since the letter I had the honour to address your Lordship on the 19th, I have had applications from the Junta of Seville and from the Governor of Cadiz, by their direction, for supplies of cloth and horses, of which they are in the greatest want. In order to obtain the license for purchasing horses in Barbary, I shall send an officer to communicate with Slowey, the Emperor's Minister; and if he grants it, I have told them that the English Government will be responsible for the payment, in such manner as shall then be agreed on. By the accounts which come to me of the French army under Dupont, I understand that it is reduced to great extremity, surrounded on all quarters by the Spaniards, and disappointed in the expectation of being joined by a corps of about 4000 men, which had advanced from Algarve with that intention. On the 13th they retired from Carmona, to a station six leagues from Cordova. The Spanish army advanced, but their head-quarters is still at Utrera.

To-day intelligence is come here that the French have made a proposal to capitulate, if they may be allowed to pass into France unmolested, which the Spanish General has rejected: indeed, such is the temper of the people, and their resentment for the indignity done to them by carrying off their King, that nothing less than unconditional surrender will be accepted.

This day two Spanish vessels sailed; one for the Rio Plata, the other for la Vera Cruz, with despatches. Vessels which may be on their passage from America are still subject to capture, which may be the cause of much embarrassment, in the state of friendly intercourse in which we now are, as we shall be taking from them their merchant-ships, while we are giving them what- ever is wanting to support the State. I have explained this to the Governor, that he may prevent the mistake into which traders might fall, by not waiting until his Majesty's Government shall order a suspension of hostilities; and I have recommended to him to send to the Canaries a despatch to prevent all vessels from sailing.

TO THE SAME.

Ocean, off Cadiz, June 29, 1808.

I have received a letter this morning from the President of the Junta, of such nature that it is necessary I should receive your Lordship's commands before I do any thing in consequence of it. I enclose Don Saavedra's letter, by which your Lordship will be informed of the intention of the Junta at Seville to invite the hereditary Prince of the two Sicilies to Spain, as Regent of the kingdom, to govern in the name of Ferdinand VII. I have thought this an extraordinary measure in the Junta to take without the concurrence or (as far as I know) the least communication with the other Councils assembled in the kingdom, and likely to create questions by the others of the right of Seville to name the Regent for the whole. Had the Prince of Sicily been a great military character, the state of the Country, which requires such a person to unite its efforts and conduct its affairs in the present crisis, might have pointed him out as a proper person to be placed at its head. Had he been distinguished for political knowledge, he might have given direction to the energies of the kingdom, and drawn the wisdom of the nation to his Councils; or had he been the next in succession after those of the Royal Family now captive in France, there would have existed some reason for the selection.

LIEUT.-GENERAL SIR JOHN STUART.

Ocean, off Cadiz, June 29, 1808.

I believe the Sicilians have at all times been firmly attached to the English, and the commons would have gladly exerted themselves to keep off the enemy. They are equal to it, if they were formed into regular bodies, properly equipped; but the Government is poor, the nobility dissipated and indifferent; and until the levies were proposed under the Prince Butera, none took the least part in the defence of the country. Although these levies have not succeeded yet, I have no doubt they will in time; perhaps they vere begun on too great a scale.

I do not know that there are many Sicilians disaffected to the Government, though there may be many disappointed with its languor, and who look to more activity as the means of ameliorating the condition of the whole. The representations that such amelioration could only be effected by the English, and the too frequent discussion of the subject, have, I believe, done much harm. It raised expectations in one class which had no foundation; and in another caused doubts and suspicions of sinister schemes. The subject, I hope, is now very fully understood. There certainly is great room for the Government, by wholesome laws, the dissolution of monopolies, and a provident use of the revenue, to change the face of the country, and banish wretchedness from out of it: but this as certainly is the business of that Government, rather than of strangers.

Ocean, oj'Cadiz, June 30, 1808.

I had the most anxious time which I ever experienced, while in pursuit of the French squadron. I assure your Lordship that no pains were spared, both to get intelligence of their route and to pursue them; but our information had always something to make the truth doubtful, and in missing them we were unfortunate. Admiral Martin, with the Spartiate, coming to join the squadron, and the Antelope's convoy, must both have passed near that squadron of the enemy; yet they were not seen.

I do not know what account I ouaht to give your Lordship of the state of affairs here. The people, irritated to the greatest degree against the French, and full of resentment at being robbed of their King, are raised to enthusiasm, and would do any thing. Their Councils, maintaining the gravity of their national character, would let this ardour cool, and do nothing. Great allowance must be made for the mode of the present Government in Juntas, all independent, and, I am afraid, not having that correspondence with each other that is necessary to their general

VOL. II. M preservation. It was long before the Junta of Seville would send to the West Indies, though I continually urged the necessity of it. A few days since, a vessel sailed to Rio Plata; and as it was important to give the Spanish settlement a proof of the connexion of Britain with Spain, the Sabrina sloop carried out to the Carraccas and Carthagena some officers with despatches for those places. I have pointed out to the Council of Government the great probability of a French squadron going to the West Indies to aid in establishing Buonaparte's authority in those parts, where his emissaries may have found the best reception, and the necessity of keeping their ships prepared to protect the Colonies: but they have, however, moved several of them up the Puntal, and some are unrigging; and now I have represented to the Governor Morla, that, on any reverse of fortune in General Castafios's army, the French may march to where those ships are, and that neither the batteries nor the town would be able to give them any protection. General Castafios's army, at Cordova, consists of 23,000 men; Dupont's, at Anduxar, of (I believe) 12,000: the French expect a reinforcement; and if Castanos does not fight them before it comes, it is not probable that he will do so afterward. This is the state in which I understand affairs to be at this moment.

TO VISCOUNT CASTLEREAGH.

Ocean, off Cadiz, July 3, 1808.

I informed your Lordship, in my letter of the 28th past, that on the 27th, the convoy of transports and troops, which had sailed for Lisbon, returned to this anchorage. Major-General Spencer, having proceeded to the Tagus before the fleet, found a state of affairs there very different from what had been represented to Sir C. Cotton, and the French force so great at Lisbon and near it, as to preclude any hope of success in landing. The General therefore returned immediately; and, after consulting with the Governor of Cadiz, it was settled that all the troops should go into the port, and such number as convenient barracks could be provided for, should land at Port St. Mary, where the General proposes to wait until Sir Arthur Wellesley arrives with the reinforcement. What service will then be determined upon, I cannot tell; for the Spaniards seem equally averse to our holding any important garrison or taking the field with them.

On considering the probability of the French sending a squadron and troops to the Spanish Colonies, whenever they were informed by their agents of the point at which they were most likely to be well received, I intimated to the Officer who is residing at Seville, the proposal I intended to make to the Junta, on the subject of their fleet being prepared for service at sea, and joining His Majesty's squadron whenever the movements of the enemy should make it necessary. The moment they found that such a proposal would be made, they ordered their ships to the upper part of the harbour, and have begun to dismantle them; and this removal of the ships was so sudden, that before my letter could arrive at Seville, they were gone up the Puntal. I enclose a copy of the letter of Manuel Gil, a member of the Junta, appointed to communicate with Major Cox on the subject, and Don Saavedra, the President of the Junta.

They state their want of funds to maintain their navy, as one reason for this extraordinary movement, so detrimental to their own security; but I do not believe this to be the true one, for the Junta have been told that His Majesty will sustain them in every measure which is necessary to their defence; and they have been invited freely to point out where the aids should be applied. Neither do I think it proceeded from any want of confidence in us; but that the Junta begin now to feel that they are not acknowledged as the Supreme Council of the nationthat their acts must be confined to the purposes of local defence that their authority does not extend to matters beyond their district; and as the disposition of the fleet is a national concern, they will not make themselves accountable at a future time for the application of it. They refer me to the Commander at Carthagena merely to evade the question here. I have, however, written to him.

Wherever the people have put themselves in action, they have proceeded to the end with a resolution and courage which shews a determination to free their Country from its invaders; and if this resolution be wanting any where, it is not in the common people. The army of Seville amounts to about 23,000 regulars, and as many peasantry as they please. The enthusiasm of the lower orders, if it were well directed, would clear the country of the enemy in a very short time; and if it be allowed to subside, they will have nothing left but a mere Spanish army.

1 informed your Lordship that, as horses were much wanted for the army, an application had been made to me, and that I had sent to the Emperor of Morocco for permission to purchase them. The officer has returned, and brought me a letter from the Minister Mohamed Ben Abdislam Slowey, the Emperor himself having marched into the interior, at the head of a great army, to quell an insurrection. I have no expectation of obtaining what I have asked: Slowey assured Captain Bullen that he would use his influence in our favour; but that, by their religion, horses were not to be sold to Christians, so that the purchase and payment were out of the question. There were, however, he observed, certain conditions which the Emperor would make known to me, and if these were acceded to, the Spaniards should not only have horses, but whatever his country produced, and they wanted. This was all he would say; but your Lordship will perceive that his object is Ceuta. If that fortress be given to him, he will grant in return whatever is asked; without it, I doubt whether he will let them have a mule. In the present state of Spain, there is no power that can be called the National Government, and no authority to make a cession of any place; and this state of affairs must remain until there be established a Supreme Council, whose authority shall extend and be acknowledged over the kingdom.

TO THE EARL OF MULGRAVE.

Ocean, off Cadiz, July 11, 1808.

I have received the honour of your Lordship's letter, giving me such information as you had then received of the French squadron. The doubts which then existed have been since cleared up, and my present consideration is, upon what scheme they may probably go next. Sicily is more secure than it has ever been, both from the increase of our forces, and the diminution of theirs in Italy. They have tried the disposition of the people in Majorca and Minorca, where their overtures have been rejected; and while our squadron is off Minorca, they cannot hope for success there.

I have no doubt that the French have long since had their emissaries and agents in Spanish America, who will not only practise the usual artifices by which they have subverted so many Governments, but be provided with proper documents from their King and captive Statesmen at Bayonne; and it is probable that, whenever a report is made to Buonaparte of a district disposed to receive the French forces, the squadron of Toulon may go thither to estabhsh his dominion. With this in my mind, I am carefully watching the Straits. The squadron is as complete as possible; and if they come this way, I shall hope to meet them, or failing in that, shall pursue them.

TO THE SAME.

Ocean, off Cadiz, July 2, 1808.

To-day I have received a letter from the Governor of Cadiz, enclosing one from the Supreme Council, in which they state, that the only reason for dismantling their ships was the want of money and stores to maintain them; but that, yielding to the arguments contained in my letter, they had resolved that all their ships should be fitted, and depended on the assistance of England to enable them to do so.

I am well satisfied with the stop put to dismantling their ships, until the affairs of their army are a little more advanced. To maintain their ships would be an immense expense. As the arsenals at Cadiz are said to be empty, they will want a great quantity of stores from England, and with the little arrangement and want of skill in their officers, they will never be effective; but they were placing them in danger where they were going to put them, and that is now prevented. In all the southern provinces of Spain they are exceedingly importunate for supplies of arms, ammunition, and money to pay their forces. In the provinces of Valencia, Murcia, Arragon, and Catalonia, their armies are continually in motion, and always with success. Here, in Andalusia, General Castaiios is perhaps more scientific, but more slow. His army lies before the enemy, but nothing is done. The castles of Figueras and Bellegarde, in Rousillon, are in possession of the Spaniards, and the French of that neighbouring province who have joined them. Barcelona is still occupied by a considerable force of the enemy, but the reinforcements which were on their way to join them have, for the most part, been destroyed; and the frigates which are stationed on the coast will do every thing that is practicable to prevent supplies coming from France. I wish much that two of the Spanish ships at Minorca would join one of ours, to sustain the frigates on that service, and will apply for them.

In all their requisitions, your Lordship will observe that they never mention men, whom they have in abundance. It is arms and money that they want. Indeed, they appear to me to be very averse from employing the troops which are here under General Spencer, and I feel convinced that they will not admit them into any garrison town of strength. From want of horses to draw their cannon, they have not advanced from Port St. Mary, and the Spanish General Morla does not appear to be very anxious that they should.

FROM THE EARL OF MULGRAVE.

Admiralty, July 12, 1808.

I have been prevented, not so much by the great pressure of Parliamentary business, and the considerable interval of time which would necessarily elapse before you could receive answers to your letters, as by my conviction that I could not add any suggestions to the judicious measures which you have uniformly taken, from replying more frequently to the very satisfactory and interesting communications which I received from time to time in your private letters. Your ready compliance with the request of the Junta of Seville for passports for their advice-boats to the Spanish Colonies, was strictly conformable to the wishes and views of His Majesty's Government, as were the facilities you propose to afford for the transport of Spanish troops from Ceuta and the Balearic Islands to Spain. Every ground of jealousy, and every appearance of distrust, should, as far as possible, be done away. It is highly important, in all communications with the Spaniards, that there should not appear any object on the part of Great Britain distinct from, much less disadvantageous to, the views and interests of the Spanish nation. No object can be of equal importance to this Country with the vigorous and persevering exertions of Spain, and that entire confidence in the zealous and disinterested aid of Great Britain, without which it is hardly to be hoped that the Spaniards will make such efforts as will be indispensably necessary to the successful conclusion of the great and interesting struggle in which that nation is engaged. I feel most highly gratified in considering that the establishment of that confidence, and the encouragement in their efforts, will depend so much upon the exertion of your Lordship's talents and zeal, and shall be happy to hear that your health has not suffered from the anxious vigilance which you have had to exercise for so many months.

FROM
MAHOMED BEN ABDESLAM SLOWEY,
THE MINISTER OF THE EMPEIIOR OF MOROCCO.
Tetuan, July 15, 1808.
To the Most High and Potent Admiral Couingwood, Commander of the Sea.

The letter which you sent to be forwarded to His Imperial Majesty reached his royal presence, and he is aware of your demand. He is also very happy to see, that, in consequence of the friendship which exists between your nation and His Imperial Majesty, others avail themselves, through you.

to mediate between us and them for their wants, which is a proof of the true friendship existing between His Imperial Majesty and you.

I am directed by His Imperial Majesty to answer you on the subject of your letter. You must know that your request is somewhat difficult for His Imperial Majesty to grant, as the Mussulmen will object to it, unless something be given as a recompense and in return for it; for it is sinful, according to our religion, and we cannot do it lawfully, except on the terms which I mention. Were it not sinful. His Imperial Majesty would have no difficulty in complying with your wishes; and you must be convinced, that nothing shall be wanting on my part to oblige you, as I know His Imperial Majesty's esteem towards you, and am always happy when I can be of service.

If you can rely on those who request this supply from you, and they will empower you to grant what you may require of them, then their request, through you, shall be granted without delay or trouble, and Consul Green will inform you of the object which is to be the reward for yielding to their request. I am very sorry that we cannot comply with this thing, which is a sin in our religion. Were it lawful, there would be no objection. Any other thing in our power we will accede to with pleasure.

TO VISCOUNT CASTLEREAGH.

Ocean, off Cadiz, July 15, 1808.

In every province of Spain, the demand for arms, muskets, pistols, c. is incessantly and urgently made. I have directed that the ships on the coast to the eastward should supply them with such arms and ammunition as they can, and have written to Sir Alexander Ball, to ask 2000 muskets from the armory of Malta, and to the Governor of Majorca, that he will employ all the forges in the country to make pikes twelve feet long, for the peasantry of Valencia and Catalonia. Cadiz at present has a body of militia of perhaps more than 2000 men; but its defence is given to the citizens, who are embodied to the number of 4 or 5000, and are training to arms with great zeal.

By a letter from General Castafios, of the 11th, at night, he was preparing to attack the enemy the next day. Some of his officers have been arrested, and sent to Seville.

Major-General Vanissa de Pedro is one of them. In a former letter, I observed to your Lordship, that, from the best intelligence 1 can get, this war is supported entirely by the common people, who, instigated by the Clergy, are worked up to the highest degree of enthusiasm. They go from the drill to the priests, who, in every street, are preaching the duty of being firm in the defence of their Country, and there is no influence so powerful in it. Amongst the higher orders there are many doubtful characters, but they dare not shew themselves.

I must inform your Lordship of a circumstance which has just come to my knowledge. The Marquess Solano, the late Governor-General, whether from the conviction of the inability of Spain to resist the arms of France, or from his engagements to that people, convened a council of general officers at Cadiz just before his death. It consisted of nine persons, who (with the exception of one only) gave their opinion that no resistance should be made to the French. The person I have named, Nanissa de Pedro, was

The Marquess de la Solano had become Marquess of Solano and Socorro, by the death of his father.

one of them, and there are others in Cas-tafios's army. General Morla, who is now Governor-General of Andalusia, and directing every thing here, was of the number. With such doubts of the principles of those high in office, your Lordship will perceive that it requires a degree of delicacy to manage well with them; but we know the ground on which they stand, and good use may be made of it; for the people, I believe, have more confidence in the British than in their own leaders.

Your Lordship was pleased to authorise me to draw bills on His Majesty's Treasury for money which might be wanted. That necessity has not occurred; and the loans and supplies to the Spanish provinces will now be in a different form. As there will be numerous, and perhaps complicated accounts to be kept, and I have at this moment business which occupies every hour and every minute of the day, and am, moreover, very little conversant in money transactions, without the smallest experience in them, I beg to suggest to your Lordship, that a proper person should be appointed to manage the accounts, and be responsible for them. Such person might be put as much under my control as your Lordship may please, as to the distribution of money in stores.

ADMIRAL SIR CHARLES COTTON.

Ocean, of Cadiz, July 20, 1808.

On the receipt of your letter of the 13th, I immediately despatched one to Major-General Spencer; and as there does not appear any service for the troops here at present, nor even, without some extraordinary reverse of fortune to Castanos, will they be wanted in future, I concluded that the General would be impatient to proceed to Lisbon, where the service seemed to be urgent. He wrote to the Junta to inform them of his intention to proceed, unless they thought his presence necessary to the defence of the province. They referred the letter to General Castanos, who replied, that the Spanish army was quite competent to resist the enemy, and that the English troops were at liberty to proceed on other service. I think the Spaniards have a suspicion of our entertaining an idea of seizing upon Cadiz.

The views of our Ministers, as they are explained to me, authorise no such measure; VOL. II. N but, on the contrary, they look to our removing, by the most candid conduct, every suspicion of a hostile or even of an interested motive, beyond that of furthering the general interests of Spain and of mankind. What we have undertaken is to give them every aid to expel the French from among them, and to establish the government of an independent nation. The reward will arise from the friendly and advantageous intercourse that may hereafter be established. This is the view and object of our Court; and whatever tends to make an impression unlike to this should be carefully avoided. It cannot be long before I shall hear from England, and supplies of money and arms come for them. That is what they want; they neither want nor wish for men.

The reports and statements which went from hence before I came, were founded on transactions passing in Cadiz while Solano lived, not upon the general principle which actuated the Country at large. The mass of people are counselled and directed by the priests, whose importance and wealth depend on the expulsion of the French. There are many of the higher orders who are not of the same sentiment, and would perhaps compound for a part of their property, rather than contend for the whole. I do not think the French will continue long in Portugal; the whole Country is opposed to them; and they have no communication either with France or Madrid.

If you can open a correspondence with Siniavin, I think it would have the effect of detaching him from the French; and if it did not, you might make him suspected by them, and cause a breach. If your ships in shore were to answer his signals with a Russian flag displayed, all he could say would not convince Junot that he has not communication with you. The last of the troops will be embarked by morning, and, I hope, sail to-morrow under the Bulwark.

FROM
FATHER MANUEL GIL TO MAJOR COX.
Seville, July 20, 1808.

I transmit to you the following project against Morocco, which appears to have had its beginning during the administration of the Prince of the Peace, Don Manuel Godoy. Setting aside its morality or immorality, of which there are various opinions, it appears that this would not be the season to put it in execution; for much time has elapsed without any thing new presenting itself. It is right that our two nations should accord; and for that reason the enclosed papers should be seen by Lord Couingwood and the Governor of Gibraltar, and we should know their mode of thinking thereon.

TO MAJOR COX.

Ocean, off Cadiz, July 21, 1808.

I have just received and read the papers which his Excellency the Padre Gil desired you to transmit to me from the Supreme Junta. I understand them to be instructions to the Governor of Melilla to give support to the rebellion of Ali Beck Abdallah against the Emperor of Morocco, in consequence of some wrongs which Spain had suffered, and which the Prince of the Peace intended to resent by fomenting the insurrection of Ali Beck. With such information as the papers afford, it is not possible to give any correct judgment of the particular case; but of the general principle I can state my ideas in a few words.

War is not a subject to be considered with levity; it is not a subject in which the personal resentment of an individual should be allowed to have any vieight; and the person who makes an honourable peace for his Country is more its friend than he who adds to its splendour by many victories in a cause which was not of strict necessity.

Wrongs to a nation, whether of insult or injustice, are not justifiable causes of war until reparation have been demanded of the offending Government, and refused. Then, indeed, war is of necessity, to defend the honour or interest of a nation, and a great nation will not shrink from it, for it is glorious to be jealous of its honourit is its duty to defend the interests of its subjects: but it is unworthy of it to bear a fair appearance to a Government, and at the same time instigate the people to rebellion, or support them in it. Such a conduct, I conceive, must at all times be derogatory to the dignity of an honourable nation; although it may be reconcilable to the crooked policy of a Frenchman of the present day.

It is known to Spain whether wrongs have been done here by the Emperor or not; but I cannot form in my mind a case that would justify the mode of revenge whicli, from what I collect from the papers, was intended to be pursued. I think also that the Supreme Junta will be of opinion with me, that although the Emperor may not deserve any unlimited confidence, it is good policy at this time not to make him an inveterate enemy.

TO HIS CHILDREN.

Oceati, off Cadiz, July 23, 1808.

MY DEAREST SARAH AND MARY, It gave me great pleasure to find, from your letters, that you were well, and, I hope, making good use of your time. It is at this period of your lives that you must lay the foundation of all knowledge, and of those manners and modes of thinking that distinguish gentlewomen from the Miss Nothings. A good woman has great and important duties to do in the world, and will always be in danger of doing them ill and without credit to herself, unless she have acquired knowledge. I have only to recommend to you not to pass too much of your time in trifling pursuits, or in reading books merely of amusement, which afford you no information, nor any thing that you can reflect upon afterwards, and feel that you have acquired what you did not know before.

Never do any thing that can denote an angry mind; for although every body is born with a certain degree of passion, and from untoward circumstances will sometimes feel its operation, and be what they call " out " of humour," yet a sensible man or woman will not allow it to be discovered. Check and restrain it; never make any determination until you find it has entirely subsided; and always avoid saying any thing that you may afterwards wish unsaid. I hope, Sarah, you continue to read geography. Whenever there are any particular events happening, examine the map and see where they took place. At Saragossa, in Arragon, the Spanish army was composed mostly of the peasantry of the country, and the priests (who take a great interest in this war,) were officers. The Bishop headed the army, and, with his sword in one hand and a cross in the other, fought very bravely, until he was shot in the arm. At Anduxar, a town upon the river Guadalquiver, the Spanish army fought a great battle, and entirely defeated the French. I hope that they will be driven entirely out of Spain very soon. Do you study geometry? which I beg you will consider as quite a necessary branch of knowledge. It contains much that is useful, and a great deal that is entertaining, which you will daily discover as you grow older. Whenever I come home, we will never part again while we live; and, till then, and ever, I am, my dear good girls, your most affectionate father.

FROM THE MARQUESS DI CIRCELLO.

Palermo, July 2b, 1808.

By the command of His Majesty the King, my master, I had the honour of addressing myself to your Lordship, and of notifying to your Excellency the determination taken by His Majesty to send his royal son, the Prince Leopold, to Gibraltar, of which I pointed out the weighty motives. So convinced is the King of your condescension, that he does not hesitate to ask another favour which is next his heart. His Majesty requests, should circumstances require the Prince Leopold to land at any Spanish port, that your Lordship will be so good as to leave one of your ships to be stationed there for his protection. Your Lordship's zeal is too well known to the

King, my master, to allow him to doubt your willingness to gratify his just wishes in this important affair, which may produce so much reciprocal benefit to both the allies; and the King will with pleasure seize every occasion of acknowledging this service from so eminent a leader of the British forces.

TO DON THOMAS DE MORLA.

Ocean, July 28, 1808.

I beg to give your Excellency my best thanks for the detailed account which you were so good as to give me of the late glorious action at Baylen; and I can assure your Excellency, that in all Spain there is no one who can feel more gratified and rejoiced than I do at all your successes. I congratulate you. Sir, in the name of my fleet and of the English nation.

The permission, however, for five or six thousand armed French soldiers to march to Cadiz and embark for Rochefort, seems to me to be so extraordinary, and so much more than they could have obtained, even from a victory, that I shall be glad if your Excellency will inform me what you understand on this subject. Every thing that can promote the interests of Spain I will cheer- fully and speedily do; but it will require instructions from England before I can allow so great a body of troops to pass to a new destination by sea. It is to be considered how large a fleet of merchant ships it will take to transport them; for if the Spanish ships of war were to go to Rochefort with the French capitulants, I doubt whether they would ever be allowed to depart from thence, except as French ships. As I have been disappointed in not having heard of the arrival of supplies from England for this part of Spain, I have taken it upon myself to raise 20,000. sterling at Gibraltar, for the service of your Country, and I will draw bills for the amount on His Majesty's Treasury. I enclose passports for Admiral Rossily and the French Naval Officers who are to accompany him to France, in which I have directed, that on their being met by English vessels there may be observed to them that kindness to which misfortune is always entitled. I hope that on their arrival in France they will be received with the same regard; but I am afraid of Buonaparte. With him, to be unfortunate is to be criminal.

Ocean, of Cadiz, Juli 28, 1808.

I am much obliged to you for your kind letter, which would have given me much pleasure if you could have informed me that you were well: but take my advice, do not be anxious about employment at sea, or let any thing disturb your mind, until your health be firmly re-established; and I doubt not that your youth and sound constitution will overcome your illness, and enable you some day to do your Country good service. You have ability to do it, and inclination, and it is your duty now to recover that health which has been injured by exertion beyond your natural strength. Your Commodore is working the gentry of the iron crown in the Adriatic; and I dare say wishes you were with him, in a good frigate. The Amphion is gone up to second him; and I expect that they will keep that sea clear. I am very glad to hear that Lord Mulgrave gave you so favourable a reception. He was acquainted with your character, which is one that every body ought to respect. Get well and firm in health, avoid all long-shore employments, and I doubt not that you will find that station in your Country's service which will be advantageous to it and creditable to you.

TO HIS EXCELLENCY

MOHAMED BEN ABDESLAM SLOWEY,

GOVERNOR OF TETUAN, AND MINISTER OF THE EMPEROR OF MO-ROCCO.

July 30, 1808.

I have received the letter which your Excellency did me the honour to write by command of His Imperial Majesty, in reply to my request that horses, c. might be purchased in Barbary for the use of the Spanish nation. This request was made by me in full confidence that the friendship which happily subsists between His Imperial Majesty and my King, the intimate connexion between our Countries, and the duty to mankind which all great sovereigns feel to rescue a gallant nation from the oppression with which it is threatened, would have induced His Imperial Majesty to grant the request which I made. I am exceedingly sorry that such conditions are annexed to the compliance with it as I cannot even propose to the Spanish Government. The Spanish nation, as your Excellency knows, was lately at war with England. We were at war because then they had attached themselves to a people who were using their power to oppress mankind, and, having no regard to justice or honour, were carrying misery and devastation into all countries. But the moment the Spaniards abandoned those pursuits, they became our friends, and the arms and treasures of our State were offered to them to assist in establishing their independence, and the rank that so great a people ought to hold amongst nations.

The same sentiments of generosity which influence my King, I am sure are not wanting in the breast of His Imperial Majesty. Your Emperor was not at war with them, the relations of friendship subsisted at all times with Spain, and it was natural to suppose that they would have applied directly to His Imperial Majesty for the aid which they required; but their treasury has been exhausted by the frauds of the French, they were unable to make payment for what they wanted, and therefore hoped to obtain it through me: I expected it from the magnanimity of your Prince, and that he would be glad to aid in humbling a nation which has grown proud in blood.

But there are other considerations which will have their weight with a wise prince, who looks forward to times to come. If the case should happen (which God prevent), that France should triumph, and ever possess the coasts opposite to Barbary, His Imperial Majesty will then be convinced how true a policy it would have been to have kept at a distance this turbulent people. Ceuta would in that case be a possession necessary to the security of his dominions: in the present instance, when in the hands of Spaniards, and with Spain in friendship with him, no danger can arise; and what is so likely to maintain friendship as acts of mutual benevolence?

I regret that granting to your neighbour this great good should be considered as in any degree militating against the tenets of your holy religion. I respect all those who are true to their faith. Mahomet was a wise and great lawgiver; he knew how fallible and weak mankind were; he knew how much they required the assistance of each other; and one of his commands to his people was, (and it is a sacred tenet in all religions,) " To do good to all." What greater good can His Imperial Majesty do than assist a loyal people in repelling an enemy who regards not the laws of God, and maintaining their existence as a nation?

I have troubled your Excellency with these observations, because your character for wisdom and benevolence is well known. You will perceive the advantages that will result to the world by giving to your neighbour all possible assistance. You will perceive that it is of much more importance to the happiness of Morocco to keep the French far from you, than it is to possess Ceuta. When I repeat to you that those aids which my Sovereign gives to Spain have no interested motives in view, you will see that it is impossible that I should make any proposal to their Government for the cession of Ceuta at this time; and I am sure you will perceive clearly, as I do, that " to do " good" will always be acceptable to God.

I have only now to beg your Excellency will use your influence with the Emperor, that the wants of the Spaniards may be supplied.

I wish you health, and am your Excellency's faithful friend.

So great was Lord Collingwood's economy of the public money, that the whole of his demand for extra-

Ocean, of Cadiz, July 25, 1808.

From the information which I have received from Captain Stewart, of the Seahorse, who is stationed in the Archipelago, I beheve that Mr. Adair will be cordially met by the Ministers of the Porte, as they have expressed an anxious desire that peace should be restored. On the subject of occupying an island in that sea, by having a garrison in it, I am really at a loss what to advise, and know not how to recommend any change which will make the islands more beneficial to us than they are at present.

Milo has a good harbour, and is well situated for a midway station: but in the summer months it is very difficult to get out of it; it has no fresh water, and a very noxious unhealthy air. There is said to be the same difficulty in getting out of the Bay of Suda, in the island of Candia, from the constant summer winds blowing from the ordinary disbursements during the five years in which he held the command in the Mediterranean, amounted only to 54, in which were included the expense of a mission to Morocco on the subject of the horses mentioned above, the postage of letters, c. 8cc.

north; and I doubt the Candians allowing a garrison to live in peace amongst them. At Paros, Scio, M tilene, and Tenedos, are good anchorages; but Paros has the same difficulty of egress that Milo has. Scio and Mytilene are too populous to have any security by a small garrison. Tenedos is laid waste, but, as a station for a squadron, is good, because, lying in the way to Constantinople, it must always be a place of great resort. In the view I have of their utility, more advantage would be derived from them in the state in which they are, than if any of them were garrisoned. A small garrison could not protect itself in any of the large islands, and would exhaust the produce of the small ones. While at peace with the Turks, it does not seem necessary; and in a state of war, it would require a squadron to protect it. The Russians had a good castle at Tenedos; but when the Turkish fleet came out, Admiral Siniavin discovered that he must either continue in the road to protect his garrison, or by going to sea, subject it to capture; and he took the first opportunity to withdraw his men, and blow up the fort. From these considerations, I cannot but be of opinion, that more ad-vol. n. o vantage may result from their remaining under the Government of the Greeks. We have had a free intercourse with them during the war, and should be still better received in peace; and this opinion I have given to Mr. Adair.

I have already informed your Lordship that the Spanish army, under the command of General Castafios, had, after two or three days' partial action, obliged that of Dupont to surrender as prisoners of war on the 20th. I understand it happened just at this time that the French General Bedel arrived, with 5000 men, to reinforce the French; and finding his friends had surrendered, and were prisoners, he entered into a treaty, and was admitted to a capitulation, the terms of which I understand to be, that they surrender their arms until they arrive at the ports of this neighbourhood, as St. Lucar, St. Mary, and Cadiz, where they are to be embarked in Spanish vessels, and, at the expense of Spain, be sent to Rochefort.

This capitulation will doubtless appear to your Lordship an extraordinary one to be granted to 5000 men by an army of 30,000, to engage to send them to France in ships which they knew they had not, and allow them to take with them their arms, which Spain so much wants. The first report that came to me was, that they were to march to Cadiz with their arms, and embark there; on which I wrote a note to General Morla. It is certainly an improvident agreement at last, and the longer they are performing it the better. When the French, by the surrender of Dupont, were reduced to a number not capable of doing harm, those which remained could not possibly have changed their position more advantageously for them than to Rochefort, from whence they may go to Biscay in a week. I have not seen the capitulation, nor have I heard that there are any conditions in it, either for the troops under the Marquess de Romana in the north, or those who were disarmed in Portugal, and are in prison there.

From the Supreme Junta I received a letter containing the two letters from General Castaiios and the Count de Tilli. This latter nobleman is one of the Junta. Castafios's letter is addressed to the " Su-" preme Junta of Government," as they have been hitherto styled. Count de Tilli styles them " the Junta of Spain and of the " Indies." I just remark this to your Lord- ship, because much has been said on the subject of the Supreme Council of Spain.

TO LADY COLLINGWOOD.

Ocean, off Cadiz, July 28, 1808.

I have just received your letter of the 25th June, out of the sea; for the Pickle Schooner, which brought it out with all the public despatches, ran on a reef of rocks in the night, and is entirely lost. The despatches, being on weighty subjects, I am afraid are all lost; your lighter letter was saved from the wreck with some others, and gave me the happiness of hearing that you were well. The Spaniards have been in great spirits since their victory; but they have rather marred the business by allowing the French to capitulate. I shall mend it for them as much as I can.

I am sorry to find my picture was not an agreeable surprise: I did not say any thing to you about it, because I would always guard you as much as I could against disappointment; but you see, with all my care, I sometimes fail. The painter was reckoned the most eminent in Sicily; but you expected to find me a smooth-skinned, clear-complexioned gentleman, such as I was when I left home, dressed in the newest taste, and like the fine people who live gay lives ashore. Alas! it is far otherwise witli me. The painter was thought to have flattered me much: that lump under my chin was but the loose skin, from which the flesh has shrunk away; the redness of my face was not, I assure you, the effect of wine, but of burning suns and boisterous winds; and my eyes, which were once dark and bright, are now faded and dim. The painter represented me as I am; not as I once was. It is time and toil that have worked the change, and not his want of skill. That the countenance is stern, will not be wondered at, when it is considered how many sad and anxious hours and how many heartaches I have. I shall be very glad when the war is over. If the other nations of Europe had resisted the French as the Spaniards have done, governments would not have been overturned nor countries despoiled. But Spain has had many favourable circumstances; they got rid of a weak court and licentious nobility. The invisible power that directs the present Government is the priesthood; the people are their instruments, whom they raise to an enthusiasm that makes them irresistible. Buonaparte has not merely the Spanish army to combat, (indeed the best of them are prisoners either in the north or at Lisbon,) but it is the Spanish nation which is opposed to him. Every peasant is a soldier, every hill a fortress. As soon as I have settled affairs here, which will be as soon as the supplies come from England, I shall proceed up the Mediterranean again, where I have much to do in many points. I hope I am working them pretty well at this moment, and that my ships are actively employed.

writes to me that her son's want of spirits is owing to the loss of his time when he was in England, which is a subject that need give her no concern, for if he takes no more pains in his profession than he has done, he will not be qualified for a lieutenant in sixteen years, and I should be very sorry to put the safety of a ship and the lives of the men into such hands. He is of no more use here as an officer than Bounce is, and not near so entertaining. She writes as if she expected that he is to be a lieutenant as soon as he has served six years, but that is a mistaken fancy; and the loss of his time is while he is at sea, not while he is on shore. He is living on the navy, and not serving in it. too is applying to go home. If he goes he may stay; for I have no notion of people making the service a mere convenience for themselves, as if it vere a public establishment for loungers.

TO VISCOUNT CASTLEREAGH.

Ocean, off Cadiz, July 29, 1808. Without any observations of my own, I beg to mention to your Lordship the substance of a curious conversation which, as I know, passed between the General Castaños and Conde de Tilli, when, after the capitulations of the French, they discoursed on the future operations of the army.

The General advised that they should immediately advance towards Madrid, and, joining or co-operating with the troops of Gallicia, which he expected to find there, get possession of the Capital, when he should propose to the other Captains-General of Provinces to assemble the Cortes by deputies from the several Juntas, and form a Council of Government for Spain. In this project he was opposed by Conde de Tilli, who asked him, what then would become of us? meaning himself and Castanos; and on his part proposed that their care should be Andalusia and Portugal, and that, leaving the Spaniards beyond the Sierra Morena to take care of themselves, they should not embarrass themselves with Cortes or Princes.

It is, perhaps, in this view of future events, (which is supposed not to be peculiar to Conde de Tilli,) that the army is not moving to the north.

My letter of the 24th informed your Lordship of the capitulation of the French army. At that time I understood it to be Dupont's division only which was to be carried to France; but it now appears that all the French, amounting to about 16,000 men, are to go. Bedel's division keep their arms. I enclose to your Lordship a copy of the capitulation, which is in its nature, and from all I have heard of it, so extraordinary, that I cannot divest myself of the idea of a French trick, and that more is meant than yet appears.

The division of Dupont, 6 or 8000 men, were in circumstances in which they had no resource but an unconditional surrender. While this was discussing. Bedel, who was in the rear of all on the road to Madrid, with between 8 and 9000 men, sent an aid-de-camp to desire that he might be included in the treaty; but his situation altered the terms of it, and lengthened the discussion. He, in the meantime, under cover of the night, seized on a Spanish regiment, and retired several miles, where the Spaniards had little prospect of coming up with him. In this state of affairs the treaty was concluded, by which not only his division, but that of Dupont also, is to be conveyed to France. The French General knew as well as the Spanish that they had not the means of sending them by sea; and I think the probability is, that, having other views, they did not wish the treaty to be executed.

This treaty has caused much agitation. I understand, from the English Officer who resides at Seville, that the Junta disapprove of it entirely, although they do not think it proper to make such a declaration, and the people, thinking it impracticable, take little notice of it yet.

On application to me for assistance to enable them to perform this service, I have told them that all aid shall be given to fitting their transport ships out for their service; but as the conveying so large a body of troops, with their arms, is a measure which may have in the end such important consequences, I cannot allow them to pass on the sea until I receive instructions from His Majesty's Ministers. This objection seems to give satisfaction, as it puts a stop to their going, without any breach of treaty on the part of the Spaniards. I have, moreover, observed that, as they have not the means of sending these people to Rochefort, the obligation ceases; for an engagement to do that which is impossible dissolves itself.

It was proposed that the Spanish army should go to Madrid; but that is deferred for the present, as it is found that they still want much arrangement with respect to their necessary equipage. In particular, canteens are wanting; for it seems when they were removed from the river they had not water to drink, which caused great distress.

FROM GENERAL MORLA.

Cadiz, August 1, 1808.

I have received the enclosed despatch from the Supreme Junta of Seville, respecting the letter which your Excellency was pleased to write to me; and your Excellency will see that the Supreme Junta is, like myself, animated with sentiments of hope and confidence in the British nation, and of admiration and gratitude to your Excellency.

FROM THE
SUPREME COUNCIL OF SEVILLE
GENERAL MORLA.

Royal Palace of Alcazar, July 27, 1808.

This Supreme Council has read, with the utmost attention, your letter of the 4th, the copy of that addressed to your Excellency by Lord Collingwood, dated on the 2d, and your Excellency's answer to it. Nothing has astonished them, as they foresaw the result, and expected no less from the generosity of the English nation, from her affection to Spain, and from the talents and penetration of the English Admiral, which they have seen displayed in the capacity with which he comprehends all our interests, and the foresight by which he would avert every danger. No Spaniard could have pleaded the interests of Spain with a warmer zeal than Lord Collingwood has done. Our gratitude to him will be eternal; and we wish his Excellency and the whole of the English nation to be persuaded of this truth.

To come to the points in question. Your Excellency, in yours of the 4th, has explained almost all our ideas, and the causes and necessities on which they are founded, and we will do no more than express them with more extension, and manifest to Lord Collingwood and Major-Ge-neral Spencer our actual situationwhat we conceive essential and in unison with the Spanish constitution and what we so ardently desire. The first of all is our existence! The weakness of the late Government, and the horrible cunning of Napoleon, appear at first to have completed the ruin of Spain. The nation, notwithstanding, believes that she can and should exist, and for that purpose has made efforts more than she thought herself capable of Spain is worthy of compassion, and deserves the assistance of all other nations, but particularly of the generous and the friends of humanity.

All the provinces of Spain have engaged in the struggle the French have suffered defeats, but are disciplinedthey are formed into armiestheir Generals are renowned and a doubt of the result, and precautions against a reverse of fortune, are, therefore, not only prudent, but necessary. The An-dalusians, whose geographical situation, and other causes, place them in the first rank, exact an incessant attention to this point, and it is our duty to pay it. Into this province entered the army of General Du-pont, and the squadron of the enemy. We have made the latter surrender, and at the same moment we flew to meet the land forces of the French. But the expenses are immense. The provinces were drained by the former Government. Is it not a kind of miracle that we have hitherto procured the necessary funds for ourselves, without extending our aid to Portugal, Estremadura, and several other points which demand our attention? Alas! these expenses continue, and the entire existence of the nation, which is our first care, becomes endangered. For this we have implored subsidies from the English nation, and we expect them with confidence: the least detention may occasion us irreparable evil. We may die, it is true, with glory, and we will sacrifice ourselves for our Country; but when this sacrifice shall be consummated, what honour can result from it to the British nation, or to any other on earth? What advantages can be derived from Spain, destroyed by French barbarity and ambition? It is, therefore, our first interest, and we will be bold enough to say it is likewise the first interest of the English nation, to avert the destruction of Spain. It is their interest that their General and the Governor of Gibraltar should anticipate our wants as far as their situation empowers them, and co-operate with us in the first, the most important, and the most sacred of all necessities, one which cannot but be evident to English penetration and policy, the support of our hope in this our hard and exhausted state.

Your Excellency is acquainted with all this, and for that reason proposed to us to disarm the squadron, to which we consented with much grief. The misfortunes suffered by our navy demand a contrary measure; the whole monarchy and its colonies require an armada. In the present circumstances, the communication of some provinces with others, the assistance which they should mutually lend, and the preservation of the Americas, render the maintenance of one indispensable. To oppose it to the naval forces of France is also necessary. Hitherto the English nation hath fulfilled this last object with a glory of which there is no example: we know she will continue it; but Spain cannot, and should not, forget the particular interests that force her to cooperate in the same object as far as she can.

We breathed, therefore, when we observed the same ideas in the letter of Lord Collingwood, and the unexampled generosity with which the English nation offers to realise them, admitting, at the same time, that these expenses will not, in the least degree, diminish the subsidies which we have demanded, and which are necessary to our existence. Arm, then, our squadrons, Spanish as well as the French which have surrendered: let the arsenal of Gibraltar provide the necessary equipments, and transfer them to our arsenal in this island, where we have artificers in abundance. Let our ships be navigated by Spanish officers and crews; above all, let them be equipped immediately, and during the existence of the present circumstances. England will have the incomparable glory (one, perhaps, hi- therto unknown in the world) of seeing a Spanish squadron on the seas at her expense. Europe will be filled with admiration, and France with terror, at this spectacle.

On the use of this force no doubt should exist between the English and Spaniards. If the naval forces of France shall render the union of our squadron, or of part of it, with the English necessary, our interest alone will be sufficient to induce this junction. If it shall not be necessary, the English nation will see that our policy demands the application of this force to the immense extent of our Americas, and to the preservation and defence of our European provinces. It will be always employed in the common cause; and we may flatter ourselves, that the English nation will do us the justice of being persuaded that we are no less ardent in sustaining that cause than we are in soliciting this aid.

We have manifested our thoughts to your Excellency, who will communicate them to Lord Collingwood, and we have no doubt but they will produce the correspondent effect. God preserve your Excellency many years.

FRANCISCO DI SAAVEDRA, c.

Joanniita, August 2, 1808.

Your great judgment and profound knowledge of our affairs make me hope that you will not imagine that what has heen done by Mustapha Pacha is agreeable to the will of the nation, or of its principal members. Among the rest, Ismael, Bey of Sarras, who thinks as I do, will set off in a few days, at the head of a strong force, to Adrianople, for the purpose of being present at what may take place. Many events will happen, and much blood be spilt, before the management of affairs will be left to Mustapha Pacha, who has been instigated to commit these acts by the insidious arts of our enemy. It is true that he at present holds the seals, but it is only by violence, and I make no doubt that affairs will soon assume a more pleasing aspect. For this reason it is necessary that there should be in my neighbourhood a sufficient naval force, of which the senior officer should receive full powers to concert and co-operate with me in all that is necessary. Your Excellency is well aware that mankind at present seem unhappily urged on by the desire to subvert

VOL. II. p and desolate. I have proposed to your Government to provide against such disposition and its necessary effects; but it is beyond my ability alone, and I cannot counteract them unless support be afforded me. Your Government, which makes daily so many sacrifices, and sends, as we hear, ships and money to the Baltic, should not be disheartened. If it could do the same in this quarter, it would be served better than it may expect, and an opportunity would be afforded me of demonstrating with honour my anxious zeal and inclination towards it. Whatever may be the event of affairs in the capital, it is evident that I shall be the object of persecution; and as I have dedicated myself entirely to your nation, I hope that it will feel a pride in protecting me, and assisting me in such a manner as may enable me to defend my person and property, and accomplish those services which I feel the greatest inclination to render.

LIEUT.-GEN. SIR HEW DALRYMPLE.

Ocean, off Cadiz, August 2, 1808. With respect to the conspiracy of Ali Beck, it is, like other conspiracies, a very dark business. It is, moreover, an old affair, for the letter of the Prince of the Peace is written in 1805, and I wondered that the Junta should take the subject into their consideration at all, as it did not involve the security of Spain, and that appears to me at present to require all their time and all their wisdom. I am always doubtful of my judgment when it differs from yours; but I cannot think that any good would be derived from discovering to the Emperor that such a conspiracy had existed. There might be injustice in doing so; for this Ali Beck may have been instigated to rebellion by the Spanish Court, and they could not impeach him without betraying their own treachery. As to obtaining the Emperor's favour by such discovery, I believe that it is too wavering and dependent on immediate occurrences to be fixed by the relation of a danger so long past. Besides, I do not think it likely that the Spaniards would gain much favour from him by the confession of a conspiracy in which their nation had taken, or were disposed to take, an active part.

The victory of General Castanos has caused, for the moment, great joy; but I cannot say that I see it in a view that makes it appear the subject of much exultation. It seems to be a departure from the principle on which a war like this should be carried on. No treaty should be made with an invader short of his unconditional surrender. They have made an arrangement which they cannot perform, and which, if they could, would be attended with the worst consequences to Spain. From all the information which I have of the subject, I consider it to be quite a French trick, and that they have obtained by art what they never could have won by the sword. Dupont was always said to have 12 or 14,000 men: in the capitulation, his division is found to be no more than 8000. Four thousand were said to be the reinforcement, and they turn out to be 6 or 7000. Is it not probable that part of Dupont's force went over to Bedel, that by this plan they might keep their arms? They probably knew then what is known to the Spaniards now, that there was no retreat for them upon Madrid. Had Dupont been compelled to surrender without terms, they could have been confined in twenty-four hours; and the Spanish army would have been at liberty to pursue their service. What is the case now? They have got the French army, who are entitled to their arms when they embark, and the Spanish army must stay to take care of them. But their embarking is altogether out of the question: one objection is, that they have not ships to put them in; another, that the people will not permit them to embark; and a third, as I have informed the Governor, that I cannot permit so great a body of troops to pass on the sea until I receive instructions from England for that purpose. But the first objection is of such weight, that, if there were no other, matters must remain as they are.

TO VISCOUNT CASTLEREAGH.

Ocean, off Cadiz, August Q, 1808.

I am very happy that His Majesty has been graciously pleased to approve my conduct in the several transactions which have occurred here. I have done all in my power to establish confidence in the Spaniards, and to give them every proof of the disinterested part which His Majesty takes in their affairs; and I believe they are perfectly assured that the British Government has no view but that of re-establishing them in their independence, nor looks to other advantages than such as will ultimately result from an alliance with a powerful nation. When I had doubts of the piinciples of certain persons in their Government, although it was proper that I should communicate them to your Lordship, there was nothing in my conduct that indicated the existence of such opinions.

I hope the supply of arms will be sent direct to Valencia and Catalonia, for their wants are urgent; and the security of Spain depends more upon Catalonia, from its geographical position, than upon any other province.

When the Moors would not allow horses to be supplied to Spain, I endeavoured to obtain mules, the sale of which is not restricted by their religion; but the Emperor, disappointed in his hopes of getting Ceuta, will not allow them to have any thing; and as the French become further removed from him, he is less disposed to be gracious.

August 12, 1808. MY DEAREST LITTLE SARAH,

Mrs. sent me lately some little observations which she had made on you and your dear sister, which gave me so much pleasure that I could not but return her my best thanks. Indeed every body speaks well of you, and I believe them, because you have yourselves promised me to be diligent, and I know you have too strict a regard to truth, and are too observant of your engagements, to be drawn from them by trifles.

When I come home, you and your sister must read a great deal to me, and as much of my reading is French, I hope you will be perfect in that language. As for the Spanish, it is very easy, and you will learn it in a very short time. My eyes are so old and so weak that you will have a great deal to do for me. I went on shore at Cadiz a few days ago, and you cannot conceive how rejoiced the people were to see me. I was received with all military honours; but, besides this, all the inhabitants, at least forty thousand men and women, came to welcome me. I would gladly have staid longer with them, but I could not, as I had to return to my ship at night. I went, however, to visit Madame Apodaca, whose husband is an Admiral, and one of the Deputies from the Supreme Junta of Seville to England, where they are gone to beg our Government will assist them in their war against the French. She is a genteel woman, about 35, which is reckoned tolerably old here, and has two very fine girls, her daughters. I wished much to visit some other ladies, to whom I am in debt for civilities, but my time would not permit. Tell dear Mary that I pray to God to bless her; and as I believe she is very good, I have no doubt that he will, and bless you too, my darling. Poor Bounce is growing very old. I once thought of having his picture taken, but he had the good fortune to escape that.

TO VISCOUNT CASTLEREAGH.

Ocean, off Cadiz, August 14, 1808.

I received a letter from Sir Hew Dalrymple yesterday, to inform me that the Duke of Orleans, with Prince Leopold of Sicily, and a numerous suite, had arrived at Gibraltar, in His Majesty's ship the Thun- derer, from Palermo. Their business, it appears, is to make some proposal to the Junta of Seville on the subject of a Regency. I was a good deal concerned at this intelligence, after my assurance to all the Juntas that the assistance which His Majesty had ordered to be given was purely to enable them to maintain the integrity and independence of Spain, and was unmixed with conditions affecting the Government; and I feared that the people would suspect that, under the guise of disinterested aid, we were introducing Princes to them for purposes distinct from our professions. I therefore wrote to the President of the Supreme Junta at Seville, and to the Governor-General of the Province, to announce to them that the arrival of those Princes at Gibraltar was entirely unexpected by the Governor and myself, and requested to be informed if their appearance in this quarter was in consequence of any correspondence which the Junta has had with the Court of Palermo. This I thought necessary to remove any suspicion of intrigue from the British Government. In the evening I learned that the Duke of Orleans was to proceed to England in the Thunderer, and that the

Prince of Sicily, with his suite, had landed at Gibraltar, until a ship should be appointed to convey His Royal Highness to Palermo again; but as I understand that Mr. St. Clair and others who formed the Queen's Councils in Sicily are the persons who composed His Royal Highness's retinue, I am not without apprehension that they will, from Gibraltar, make proposals to the Junta at Seville. If any inclination be shewn to accede to their proposals, it may produce discussions not favourable to the common cause with the other Juntas, whose sincere attachment to this is problematical.

I have this moment received a letter from General Morla, in reply to mine of yesterday, on the subject of the Princes. Captain Legge, who was charged with the delivery of my letter to the Governor, informs me that he appeared exceedingly embarrassed by their arrival, that he could not understand how they could be brought thither in an English ship of war without the privity of the Court of London, and that if they come to Cadiz, he will not allow them to land until he receives the instructions of the Junta. Mr. Drummond will no doubt explain to your Lordship the views of the Court of Palermo in sending this Prince to Gibraltar.

General Dupont and some French officers were brought to Port St. Mary's yesterday, for the purpose of embarking in one of the ships of war for their security. The mob attacked them, and took from them their baggage, in which was church plate and other valuable plunder. General Dupont was wounded in the head, and at last got off to a Spanish ship. I mention this circumstance to your Lordship, as it shews the intention of the people to pay no regard to the capitulation, but to oppose its execution, if the French troops are brought near the sea.

A number of Spanish vessels are said to have sailed from ports in the Bay, with despatches from Joseph Buonaparte to the different colonies. The colours they sail under are Spanish, in which an eagle is substituted for the lion quartered in them.

TO THE MARQUESS DI CIRCELLO.

Ocean, off Cadiz, August 15, 1808.

I have received the honour of your letter, and your Excellency may trust, that in all things which relate to Prince

Leopold's convenience and comfort, my inclination, as well as my duty, will lead me to be strictly attentive; and in the event of His Royal Highness passing into Spain, what His Majesty has desired shall be done, and a ship appointed to attend him. I am well satisfied, my Lord Marquess, that the King, my master, will approve of every step which may advance the interests or add to the convenience of any branch of the Royal Family of the two Sicilies.

His Royal Highness the Duke of Orleans, whom I have had the pleasure of seeing, informed me of the purpose for which Prince Leopold had taken this voyage, and His Highness was so well satisfied that, in the present state of affairs in Spain, there neither exists a power to which Prince Leopold can address himself, nor which can, with any advantage to the future settlement of the Government, address the Prince, that His Highness has proceeded to England to confer with His Majesty's Ministers. It has been a principle observed by the British Government, and the orders given to their officers are founded upon it, that every possible aid be given to the loyal Spaniards in the glorious contest in which they are engaged with the invaders of their Country. Men, money, arms, whatever succour they may want, and Britain can produce, are offered to them. It is given with a free and liberal hand, that they may be enabled to establish their King and maintain their independence; but whatever has the appearance of interfering with their Government, or the temporary modes of administration which circumstances may make it necessary to adopt, has been strictly avoided.

Your Excellency knows that there is not in Spain any supreme head which has authority over the kingdom at large, the provinces having hitherto been governed by the Supreme Juntas. It is proposed that a General Council shall be formed, to have authority over the whole; but until such Council be established, it is difficult to determine where a foreign power should address itself as to the organ of the Spanish nation. I am not a politician. Your Excellency may well believe that the habits of my profession unfit me for studies so abstruse; but I think your Excellency will perceive all the consequences that must be the effect of proposals to any body of men having merely a local authority.

I have swerved from the subject which I proposed for my letter. It was merely to assure you, Sir, of the careful regard which I shall pay to every thing that is connected with the interests or happiness of the Prince, and of the pleasure which I shall always have in complying with His Majesty's commands.

A very great number of letters were at this time addressed to Lord Collingwood from Spaniards of all classes. Among them was one from Don Pedro Ripolle, the Curate of Beniva, in Valencia, in which he descanted at much length on the legality of the Spanish resistance to Joseph Buonaparte, and supported his arguments by various extracts from the works of Grotius and Vattel. The following is Lord Collingwood's answer.

TO DON PEDRO RIPOLLE.

August 14, 1808.

The right of making war belongs only, it is true, to the Sovereign; but if, by taking the Spanish Princes out of the country, Buonaparte thought that he had dissolved the only power which could lawfully oppose him, he was mistaken; for on the removal of the Princes, the sovereign power reverted to the source from which it sprungthe people; and the act of their delegates is legitimate sovereignty. The justice and necessity of the war in which Spain is engaged with the French are so obvious, that there can be no need of referring to the opinions of learned civilians for its support. When the rights of a nation are threatened, and its territory insidiously invaded by an army professing friendship, but pursuing a conduct which manifests a design to seize upon the Government, it becomes the imperious duty of the Sovereign to resist by arms. But when the Prince himself, who is the organ of the nation's sovereignty, is seized, and induced, while in captivity, to sign renunciations and abdications, it would be ridiculous to suppose that such instruments could have any validity. Your King was under circumstances in which he could not exercise a free will; but even if it had been otherwise, the case with respect to Spain would not have been altered. The Prince may retire from the Government, but no public law or constitution in Europe an give him the right to transfer the people to another Sovereign; for they are not his property, but he was their King. He was the King of the Spanish nation; and when he is removed from them by fraud, his authority can only devolve to a Council of State, which shall represent the nation at large, and have a sovereign power over all its members. The Junta of a province, though of the first necessity for the immediate defence of such province, and for preventing that anarchy which must arise in the absence of all Government, can, as I conceive, be considered as a legitimate authority for no longer a time than is necessary for the assembling of a General Council. For one part of Spain to make laws and regulations for the rest, which is not subject to it, and over which it has no control, would be as absolute a dissolution of the Government as the enemy could cause by any partial conquest which he may achieve.

Spain is a monarchy in which hereditary succession is established; and if the King and the Princes next in succession to the throne be in captivity and unable to govern, that is no reason for change in the form of Government for a longer time than is necessary to call to the Regency the Prince who shall be chosen, or is next in succession to the captives. The nation is only in the state in which it would be during infancy or other incapacity of the Sovereign. It becomes a great nation to restore, without delay, the form and spirit of its Government. When they have such an enemy to contend with, it is necessary that the unity of the State, which constitutes its strength, should be as little interrupted as possible: it is necessary for its communication with Foreign Powers; and it is, above all things, necessary for the direction and concert of its own forces, which can never act in co-operation but when the whole is directed by one power.

TO LORD RADSTOCK.

Ocean, off Cadiz, August 15, 1808.

I am much obliged to you for your kind and friendly letter, and for the true interest which you take in my affairs. No person can devote himself more to them than I have done, and do. The power that God has given me I exercise to the utmost: for that I am accountable, beyond that I am not. When I look back, I have nothing for which to reprove myself: but it is a matter of curiosity to observe how much

VOL. II. Q things depend upon what we call chance. The Standard arrived at Syracuse on the very evening that we sailed in the morning; or, instead of going off to Maritimo, I should probably have gone to Corfu with my few ships. I am here engaged in a service of great delicacy and very high importance. The Spanish people are making the most glorious efforts to expel the enemy from their country; but I am afraid their Juntas, by their cabals and contentions for superiority, will cause an anarchy that will be more dangerous to their country than the French. There is no combination of their force, and the Provincial Governments appear to me to keep as much aloof from each other as possible, lest they should be thought to concede any part of their authority. The Junta of Seville assumed powers and titles that gave great offence to the others, and caused dangerous discussions; but they seem now to have retracted them. To the eastward, they are in great want of cannon. Here is their foundery, and they have the most abundant store; yet they will not send them any. I have told them a ship of war shall carry the guns, and the Governor replies, that they are an ingenious people, and have abundance of resources. In a word, there never was a nation more disjointed, and I consider its safety as very doubtful. If they do not constitute one sole Government, which will combine the powers of the Country, it will be lost. These subjects, and my cares for them, are wearing me to death; but much that I see in the world reconciles me to its approach, whenever it shall please God. If men were honest and just, all difficulties would be overcome; but of those very people who are conducting the defence of their country, one scarcely knows whom to trust. I am anxious to go up aloft again, where I hope something good may offer. I expect we are doing something in Italy; but there is no stuff to work upon there, the people are licentious, the nobles unprincipled, and all without those qualities that can give them importance in any circumstances of difficulty or danger. It is a superior army alone that can effect any change, or maintain it. Dupont has at last got a safe retreat in St. Sebastian light-house, or the fort near it. So enraged are the populace against the French, that they could only be removed into the town during the night.

Ocean, of Cadiz, August 15, 1808.

I have received your letter on my portrait; but I think, when you see the original poor creature, you will be reconciled to the picture. I have laboured past my strength. I have told Lord Mulgrave so, and I hope they will think of relieving me, that I may come and enjoy the comforts of my own blessed family again, and get out of the bustle of the world and of affairs which are too weighty for me. God bless me! how rejoiced will my poor heart be when I see you all again. Last week I went ashore to Cadiz, and was received with great acclamations. The volunteers, who are gentlemen of the city, were turned out to receive me, and all the officers of the district were assembled. The cavalry cleared the streets for us to pass through. About 40,000 people assembled to welcome me, and the whole city resounded with the cry of " Viva King " George!" " Viva Collingwood!" I was much pressed to stay on shore; but when people have a great deal to do, short visits are more suitable than long ones. After a visit of three hours, and a collation at the Governor's, I returned to my ship.

I have another great puzzle come to me. The Queen of Sicily has sent her son, Prince Leopold, to Gibraltar, to propose himself to be Regent of Spain. It appears to me to be extreme want of knowledge of the state of Spain. If it had not been a Queen that did it, I should have called it folly; but as Sidi Mahomet Slowey, when telling me in his letter what the Emperor had determined to do, says, "You know Emperors and Kings " are a great deal wiser than other people," I suppose the rule applies equally well to Queens. The Duke of Orleans came down with him; and the day before yesterday I discussed the subject fully with His Highness, much to his satisfaction, and he went off to England with a light heart.

The Duke professed to be much taken with me, though I had to argue against his object, and to put him from his purpose. He said, when we parted, that he should never forget the day that made him acquainted with me. The service is become very arduous. I cannot tell you all about it in a letter; but some long winter's evening I will give you the whole history.

Ocean, off Cadiz, August 16, 1808.

General Castanos meant himself to go to Madrid, where he hoped to meet Cuesta and the General of the Valencian army, and with them settle some plan of general operation, which becomes hourly more necessary. I hope they will also propose some General Government for the Country; without it, anarchy and dissension must inevitably take place.

I am informed, that after the capitulation of the French on the 20th ult., on some assumption of power by the Junta of Seville, that of Grenada refused to acknowledge their authority; and on its being debated in what manner those of Seville should assert their right of supremacy, it was determined, by a majority, that the army of Andalusia should be sent to reduce them to obedience.

General Castanos, who was present at the debate (though he was not a member of the Junta), came forward and declared, "That " he had heard with grief and astonishment " their debate and resolve. He observed, " that he commanded the army they alluded " to, and begged to set them right in one

"point, that it was not the army of Anda-" lusia, but part of the military force of " Spain, assembled for the purpose of ex-" pelling the invaders from their country; and while he commanded it, it should not " be employed against the loyal subjects of " the King, or for carrying on a civil war " of one province against another." Before this circumstance, it was stated currently that the army of Andalusia was not to pass the mountains. Since, in a letter which I have received from the President, the Junta is called " the Supreme Junta of " Government," Spain and the Indies being left out.

TO THE SAME.

Ocean, off Cadiz, August 16, 1808.

I have just received a letter from Don Francisco de Saavedra, the President of the Supreme Junta of Seville, to inform me that they knew nothing of the coming of Prince Leopold to this quarter until the letters from Gibraltar mentioned his arrival.

I am not informed of what His Royal Highness proposes, whether it be to remain at Gibraltar and wait the answers to the letters which he may have sent to England, or to return to Sicily; but I am quite assured that his presence at Gibraltar will not promote their views. They left Palermo without any knowledge of the state of Spain; for several of the nobles who attend His Royal Highness are French, and there is no Government here which can give protection to any Frenchman from the insult of the populace.

When the Duke of Orleans came here on Sunday, in the Thunderer, I waited on him. His Highness expressed a great desire to stay here, with a view of giving his support to the claims of the Prince Leopold, whatever they were; but I informed him, that my orders from His Majesty's Ministers were to give every assistance to the Spanish people to defend their country and maintain their independence as a nation; that there were no stipulations respecting their Government, or the mode in which they might conduct their aifairs, which were left entirely to their own wisdom and energy; that I understood that the Junta had no correspondence with any other nation than England; and that His Royal Highness would perceive the impossibility of any propositions going to Spain from the ships or from the garrison, until it was directed by His Majesty's Government. I observed to His Royal Highness that, had the case been otherwise, and had His Majesty sanctioned the measures proposed, there did not appear to me to be any power in Spain at this moment to which Prince Leopold could address himself. Would he make his proposals to a Provincial Junta? The proceedings of a particular Junta might not be approved by the rest, and thence discussions would arise to the prejudice of the cause which he meant to support. If His Royal Highness addressed the people at large, he opposed the constituted authorities. And even had there been one sole Council of Spain, the acknowledged organ of the nation, I presumed to give His Royal Highness my opinion, that any proposal which His Sicilian Majesty had to make to Spain in behalf of himself and his rights, would have gone to such Council with more importance and more dignity from his Court at Palermo than by the mode which they have taken. This reasoning seemed to satisfy the Duke that nothing could be done at this moment; and he resolved to return to England, and refer himself to His Majesty's Ministers on the subject.

I enclose to your Lordship a letter which I have received from the Dey of Algiers, complaining of the conduct of the Malta privateers in not respecting his flag and passports. It is to indemnify himself for his losses that he is sending his cruisers to the Coast of Sicily. Their success has encouraged the Emperor of Morocco to send his ships, which have lately been fitted, to the same quarter; so that these subjects of contention beget evils which are likely to be very injurious to Sicily, and to keep us in continual discussion or explanation with the States of Africa. I have observed nothing in the conduct of the Dey but what is temperate, and indicating a desire to preserve harmony; and I think it would be advantageous to the general interests, if the same disposition were more manifest in the Admiralty Court at Malta.

FROM VISCOUNT CASTLEREAGH.

Downing Street, August 19, 1808

Your Lordship's several despatches have been received and laid before the King. I am to convey to your Lordship His Majesty's entire approbation of your Lordship's remarks upon the communication made by the Junta of Seville of the designs of the Prince of Peace against Morocco of the sentiments you have expressed to Sir John Stuart of your instructions to Rear-Admiral Thornborough and of your decision respecting the loan of 20,000. which you have advanced to the Spanish Government.

The peculiar circumstances of Spain, under a change of affairs so total and so unexpected, have naturally produced events of the most important as well as curious nature. I am, therefore, to express the satisfaction which His Majesty's Ministers feel from your descending to minute particulars and anecdotes, which throw much light upon the state of the public mind, and give great assistance to His Majesty's Government in forming their opinions; and I trust that your Lordship will not discontinue communications of so interesting a nature.

TO VISCOUNT CASTLEREAGH.

Ocean, of Cadiz, Aug. 21, 1808. I had yesterday a long conversation with General Morla on the state of affairs in Spain, on which he spoke his sentiments very freely, and convinced me that his opinion of the condition of the country, and of the persons who conduct the government in this part of it, nearly corresponds with what I had before heard, and communicated to your Lordship.

He observed, that the Juntas were found to be totally unequal to the government; that they were men, for the most part, unused to public business, and many of them of such a character that, but for circumstances like the present, they could never have been engaged in it; but they had tasted of power, and though every day's experience proved their unfitness, their ambition was gratified, and they resisted any proposal that was likely to put a period to it; that the best hope of the country was in a General Council of the kingdom, which might form a Regency, or some regular administration of all the departments; that at present all vwas anarchy, and that every day threatened contentions which might have disastrous consequences. All the Juntas seemed to confess the necessity of a Council whose authority should embrace the kingdom, and made proposals, and offered plans, for the purpose; yet no progress was made in what was so desirable: and it was his opinion that they never would get any farther in it until England should send a Minister to Spain, who might suggest to them some mode of proceeding by which they could attain what they all professed to desire.

I told him that I heard a Minister had been nominated; but it appeared to me to be a matter of considerable difficulty to determine to what part of Spain, divided as it now was, such Minister could be sent without risking jealousies in the provinces; and this, for aught I knew, might be the reason why none had yet arrived. He admitted the difficulty, yet thought that a Minister might be sent to Spain without being resident with any Junta, but in a town, as at Cadiz, from whence he could communicate with them all. The Spaniards had confidence in His Majesty's friendship towards them, and knew that it was the interest of England that they should prevail against France, and establish their independence of her; and any proposal which was made for this purpose he thought would be well received by the people at large, and might be the means of establishing what he despaired of without such assistance. He quoted what had happened in Leon as a proof of the necessity of speedily getting the better of this provincial independence. The Gallician army had refused to join General Cuesta, and had fallen back towards their own province, which obliged Cuesta to retire from the French. I believe he might have given an instance of difference of opinion in the provinces nearer home, I am at present very anxious to hear from Portugal, before I go up the Mediterranean, which I propose doing immediately, leaving Rear-Admiral Purvis here with a few ships, to cruise off the coast to protect the trade, and prevent the French prisoners from being sent away, until the instructions of His Majesty's Government be received on that head. I have reason to believe that allowing them to depart would make this province very unpopular in Spain, and that my interference to stop them has given universal satisfaction.

The Catalonians have been supplied with such small arms and ammunition as the ships could spare, but they are still in extreme want of those articles. General Morla promised yesterday to send them twelve small field pieces, for which I shall, if possible, fit carriages on board my ship, while on the

Passage up the Mediterranean, and convey them to that province.

TO LADY COLLINGWOOD.

Ocean, off Cadiz, August 25, 1808.

I am not ill, but weak and nervous, and shall think seriously of going home, for the service I am on requires more strength of body and mind than I have left me in my old age; and in future I shall think only of my comforts, and how best I can make every body about me comfortable and happy. I have been several times on shore; and whenever I went was received with a kindness by every body that was quite delightful. On Tuesday last the Governor gave us a most magnificent entertainment. There were not many people, but all of the first rank. I would gladly have had him on board my ship, but I could not go into the port, and it was too far for him to come off. We went to an opera, which, on the occasion, was in gala. Nothing could be more gratifying than our reception there. The audience clapped for a quarter of an hour when we went into the Governor's box, and every mark of attention that was possible was paid to us.

I can only say, on the subject of letter, that in the first place it is entirely a mistake to desire to send their son with me, for mine is the only ship in which no attention is paid to the youths. I have so little time to give to them, that I seldom see any of them, and do not know the names of three midshipmen in the ship. In the next place, he is a great deal too young. He cannot be educated so early for an officer; and there is nobody here to teach him. And thirdly and lastly, I shall go home as soon as I can, and never after have any thing to do with ships. I would recommend them to send him to a good mathematical school, and teach him to be perfect in French and Spanish, or Italian; and if he spend two years in hard study, he will be better qualified at the end than if he came here. If parents were to see how many of their chickens go to ruin by being sent too early abroad, they would not be so anxious about it. God bless you.

TO THE HON. WM. WELLESLEY POLE.

Ocean, August 26, 1808.

I beg to represent to you that I have been for some time past in a very weak state of health, which I believe may be attributed to the long time I have been at sea, with little intermission; and as the service at this time requires all the strength and spirits that can be applied to it, I would beg that you would lay my request before their Lordships, that they will please to relieve me from service for such time as will be necessary to restore my health and strength in England.

I feel great repugnance in making this application to quit my station; but I hope their Lordships will be satisfied that it proceeds from the same sense of public duty which made me formerly desire to serve.

TO THE EARL OF MULGRAVE.

Ocean, August 26, 1808.

As my strength and health are very much impaired, and as I attribute it in some measure to the long time I have been at sea, and to the anxiety of mind which I continually feel for the service, 1 have very reluctantly written to the Admiralty to pray that their Lordships will be pleased to relieve me. But sentiments of public duty demanded this from me, and at every period of my life the public service has been

VOL. II. H paramount to all personal considerations. When I am recalled, it would be a great satisfaction to me if your Lordship would promote one or two of my Lieutenants. They are respectable officers, and will be creditable and useful to the service. Your Lordship knows how little opportunity I have had of serving them: most of them have been with me near three years, and the only one whom I have advanced, Captain Clavell, was made on the death of Captain Secombe.

The affairs of Spain in this quarter being as much composed as they can be until a general Government for the country be formed, I am proceeding up to Toulon, to join the fleet, and see what can be done in Italy, The eastern provinces of Spain require great attention, and all the assistance that can be given them; for the French continue to advance their forces by that entrance, and the Spaniards possess no regular appointed army that can reduce Fi-gueras, and I am afraid they will not have one until they have a Government. We have given them all the arms that can be collected, but they are still much in want.

Admiralty, September 6, 1808.

Your letter of the 2(1 August (which has been long on its way) serves to confirm all the opinions which are entertained here respecting the affairs of Spain. Upon hearing of the nature of the capitulation with Dupont, I thought it expedient to suspend (to such extent as you should think necessary) the recall of ships from the fleet under your command, as well on account of the necessity of having a naval force sufficient to support the principle which you had so justly stated, of the impossibility of suffering so large an armed French force to pass the sea, as to prevent any part of that force going in ships of war which might be detained in a French port, and equipped to act against this Country. The consideration of the exigencies of the service, and the object of economy in the relief and repair of such ships as may require to be sent home with that view, cannot be better provided for than by the full discretionary instructions which the change of circumstances has induced this Board to send out to you.

I read with great uneasiness and regret the concluding part of your letter, in which you express some doubts of the continuance of your health to the end of the war, and I earnestly hope that the service of the Country will not suffer the serious inconvenience of your finding it necessary to suspend the exertion of your zeal and talents. It is a justice which I owe to you and to the Country, to tell you candidly, that I know not how I should be able to supply all that would be lost to the service of the Country, and to the general interests of Europe, by your absence from the Mediterranean. I trust you will not find the necessity, and without it the whole tenour of your conduct is a security that you will not feel the inclination, to quit your command while the interests of your Country can be so essentially promoted by your continuing to hold it.

TO LADY COLLINGWOOD.

Ocean, off Toulon, September 20, 1808.

I am returned to watch the French in this port; but it is impossible to devise or form the smallest judgment of what they will do, or what project they may have in view; so that all 1 can do is to watch them on this stormy coast. Since I have been here, we have only had two days of weather in which boats could pass from ship to ship; and so you may judge with how little effect this service can be done. It is not practicable, but this the people on shore cannot comprehend; and I fear in the perseverance both ships and men will be worn out. I will do what is possible. It would be a great relief to get hold of them before the winter be advanced. I told you I had written to the Admiralty to request that I might come to England, having very much failed in my health, and being fit only at present for a life of quiet. I hope Smith will stay with me when I go on shore, for he is quiet and well educated, and suits me very well. I have not had occasion to find fault with him these four years; indeed never.

I am endeavouring to make commotions in Italy against the French; but the people there are enervated by their licentious manners. They have not the Spanish spirit; indeed in Spain it is more in the common people than in the superior orders.

I wish were on shore. As to his being an officer, it seems entirely out of the question. That would be sporting with men's lives indeed.

THE VIZIER ALI PACHA OF ALBANIA.

Ocean, off Toulon, September 22, 1808. MOST EXCELLENT PACHA, I have, on my arrival off Toulon, received the honour of your Highness's letter of the 6th August, and learned with great concern those melancholy events which have lately taken place at Constantinople, because they seem to indicate a return of the French influence with the party which proceeded to such violent measures measures which can only produce disorder and anarchy, and which are never necessary to the support of legitimate power. That Mustapha Pacha Bairacter should have suffered himself to be seduced by the artifices of the French and Russians, who are the enemies of his Country, is much to be lamented. Whatever views of personal aggrandizement he may have in this act of treachery to his Sovereign and his Country, he will never accomplish them, because the very act shews him to be a man who does not possess a mind informed of the real state of the nations of Europe, or a head capable of foreseeing the result of his own deeds. He should have known that every European state is anxious to give to mankind that peace which ought to subsist among wise nations; that the harmony of the w orld w'as first destroyed by the convulsions which happened in France; and that the restoration of it is prevented by the ambitious projects of one man, who, being unhappily possessed of extraordinary talents, turns them to abuse, and, for the aggrandizement of himself and his family, makes France to groan beneath his tyranny, and would hold all Europe in disgraceful bondage. England has ever had a perfect view of the dire consequences which must result from the establishment of such a power, and has uniformly opposed it. This, too, was the duty of all Sovereigns, for they are the guardians of their people's happiness, and ought to have resisted those whose object was to destroy it. What, then, can Mustapha Pacha and his party propose to themselves by an attachment to France? Would they increase the power of France? France is, unhappily, possessed of power but to abuse it. Do they expect advantages to be obtained for Turkey?

Let them cast their eyes round Europe, and behold the wretchedness of those miserable States which have entertained the fantastical idea that good was to be derived from such a character as the present ruler of the French. Before I received your Highness's letter, detailing these affairs, I suspected, from the frigates sailing from the Dardanelles, that some change had taken place at Constantinople. I had communicated the sentiments of my Government to the Capitan Pacha, who knew our sincere desire for an honourable peace, and I had requested that he would prevent any circumstance which might interrupt it, by keeping his ships within the Dardanelles until the Ministers had concluded the treaty. We did not seek these ships, but they came to seek us. We are at war, and the consequences were inevitable. Mr. Adair, a skilful Minister, a man of wisdom and temperance, is gone to the Dardanelles, with full authority from our Government to treat with the Minister of the Porte, and conclude peace. If the new state of affairs at Constantinople cause any impediment, I shall deeply lament it; but I shall always give to your Highness's friendly sentiments towards England that value which your wisdom and correct judgment of the real interests of our two countries has stamped upon them.

Your Highness will be glad to hear of the reverses which the French have lately met with. It seems to be the beginning of their depression, and holds out some hope that the calamities which they cause will cease. Your Highness is informed of their treachery in Spain how they corrupted the Spanish Ministry, marched her best troops into distant countries, made them instruments for enslaving Austria, Prussia, Denmark, Sweden, and Portugal, and removed them from Spain, which they were born to defend. When they had drained the country of its resources, there was nothing wanting to their perfidy but to seize on the persons of the Princes, and of those nobles on whom the Government seemed to rest. These indignities, these violations of every right, roused the native and inherent spirit of the nation: all Spain arose to assert its independence. They were not discouraged by a numerous French army in the heart of their kingdom, commanded by Buonaparte's veteran Generals, by the absence of their best troops, by finding their arsenals empty, and every munition of war removed or in decay. It was their Country which they were to rescue from the tyranny of a perfidious invader, and their patriotism surmounted every difficulty. It was against oppression and injustice that they struggled, and they found in England a powerful and faithful friend. In every action which they have had with the enemy they have been victorious; and the people, whose occupations had been hitherto in tillage and the arts of peace, became in a short time skilful in war. At Baylen the whole French army was taken. At Saragossa, Valencia, and Ge-rona, to which towns they laid siege for a length of time, they were repulsed at last with the loss of most of their force. The French General Junot kept possession of Portugal until the arrival of the English troops, who fought with him on the 21st of last month, and his whole army surrendered as prisoners. They still hold possession of Barcelona and Figueras, because a sufficient force has not been brought against them; but they are in misery, and content themselves, like other evil spirits, in doing all the mischief they can.

I have given your Highness an account of these transactions, because I believe you will be glad to hear that the progress of a power which has caused so much desolation in the world has met with a check, and because they afford a memorable proof, that whenever the inhabitants will oppose a firm resistance to France, they will insure success. Let not, then, the Sublime Porte be deluded by the French, and their vain boast of invincibility. The integrity and independence of Turkey should depend on itself, not upon a frail alliance with a deceitful nation. The dignity of the Ottomans would be injured, and the splendour of the Sublime Porte tarnished, by a dependence on a power whose injustice has made it the opprobrium of Europe. I pray God to give wisdom to the Turkish Councils, that they may avert so great an evil. Your Highness requests that large ships may be sent to your coasts; but at this moment it cannot be done, because the French have at this port, Toulon, where I now am, a large force ready for sea; but I hope the frigates in your neighbourhood are vigilant and active against the enemy, and that soon your interests and ours will be the same.

Admiralty, September 25, 1808.

I have received with great regret your private letter of the 26th of August, explaining to me the grounds on which your public letter, requesting to be relieved, had been written. I lament to learn that your health and strength have been impaired from the long and uninterrupted exertions by which you have so ably conducted the delicate, difficult, and important duties of your command. Upon a former intimation of the injury which your health had received, I took the liberty of pressing strongly upon your Lordship's consideration the importance which I attach to your continuance in a situation in which, through a variety of great and complicated objects, of difficult and delicate arrangements, of political as well as of professional considerations, your Lordship had in no instance failed to adopt the most judicious and best-concerted measures. Impressed as I was and am with the difficulty of supplying your place, I cannot forbear (which I hope you will excuse) suspending the recall which you have required, till I shall hear again from you, whether, under the diminished difficulties of your command, you are still of opinion that a longer continuance at sea would be injurious to your health, which I should feel it a public, as well as a personal duty, to consult. Should such be your determination, I am not without hopes that the service may yet derive material advantage from the exercise of your Lordship's talents, without any impediment to the restoration of your health, if the eventual proposal which I am about to submit to your Lordship should be consistent with your arrangements, and receive your assent. I have it in contemplation to relieve the officers commanding at the several ports who have been more than three years on that duty; and in making my arrangements, I should consider it as highly advantageous to the service if your Lordship would take the direction at Plymouth, which is, in a great degree, the centre and spring of the most active points of naval operations. I shall await your Lordship's answer, in the hope that I may have the advantages of your able assistance in one or other of the two commands at Plymouth, if the Mediterranean should no longer be consistent with the material considerations of your health.

Upon receiving the names of the Lieutenants whom your Lordship is desirous of promoting, I shall pay attention to your wishes in that respect.

HIS EXCELLENCY ROBERT ADAIR, ESQ.

Ocean, off Toulon, October 2, 1808.

I have received a letter from Lord Mulgrave, informing me that a quantity of artillery, c. will be sent out, to be supplied to Ali Pacha, in the event of his commencing hostilities against the French. I have always encouraged the Pacha of Albania to expect assistance in expelling the French from his territory whenever he declared himself their enemy; and he was last summer most desirous that we should attack St. Maura, and having reduced it, give it to him. Although we were at war with the Porte, I offered him the assistance of ships to act against it, and co-operate with him when he attacked with his army; but he always declined any measure of actual hostility against the French to be committed by himself. By Seid Achmet Effendi, whom he has sent to London, I find he has particularly desired that he should be assisted in reducing Parga. From all the accounts I have of that place, I think that to take it may require more of the art of war than the Vizier's Generals possess. It has a port for small vessels, on the outside of which is deep water, and where ships certainly cannot lie in winter. The cliff is stated to be about as high as Europa Point, at Gibraltar. The town stands upon the acclivity of an easy hill, on the summit of which is an old citadel, but of what strength is probably not much known, though its situation commands the town. The fortresses were in a ruinous state, until the reserve which Ali Pacha has lately observed to the French induced them to strengthen the works by some new batteries towards the sea. This is the best account I can get of Parga; and I think, if he were to bring his forces against it at a season when the ships could anchor near it, it would probably be soon reduced; but one of the greatest obstacles is, the disposition of the inhabitants, who, being Christians, have always shewn an abhorrence to the

Turkish rule. It is of importance to All Pacha to possess it as a sort of frontier town; for I understand that his authority is very ill established between that and De-mitri. He has scarce any control over the people of that coast, nor have his forces ever been able to assert his power, or enforce his laws. He has there but a very nominal superiority, which you know is the case in other parts of Albania, and very common in the Morea.

Lord Mulgrave desired me to communicate to you my sentiments on this subject, as in the course of your negotiation you may have occasion to advert to it. It is doubtless of great importance to dispossess the French from every part of that coast; but St. Maura appears to me of the greatest importance, from the circumstance of the pass between it and the main, in which there is said not to be more than three or four feet of water, and through it all the coast vessels from Petressa, the Gulph of Lepanto, and ports to the southward, pass, to avoid the cruisers. The possession of St Maura would limit the French intercourse very much; that of Parga would not pre- vent what is carried on, in despite of the Pacha, between Corfu and the coast immediately opposite.

I have had great anxiety of mind lest the changes which are said to have taken place in the Government at Constantinople may have caused difficulties to your important mission.

TO VISCOUNT CASTLEREAGH.
Ocean, off Toulon, October 12, 1808.

I have received the honour of your Lordship's letter of the 19th August; and I beg to express to your Lordship how truly gratified and happy I am that the conduct which I have observed on the several subjects therein mentioned should have met with His Majesty's approbation, and that my statement of the events which have happened in Spain should be in any degree useful to His Majesty's Ministers.

I have also received your Lordship's letter of August, conveying to me the senti-ments of His Majesty's Ministers on the capitulation of Baylen, and the commands of His Majesty as to the manner in which the provisions of it may be carried into execution. I have written a letter to the Supreme Junta

VOL. II. s of Seville, to be sent to them by Rear-Admiral Purvis, whenever they shall make application for the passports; in which letter I have asserted His Majesty's just rights as an independent belligerent power; pointed at his reason for conceding to Spain a permission to send their prisoners away as arising from His Majesty's admiration of the military talents of their General, and the loyalty and courage which animated his army and the people of Spain; and prescribed the manner in which they may be sent, and to what ports in France.

MOHAMED ALT, PACHA OF EGYPT.
Ocean, off Toulon, October 16, 1808.

I had the honour to receive your Excellency's letter; and it gave me much pleasure to find you disposed to friendship, and manifesting that disposition by offices of kindness towards the English in Egypt. It has always been the wish of my King to preserve peace with all countries. The respect which the two nations bear to each other, and their mutual interests, would have insured the continuance of their friendship, if it had not been interrupted by the insi- dious arts of France; but it is worthy of your

Excellency's attention to mark the object and ultimate design of those perfidies by which she accomplished the rupture. It was not England that was affected by a war with Turkey. The security of England from the assault of foreign powers, her wealth, her commerce, and the happiness of her people, were not impaired; yet was it a subject of lamentation that an ancient ally should listen to the faithless representations of our common enemy, and a great people pursue measures that must inevitably lead them to their ruin. But it was the subversion of the Ottoman Empire in Europe which the ambition of Buonaparte contemplated, and the intrigues of his Ministers prepared. It was the boundless pride of the French Ruler which inflamed him with the desire of seating himself upon the throne of the Sultans; but, happily for mankind, God has been pleased to will it otherwise.

I conclude that your Excellency has been informed of what has happened in Spain, that Buonaparte, under pretence of defending that kingdom against the English, who were not attacking it, corrupted the Spanish Ministers, marched a great army into the country, was put, by the treachery of one Godoy, the Spanish Minister, in possession of many places of strength, and having established himself in Spain, appointed one of his brothers to be its King, telling the Spaniards that it was their happiness alone that led him to give them a new ruler, that he thought their King was not a good one, and therefore gave them a better. This man would probably say the same thing to your Excellency were he ever to be established in Europe; or perhaps, as the sanctity of religion has no respect from him, he would tell you that he did not approve the doctrines of your prophet, and would name you another object for your veneration. Under the pretence of settling the Government, he seduced the King, his family, and numbers of the nobility, to meet him at Bayonne, from whence he sent them prisoners to France, where they remain. The Spanish people a brave and noble-spirited race of menhad seen the misfortunes of their Government with pain, but obeyed the laws while there was an authority in Spain to administer them. But when their Princes were stolen or imprisoned by Buonaparte, they saw themselves on the eve of suffering those devastations which all other unhappy States have experienced wherever the French have prevailed. The whole nation rose in arms to save their Country; and in every battle which the French have fought with the Spaniards they have been driven from the field, or have sought for mercy in submission to their conquerors. A great army, commanded by Dupont, Bedel, and other French Generals of note, after a battle, in which they lost many men, laid down their arms. At Sara-gossa, the inhabitants, who were not soldiers, beat the French sixteen times in as many assaults which they made upon that city. At Valencia and Gerona they were, in like manner, driven away. In the mean time, the English army landed in Portugal, and having beaten the French under General Junot in two battles, on the 17th and 21st of August, compelled them to quit Portugal, and restored that country to its lawful Sovereign. The Russian fleet which lay in the Tagus surrendered, and are sent to England. Great numbers of the foreigners who were in the French army are deserting from it, and some of my ships are employed in carrying them to their own countries.

I have thought this account of affairs in

Spain and Portugal would be satisfactory to your Excellency; and as you will never hear the real truth from the French who are in your country, this may serve to guard you against their misrepresentations. The English Embassador is gone to the Dardanelles, and I hope before you receive this, you will have heard of the restoration of peace.

I wish you health, most excellent Pacha, and have the honour to be your friend.

HIS MAJESTY'S CONSUL-GENERAL

AT ALGIERS. Ocean, of Toulon, October 26, 1808.

I am sorry for the English merchants who were so unfortunate as to be taken in a Portuguese vessel; but the Dey is at war with Portugal, and Englishmen being in a ship of that nation cannot be understood to give her protection from capture. The Algerines, in hoisting English colours when in pursuit of their enemy, only did that which is a common practice with all nations who are at war. It must be considered as deceiving their enemy, which they have a right to do, and not the Englishmen, whom they had no reason to expect to find there.

The cargoes of ships of those States with which another State is at war are confiscate, unless they be the property of the subjects of a nation which, by treaty, has secured the restoration of it. I believe there is no such provision in our treaties with Algiers. It is provided, in the 19th article of the treaty of 1698, that British subjects are to be treated with kindness, and their baggage preserved entire to them; but I do not understand this protecting article to secure their property, if the ship's cargo be theirs. It may appear, at first sight, extraordinary, that the securities given to the property of the subjects of the two nations are not reciprocal; for the persons of British subjects, taken in the ship of a nation at war with Algiers, and their property only, are protected; but Al-gerine property, even if it extend to the whole cargo, is to be restored. AVhatever restitution of property the Dey may make, on your application, should be considered as a proof of his friendship to the British nation, and his desire to do equal justice; but his withholding such favour does not afford a just cause of complaint.

I have said that this inequality of rights appears at first sight extraordinary, but I believe it to be the true meaning and intention of the treaty, and for the following reason: In the year 1660 the Navigation Act was passed, which had for its principal object the increase of British shipping, and the restraining merchants, in their commercial intercourse with foreign countries, from using ships which were not British. All subsequent acts and treaties with Foreign Powers kept this important object in view. Every security which could be devised was given to property embarked in British ships and those which were admitted to the same privileges, while the same security was not given to what was embarked in foreign ships; and this principle seems to have been in the contemplation of the Ministers who made the treaty with Algiers, and is the cause of the inequality of the security.

TO THE KING OF NAPLES.

SIRE, Ocean, of Toulon, October 27, 1808.

The letter which your Majesty has done me the high honour to address to me has inspired me with the most lively sense of gratitude for your Majesty's gracious condescension, and with the most perfect gratification that my humble services should in any degree merit your Majesty's approbation. It is the duty of every officer of my Sovereign to be vigilantly regardful of whatever relates to your Majesty's interests, or to those of your Royal Family; and I have the pleasure to say, that their anxious desire perfectly coincides with this duty. I should consider it as a great misfortune to me, were any circumstance to remove me from this country before I had paid my personal homage to a Prince in whose service I have, in some degree, considered myself since I came into the Mediterranean, and to Her Majesty; and I hope your Majesty is assured that it has been my careful regard to my public duty which has alone prevented me so long from having that honour.

With my prayers for your Majesty's happiness, I have the honour to be,: c.

TO THE MARQUESS DI CIRCELLO.

Ocean, of Toulon, October 27, 1808.

I have to express to your Lordship the gratification I feel in the expression of approbation which His Majesty has been pleased to signify of my attention to Prince

Leopold. The interests of His Majesty and of every branch of the Royal Family have ever been near my heart. While the French were in force to undertake any enterprises, it was my duty to be near them; and although I have not had the good fortune to meet the enemy, I hope I have prevented their taking any measures which would have been detrimental to the general interests of our countries.

While I am writing this letter to your Excellency, which was meant alone to express my obligation to you for the confidence which your Lordship has placed in me, I cannot forbear mentioning a circumstance which has occupied much of my consideration.

The Dey of Algiers, on some report being made to him of rigorous treatment to Alge-rines in Sicily, had ordered all the severities of slavery to be exercised on the Sicilians who are in his power. I desired the English Consul to use his influence in their behalf; and by a late letter, I learn from him, that the Dey has promised to desist from persecuting them, whenever he hears that his people are treated with lenity, and has already, in some degree, mitigated the severities to which they had been subject. Well assured, my Lord, that your ears are ever open to the cause of humanity, I mention this subject to you, in behalf of the unfortunate Sicilians. Tunis and Algiers having lately made peace with each other, I can already perceive, in those States, a disposition to be active on the sea; and it will require a very particular care and vigilance on the coasts of Sicily to prevent their committing depredations.

HIS EXCELLENCY R. ADAIR, ESQ.

Ocean, off Toulon, October 29, 1808.

I have lately received letters from Egypt, giving a relation of the state of affairs in that country; and I must state to you what is the impression which the general tenor of those letters, and of others which I had before received, has made on my mind.

At all times, M. Drovetti, the French Consul, has been very zealous to ingratiate himself with the Pacha; but particularly since there was the appearance of our nego-ciating for peace with the Porte, he has been industrious to reconcile the differences of the Beys, aftd bring the whole to a friendly correspondence with the Pacha. They have lately re-organised their troops, reviewed the defences of the coast, erected new batteries at Alexandria, Rosetta, and Damietta, provided armed vessels for the river, and are in a state of activity not usual for those people at any time, certainly not when there is no appearance of hostility against them. Drovetti's influence is predominant at Cairo; and I am strongly impressed with the opinion that, should peace be concluded by your Excellency with the Sublime Porte, Egypt will still maintain its connexion with France, or, at all events, will act in despite of the Supreme Government of the Porte.

Monsieur Drovetti knows that, in such a case, the Pacha will soon want assistance, and has doubtless promised him that of the French. Their armies would then probably be admitted into the country in small parties, as they could conveniently send them, and would be received as friends; for the minds of the inhabitants are prepared to consider them in that light by numerous publications printed in the Turkish language in France, and dispersed throughout the country.

I have troubled your Excellency with this conjecture on the state of Egypt, as it may not be useless to you in the service in which you are now engaged.

TO THE EARL OF MULGRAVE.

Ocean, off Toulon, October 30, 1808.

I have received the honour of your Lordship's letter of 6th of September, and it has afforded me the highest gratification to find that the conduct I have observed in the several occurrences that have presented themselves to my attention has met with your Lordship's approbation.

I can always assure your Lordship of my zeal and diligence in my duty, and of the exercise of my best judgment in the service of my King and Country. I never have had, I hope I never shall have, a desire to shrink from it while I have health and ability to perform it; but my life has been a long one, and an anxious one to a mind which never engages in any thing with indifference. I have not any particular ilhiess; but am become exceedingly weak and languid, and often find myself too much disordered to exert myself as I wish to do, and as my situation requires. It was this consideration that induced me to make the request to the Board of Admiralty, which I have done since writing to your Lordship; and now that I have explained my motive and reasons, I have only to add, that my best service is due to my Country as long as I live, and I leave all else to your Lordship's consideration and convenience.

TO LORD RADSTOCK.

Ocean, off Toulon, November 1, 1808.

That system of Acting-Captains is a dreadful bar to good order in the Navy, and there are many other things which well-meaning people, in the kindness and benevolence of their hearts, think very necessary. I dare say they are gratifying to their feelings; but with a view to public service they are highly detrimental. When one considers, that in all great bodies of men who are in any profession, a large proportion of them engage in it more from motives of individual interest than from public spirit, all laws, rules, and regulations, should have this principle in view, and the interests of those who really serve should be advanced. It is not the case, which is the reason that the ships have very inexperienced youths for their Lieutenants, and the Surgeons have a premium, in a large half-pay, for going ashore.

I could say a great deal on this subject, if I were not afraid it would impress you with an idea that I am hard-hearted, which indeed I am not. The difficulty in getting officers is such, that the subject has been much upon my mind. Few line-of-battle-ships have more than two or three officers who are seamen. The rest arc boys, fine children in their mothers' eyes, and the facility with which they get promoted makes them indifferent as to their qualification. I have been made very happy in finding that my conduct, and the principle by which I was governed through some very delicate and interesting discussions at Cadiz, have been much approved by His Majesty's Ministers. My only object in this world is the interest of my Country; and if I go wrong in my endeavours to maintain it, the error will be in my judgment, and not in my heart.

For Spain, I hope that its affairs will mend, now that they have got something like a Government. This province of Catalonia is still dreadfully languid in its operations, although the spirit and enthusiasm of the people are equal to that of any part of Spain. They all want leaders, and here, unhappily, they have none but a fat unwieldy Marquess, who, if his principles are good, has a very limited ability. You know more of Portugal than I do; but, from what I hear, we have mistaken the principle of action which is to put it out of the power of the armies of France to be combatants. In the present state of things, perhaps they were less injurious in Portugal than they will be in France. Sir H. Dalrymple is an honourable and a very sensible man; and how it was managed I do not know.

I have been indifferent lately, growing very weak and infirm in my limbs, worn out, I believe, by the weight of years. I hope to keep the complaint out of my head a little longer; but as God wills.

I wish you health, my dear Lord, and every happiness.

TO THE SAME.

Ocean, November 7, 1808.

I am sorry that I had not the means of keeping Captain Waldegrave here, but really the thing is not a great consideration; for of pecuniary advantage there is very little, although a great deal of very hard and laborious service. The only trade of the enemy is in small boats going along shore with a little oil and earthenware, a great number of which have been destroyed, as the only means we have of making the inhabitants feel the pressure of war. You may depend on it, the hearts of the States of Europe are with us, and that the fear alone of the French army prevents them all, even Russia, from taking an active part. I have kept the fleet complete in all things, through a very boisterous season; but it keeps my attention constantly on the stretch, and I am not strong as I once was. The Spaniards are very languid in Catalonia. I brush them up, but they are not the brighter for it.

TO LADY COLLINGWOOD.

Ocean, of Toulon, November 8, 1808.

You cannot conceive how I am worried by the French; their fleet is lying in the port here, with all the appearance of sailing in a few hours; and God knows whether they will sail at all, for I get no intelligence of them. Their frigates have been out in a gale of wind, were chased by some of our ships, and got in again. We have had most frightful gales, which have injured some of my ships very much; but now that the Alps have got a good coat

VOL. II. T of snow on them, I hope we shall have more moderate weather. I have a double sort of game to play here, watching the French with one eye, while with the other I am directing the assistance to be given to the Spaniards. The French have a considerable force at Barcelona and Figueras, by which they keep the avenues open for Buonaparte to send his army whenever he is ready. The Spaniards have much to do, more than the people in England are aware of. I have, however, from the beginning, given the Ministers a true view of the state of affairs in Spain. It is a great satisfaction to me to find that every thing I have done has been approved by Government; and the letters I receive from the Secretary of State always communicate to me His Majesty's entire approbation. I have heard from the Governor of Cadiz and others, that some of my papers, addressed to the Junta of Seville, on the conduct which the Spaniards ought to pursue on certain occasions, have been very much commended. Perhaps you may think I am grown very conceited in my old age, and fancy myself a mighty politician; but indeed it is not so. However lofty a tone the subject may require and my language assume, I assure you it is in great humility of heart that I utter it, and often in fear and trembling, lest I should exceed my bounds. This must always be the case with one who, like me, has been occupied in studies so remote from such business. I do every thing for myself, and never distract my mind with other people's opinions. To the credit of any good which happens I may lay claim, and I will never shift upon another the discredit when the result is bad. And now, my dear wife, I think of you as being where alone true comfort can be found, enjoying in your own warm house a happiness which in the great world is not known. Heaven bless you! may your joys be many, and your cares few. My heart often yearns for home; but when that blessed day will come in which I shall see it, God knows. I am afraid it is not so near as I expected. I told you that I had written to the Admiralty that my health was not good, and requested their Lordships would be pleased to relieve me. This was not a feigned case. It is true I had not a fever or a dyspepsy. Do you know what a dyspepsy is? I'll tell you. It is the disease of officers who have grown tired, and then they get invalided for dyspepsy. I had not this complaint, but my mind was worn by continual fatigue. I felt a consciousness that my faculties were weakened by application, and saw no prospect of respite; and that the public service might not suffer from my holding a station, and performing its duties feebly, I applied for leave to return to you, to be cherished and restored. What their answer will be, I do not know yet; but I had before mentioned my declining health to Lord Mulgrave, and he tells me in reply, that he hopes I will stay, for he knows not how to supply my place. The impression which his letter made upon me was one of grief and sorrow: first, that with such a list as we have, there should be thought to be any difficulty in finding a successor of superior ability to me; and next, that there should be any obstacle in the way of the only comfort and happiness that I have to look forward to in this world. The variety of subjects, all of great importance, with which I am engaged, would puzzle a longer head than mine. The conduct of the fleet alone would be easy; but the political correspondence which I have to carry on with the Spaniards, the Turks, the Albanians, the Egyptians, and all the States of Barbary, gives me such constant occupation, that I really often feel my spirits quite exhausted, and of course my health is much impaired: but if I must go on, I will do the best I can. The French have a force here quite equal to us; and a winter's cruise, which is only to be succeeded by a summer one, is not very delightful, for we have dreadful weather; and in my heart I long for that respite which my home would give me, and that comfort of which I have had so little experience.

I hope your father and sister are well, and far happier than I am; but tell them that, happy or miserable, I shall ever love them. who was making a fortune, has behaved so ill, that he is to be tried by a court martial: but there are some people who cannot bear to be lifted out of the mud; it is their native element, and they are no where so well as in it.

TO THE MARQUESS DI CIRCELLO.

Ocean, of Toulon, November 13, 1808.

The capture of Capri by the enemy gave me very great concern, because of the effect which every success they have naturally makes upon the public mind, and as it is an indication of more activity in that quarter than they have shewn lately. Your Excellency may depend upon it that my cares are ever awake for the safety of Sicily, and I have been for some time preparing to send ships to its coasts; not, indeed, having it in my contemplation that they were necessary to its defence, but that they should be ready to co-operate in any offensive operation which might be judged advisable. The condition of the fleet, which has made it necessary to send several ships into port for repair, and the attitude of readiness which the enemy preserves in Toulon, have alone delayed this disposition.

To watch the enemy's ships, there has, at all times, been stationed three vessels of war, which were supposed to be superior to any they had at Naples; and considering the numerous points, all which require to be occupied, at all of which they are asking for an increase of force, your Excellency will perceive the reason why a large force was not stationed where the enemy appeared to have very little; for I never heard that any preparations were making at Naples, until I was informed of this appearance off Capri.

But Sicily is one of the most important objects in my view, and all the force I can possibly collect shall be assembled for its safety. I have sent Admiral Martin with two ships of the line; he is ordered also to keep the Renown, which 1 expect he will find at Palermo. I could not commit this service to a more intelligent and zealous officer; one who, besides his exactness in all his public duties, has the additional stimulus of his attachment and respect for Sicily.

Your Excellency observes that, now we are at peace with Spain, a larger disposable naval force will remain to me: at first view it is a very natural conclusion, yet the very reverse is the case. The Spaniards, for want of national funds and the means of supporting their army, have found it necessary to unburden themselves of the expense of their navy, and their coasts near the enemy all demand our protection with most pressing importunity. The Castle of Rosas has been repaired, and partly garrisoned from the ships which, lying in that bay, have alone prevented it from falling into the hands of the enemy. Even at Cadiz, where 1 (considering the security of that district as established) left a very small force, the Governor has applied for more ships, to restrain the turbulent disposition which has shewn itself amongst the French there. Since the troops were drawn from Majorca and Minorca to reinforce the army on the Continent, those Islands cannot be considered in a state of security but by the presence of a fleet which can restrain the enemy's; add to which, ten sail of the line are gone to England.

I mention these circumstances to your Excellency to remove the idea that the late events in Spain have relieved the pressing duties of the squadron; but however numerous they may be, I shall always consider Sicily as one of the most important.

TO THE MOST ILLUSTRIOUS LORD,
AMET, PACHA AND DEY OF ALGIERS.

Ocean, off Toulon, November 15, 1808. MOST ILLUSTRIOUS LORD,

As soon as His Majesty's Consul, at your Highness's residence, informed me that a representation had been made to you that your subjects, who were captive in Sicily, were treated with rigour and unnecessary severity, I lost no time in making inquiry on this matter, and have received an answer from the Marquess di Circello,

Minister of State to His Sicilian Majesty. This Minister, as your Highness, without doubt, ah'eady knows, is esteemed to be an honourable, just, and humane man, and, from his report, I think I can assure your Highness that the accounts which have been given of the treatment of the Algerines in Sicily have been exaggerated. He tells me that he ordered strict inquiry to be made into their situation, and directed that no severities should be exercised on them beyond what the public safety made necessary, and that measures should be taken to ameliorate their condition as much as possible. This resolution is worthy of a wise man, who can compassionate the misfortunes even of his enemy; and I doubt not that the same rule of conduct will be ordered by your Highness to be observed towards the Sicilians, That they are in your power will be a sufficient motive to your noble mind to take them into your protection. In considering the case of the Algerine captives, I could not overlook the unhappy condition to which two countries, which possess so fully the means of happiness for their inhabitants, are reduced by the continuance of war, where there is no quarrel, a war which had its origin in ancient prejudices, which are long since worn out, and continued by habit, the prosecution of which brings nothing but misfortune to the subjects, and is in direct opposition to the best interests of both countries.

I hope your Highness will allow me (who, feeling that respect which is due to the illustrious friend of my Sovereign, would be glad to see your name exalted as the founder of peace and happiness in your country,) to bring this subject to the consideration of your enlightened mind, and to consider of the means by which peace and the blessed intercourse of friendship might be established between two powers who are so much enabled to render mutual benefits.

In making peace, your subjects will be secure from the danger of an unhappy bondage; you will open the avenues to a social intercourse with your nearest neighbours, and your ports to a commerce that will fill your treasury with wealth.

Your Highness knows how precarious and doubtful are the enterprises of your cruisers, seldom being successful enough to pay the expenses of their equipment; but there will be no doubt in the enterprises of your merchants. You may consider every ship that will enter your port as bringing riches to your state; and no country is more conveniently situated for your commerce than Sicily. The true policy of such a measure will be apparent by observing what has passed in other countries.

The Sublime Porte having experienced the benefits which arise to the subject and to the state by preserving peace, never would have abandoned it but on the instigations of the French, whose ruler, having views on the Turkish Empire, saw his wicked plans advanced by reducing the power of Turkey, and involving it in war, which, although not a very active one, was exceedingly destructive to the Ottoman Empire, exhausting its treasure, and suspending the commerce which was the source of it. But the wisdom of the Sublime Porte soon discovered how great an evil had been brought upon them; and the measures which they are taking to restore peace will, it is hoped, be effectual. Through how many ages did the Emperor of Morocco wage an implacable war against

Spain? But time and experience opened the eyes of those Governments to the true interests of their respective countries.

Their enlightened understandings saw the absurdity of continuing those violences to the human race, when the original cause of their warfare had so long ceased; they made peace, and have since carried on an intercourse of friendship highly advantageous to both their countries; they have forgotten all former animosities, and a Moor at Cadiz is as well received as an Englishman. The misfortunes of your people in Sicily brought this subject to my consideration. In submitting it to your Highness, I have great hope that, directed by wdsdom, you will discover the means of blessing the two countries, and establish your name as the friend and benefactor of both, by making peace.

TO J. E. BLACKETT, ESQ.

Ocean, at Sea, January 1, 1809.

On the return of your birthday, I must send you my best wishes for your health and happiness.

My ship is in bad condition. I have worn my patience out, in endeavouring to get to Gibraltar, and the adverse winds now oblige me to go for Malta. Many misfortunes have befallen me; and the state of my health, decayed from anxiety and care, unfits me to contend with them. I have applied to come to England, and he relieved; to which the Ministers are very averse: but I am unequal to continue those labours which I have hitherto borne, and I hope they will relax. While able, I have not shrunk from the task, and should now be allowed to retire.

FROM THE EARL OF MULGRAVE.

Admiralty, January 3, 1809.

I cannot easily express to your Lordship the satisfaction with which I have received your letter of the 30th October, intimating your consent to continue in the command of the Mediterranean station. If the appointment of any particular officers, of whatsoever rank, to serve in the fleet under your Lordship's command, will tend in any way to render the arduous and important service committed to your direction either more easy and agreeable to yourself, or the attainment of the various and complicated objects which engage your attention more certain and effectual, I will take care to make arrangements for placing under your command those whom you may select, with every possible attention to the officers who may be withdrawn for that purpose.

That excellent man and highly distinguished officer, Lord Gardner, was lost to his family, his friends, (among whom I was proud to be classed,) and to his Country, last Saturday, at Bath. Your Lordship's eminent services and high professional character pointed you out as a worthy successor to the dignified distinction of Major-General of Marines, and I have great satisfaction in acquainting you that I have received His Majesty's commands to notify to you, that His Majesty has been graciously pleased to appoint your Lordship to be Major-General of Marines, vice Admiral Lord Gardner, deceased.

TO LORD RADSTOCK.

Ocean, in the way to Malta, January 4, 1809.

The termination of the affairs in Portugal was not such as I thought it probably would have been; for, in any event almost, it would seem to have been better to have kept the French in Portugal than to have let them loose. This, however, depends on particular circumstances, of which I am not possessed; and I cannot help thinking that the outrageous clamour which was made in England against Sir H. Dalrymple, c.

before any of the circumstances were or could be known, is, in every point of view, the worst part of the business. It was this which gave a triumph to the enemy that they could no where else have found, it was this which raised their reputation amongst all foreign nations. Had they been represented as beaten, pursued, humbling themselves before the British arms, and turned ignominiously from a country which they had despoiled, (which was, in fact, the case,)' they would have lost credit in the eyes of Europe, instead of having their fame for skill and ability exalted and proclaimed.

I do not mean to be the advocate of the measures taken; for I know not enough of the circumstances to enable me to judge of them, and yet as much as many of those who caused the clamour. Every day the service will become more arduous, and perhaps offer more occasions for trying the temper of the people, who cannot easily be reconciled to reverses. It is so easy to form plans over a bottle of wine, and to make an estimate of the advantages to result from them, that I do not wonder that such people should often meet with disappointment.

My weak eyes and feeble limbs want rest; my anxious breast has not known an hour's composure for many months. In Spain every thing seems to fail. In short, they have not an organized army to act against the legions of France. My ships have done every thing possible to enable the Spaniards to maintain the castles at Rosas; but I hear they have surrendered. The Spanish army would do nothing, no argument could move them from Gerona, to raise the siege. Every day brought an excuse: they were ill armed they had not provisions they were without clothes in short, they would not come. To the Captain-General I represented what must inevitably be the consequence of this delay. I shewed him Catalonia lost, if he did not raise the siege, which was carried on by a gang of Italians, who were ready to run away if they had been attacked. Captain West, at Rosas, and Lord Cochrane, in Trinity Castle, distinguished themselves very much: indeed, the defence which Lord Cochrane made, even after the breach was practicable, redounds highly to his honour and reputation as an officer. These events kept me off' Toulon, that no aid should go from thence. The storms were unceasing, and at last drove us, by their violence, quite away. This ship has suffered very much: she is bolted with copper, and might as well be bolted with lead. She had like to have gone to pieces. I am now on the way to Malta, to secure her with iron bolts; but she will never be good for any thing until she be docked in England, and secured with iron. Your nephew is a Lieutenant of this ship: he is a fine young man, and I like him very much.

TO THE EARL OF MULGRAVE.

Ocean, Malta,. Januanf 10, 1809.

In the last month I received the honour of your Lordship's letter of the 25th September. Nothing could be more gratifying to me than such a testimony of your Lordship's approbation of the measures which I have taken to promote the public welfare on the several occasions which have come within my cognizance. My long continuance at sea has made me very i'eeble; and the fear of my unfitness, which I know

VOL. II. u people are often the last to discover in themselves, induced me to make the application. My situation requires the most vigorous mind, which is seldom possessed at the same time with great debility of body. Since my letter of the 30th October to your Lordship on this subject, the vexations which I have had on account of the affairs in Catalonia, and the violent stormy weather, which has done much injury to some of the ships, particularly to the Ocean, have increased my infirmity; but on this subject I have nothing to add to what was said in that letter. I have no object in the world that I put in competition with my public duty; and so long as your Lordship thinks it proper to continue me in this command, my utmost efforts shall be made to strengthen the impression which you now have; but I still hope, that whenever it may be done with convenience, your Lordship will bear in mind my request. On the subject of Plymouth, I have only to say, that wherever I can best render my service, I shall be at your Lordship's command, I would not have requested to be recalled from hence on any account but that which I have stated; and when my health is restored, I shall be perfectly at your Lordship's disposal; but with the little that I have ever had to do with ports, I should enter on that field with great diffidence.

TO THE SAME.

Ocean, at Malta, Ja7mary 21, 1809.

This winter has been, and continues to be, unusually boisterous. The unremitting gales have done much injury to the ships which were at sea, and many are here for their repair. The Ocean, I hope, will soon be made as firm as she can be without a dock, but that is necessary to make her perfect. The state of the enemy and Spaniards at Rosas kept me longer out than I would have staid; but it was necessary, to prevent the French army receiving any assistance from Toulon; and had the Spaniards moved to raise the siege, they might have done it. The French army was not more than 10 or 12,000 men, most of them Italians; and by the Spaniards' account, they had to oppose to them near 30,000, between Villa Franca and Rosas; but not the smallest effort was made to give obstruction to the enemy.

I believe I have before mentioned Ge- neral Vives to your Lordship as an officer in whom the Spaniards themselves had not much confidence. He was a dependant of the Prince of the Peace, and his fortunes were raised by that Minister. The objections he made to sending troops from Majorca incurred the displeasure and suspicion of the Supreme Junta; and yet, when they removed him from the islands, they appointed him Captain-General in Catalonia, one of the most important posts in Spain. At the moment when letters were written to me from Madrid of the suspicion entertained of him by the Supreme Junta, and I was requested to call on him to declare the part which he meant to take, whether hostile or loyal to Spain, the Junta were writing to him in the most flattering terms, which letters he published in the province. Rosas was very important to them: they cannot recover it again but with great difficulty.

I received by the Camilla a copy of the instructions given to Captain Leake, for his conduct in the interview with the Pacha of Albania. I hope I shall have an opportunity of seeing him before he proceeds to that coast. A great deal of caution is necessary in treating with the Pacha, from what I have collected of his character. He possesses consummate art and subtilty, is powerful, and has a thirst for power. The Russians supported, as the French now do, the neighbouring Pachas and Agas, with the view of restraining him. His anxiety to possess Parga is more for the purpose of controlling the neighbouring Agas, than of extirpating the French, with whom I have a suspicion that he was carrying on a friendly correspondence last year, when to us he was professing himself their inveterate enemy. I have heard that he negociated with the French General for the possession of Parga, at the moment when he was entreating us to take St. Maura and give it to him. His negociation failed, and then he resorted to other means to obtain it. My language to him has always given him assurance of our friendship, and that whenever the state of the Porte will authorise him to commence hostility against the French, he shall have every assistance which the squadron can afford him. I apprehend he will have more than the French to oppose; for the Greeks have a much greater dread of him than of the French, and will exert themselves for the independence of their respective coun- tries. It is difficult to form a just notion of the policy and complex interests of such a number of little Governments, ruled by Pachas and Agas, along the coast, all subject to the Porte, but all jealous of their independence of each other; ready to oppose any invader of their Country; and most of them more afraid of Ali Pacha than of the French, and only holding intercourse with the latter, as they enable them to resist his projects.

In the Seven Islands, the people, oppressed by the exactions of the French, have amongst them men who form projects for the emancipation of their Country and the restoration of the Republic, looking to England for the means of men and money to accomplish them. One of those at Vienna lately sent me a copy of his plan. It appeared to me to be the indigested scheme of a person who wished to have some appointment in the British service. I evaded his proposal, as not being convenient to be undertaken at the present moment, and recommended that a person of so much influence in his country as he stated himself to be, should, by his presence in the island, support the interest which he espoused, and wait a favourable opportunity. This, by his reply to me, he seems to consider as an instruction from me to organise a revolution, in a country where I understand he has but a second-rate influence, and which itself possesses no means whatever. I mention this to your Lordship as an instance of the flimsy foundation on which people, distressed by their misfortunes, would build their hopes, and who, having lost all, would grasp at any shadow. There are often such projectors; at the same time, I believe they would all unite even with the French to oppose All Pacha.

TO THE MARQUESS DI CIRCELLO.

Ocean, at Malta, January 24, 1809.

Soon after I received the honour of your Excellency's letter, in which you observed that there was nothing which His Sicilian Majesty more desired than that peace should be concluded with Algiers, I had occasion to write a letter to the Dey, in which I brought this subject before him. I endeavoured to shew him the honour he would derive from terminating a war which had so long existed, and which had its origin in ancient prejudices of which his sagacious mind could not but see the fallacy; that his predatory expeditions were unworthy of a respectable Government, and failed in their view of profit, as his equipments always cost more than his successes reimbursed; and that in making peace, he would open to his subjects a field for commercial speculations that would bring wealth to his treasury and respect to the Regency. I used all the argument I could devise, to shew him that his honour and his interest would be advanced by terminating a war which brought only misery to the subjects of both countries. The proposal was stated to arise from my own feelings for the misfortunes of the subjects of two States, both in amity with my Sovereign, and brought to my consideration by his complaint of the sufferings of his people at Palermo. The letter was delivered to the present Dey by the British Consul; he seemed to be particularly attentive to the subject, but said he could give no answer until he had consulted the Divan. They were assembled, and the day following, the Consul had an audience, when the Dey declared his willingness to make peace with Sicily, on condition of the payment of sums of money which were cer- tainly very extravagant. He required a million and a half of dollars on the conclusion of the treaty, and a tribute equal to that which America pays: the prisoners to be released on both sides. On the Consul stating the impossibility of a country whose finances had suffered from the pressure of the war, paying so large a sum of money, the Dey reduced his demand to a million of dollars, and half the tribute which America now pays. He professed a desire that peace should be settled, but stated that he did not feel that he had the power to agree to it without a pecuniary gratification. His subjects expected it, and it was a condition which could not be dispensed with.

I have now, my Lord Marquess, related to your Excellency what has passed on this subject. The Court of Sicily thus far have had nothing to do with it; they are not engaged in any degree. It was confined to my individual opinion, stated for the purpose, indeed, of discovering his sentiments, because if I could turn them to the advantage of Sicily I should be gratified.

HIS EXCELLENCY ROBERT ADAIR, ESQ.

Ocean, at Malta, January 27, 1809.

I have to acknowledge the honour of your Excellency's letter of the 6th instant, informing me that you had concluded a treaty of peace and amity with the Turkish Government, and beg to congratulate your Excellency on the happy termination of your negotiation.

I shall at all times have pleasure in paying every possible regard to your requests or suggestions. No officer is in higher estimation in my mind than Captain Stewart, because I have experienced his ability and judgment wherever he was employed, and know that he is suited to the most important services. With this impression, I shall be glad to appoint him to a station where he himself will feel confidence.

LIEUT.-GENERAL SIR JOHN STUART.

Ocean, at Malta, January 29, 1809.

There was a period, the beginning of November, when a British army in Catalonia would have been extremely beneficial to their cause, when they would by their example and countenance have given a confidence to that people, and, perhaps, have induced them to advance and put a stop to the operations of the enemy against Rosas; but, at the same time, had the Captain-General been as determined in his non-resistance of the enemy, and made as little use of the Spanish troops as he has done, the force that could have been detached from Sicily would not have been sufficient to arrest the enemy. Rosas surrendered, I believe at discretion, on the 5th December. The ships which I had sent to that bay had given them all the assistance in their power; but on the part of the Spanish army, which, between the head quarters at Villa Franca and Rosas, amounted to little less than 30,000 men, no effort whatever was made to raise the siege. The consequence has been, that the French army, composed mostly of Italians, have overrun the country. I have not had any correct account of their operations; but both parties, I understand, have in their turns been defeated and victorious. The last account which Admiral Thornborough had received at Minorca was.

that Tarragona was threatened, and the Spaniards determined to defend it.

When I directed Rear-Admiral Martin to proceed to Sicily, in aid of its defence, I did not give him instructions for any distant service, on which the troops might be engaged, as the tenor of your letter of the 28th October shewed that none such was in contemplation; but, on the contrary, that Sicily required all the force and every security that could be given to its defence. At the same time, my own opinion is, that those threats and menaces of the French General against Sicily were for the purpose of drawing our attention to an object distant from the point of their real operations; and that the reports which have been since circulated are only a continuation of the same system. All the ports in the Adriatic have been examined, and there does not appear, nor ever has there been, in any of them the sign of an armament; and by very good intelligence from Trieste, the Russians are exactly in the same state in which they have been this year past. Three of them are exceedingly rotten, and only the Turkish ship is fit to go to sea. I have heard that it has been proposed to sell them; yet at the time there was a report at Trieste that they were to be fitted for sea, and that Count Tolstoy was gone there to make the necessary arrangements. I thought it likely that this was given out with the view of getting their frigates from Venice before any rupture should take place with France, which is not an improbable event to happen.

I enclose to you, Sir, the copy of a letter from Decres to Buonaparte, in which he states the number of ships which will be ready at Toulon in a short time, and the measures he proposes for completely manning them.

The first danger which Sicily has to apprehend is, I believe, from that fleet, and the army that may come in it: it is, therefore, absolutely necessary that a squadron should be composed of sufficient force to oppose them. To form such a squadron will require all the ships on this station, which must be collected in due time, excepting only such as may be necessary for the convoy of troops which you may think proper to send to Catalonia. Whenever this ship is repaired, I shall be impatient to join the squadron; but it would be a great satisfaction to me first to confer with you. Sir; and as I wish also to see Mr. Mellish at Palermo, I purpose going thither when I leave Malta. The winter has been particularly severe at sea. This ship, which I thought a strong one, is quite ruined for present service, and must go to England when the season will admit; and there are near half the small ships of the station under repair in port.

HIS EXCELLENCY ROBERT ADAIR, ESQ.

Ocean, at Malta, February 2, 1809.

Your letter of the 18th November having been sent down to Gibraltar, did not reach me until yesterday, and I am very glad that all the impediments which were apprehended at that time from the violent commotions in the Turkish Government have not prevented the success of your ne-gociation, of which I was informed by your later letter, before the present one came to me. Indeed, from the assurance of Ali Pacha that the negociation would terminate favourably, I had little doubt of it; for that chieftain is known to have great influence at the Porte, and to be very much engaged in the politics of its internal government.

Bairacter was his enemy, and the removal of that person from power did not probably cause delay. The Turks wished, in making peace, to have terms the most favourable to them, and would, no doubt, have been glad to have had compensation for their losses, and their ships returned. They protracted the discussion, in hope to obtain them; but never intended to let you depart from the Dardanelles without concluding a treaty, for which they had for a year past expressed so much impatience. The suspension of all hostility in the Archipelago during the discussion had my perfect approbation. The Turks had expressed a desire to renew their ancient amity with England; and as nothing could more effectually mark the same disposition in the British Government than a cessation from war while the terms were settling, I gave an order to all ships going to the eastward to that effect. In Captain Stewart's judgment I have such confidence, that I am sure if there had been any thing objectionable in that measure, he would have represented it to your Excellency.

With respect to the protection to be given by us to the Turks in the Archipelago, it cannot be better done than by keeping the enemy's fleet at Toulon in our view. The frigates and small vessels will be frequently coming up with despatches and convoys; but to detach larger ships to the Archipelago is not possible in the present state of the French squadron, which is strong, and daily increasing; while ours, from the severe storms of this winter, has suffered very much, and several of the ships, of which my own is one, are scarcely fi o go to sea.

I wish it were in my power to send you a good account from Spain. In Catalonia every thing seems to have gone wrong since the fall of Rosas. The French are not very numerous; the Spaniards are in considerable force, yet are dispersed and panic-struck whenever the enemy appears; notwithstanding which, I believe the people to be as loyal to their cause as in any part of Spain, but unorganised and ill-conducted. It has very much the appearance of want of integrity in their leaders. All I can do for them is to prevent the communication by sea; and as many ships are allotted to that service as I can spare. The French passed on to Barcelona, without assaulting Gerona, leaving it insulated, as it were, in an enemy's country; and, having dispersed the Spanish cordon, advanced to Tarragona, before which town they now are, with about 5000 troops, while in Tarragona the Spaniards amount to 14 or 16,000 men. General Vives is superseded in the command; and Reding, who is a Swiss, is now at the head of that army.

TO THE HON. MISS COLLINGWOOD.

Ocean, at Malta, Februart 5, 1809.

I received your letter, my dearest child, and it made me very happy to find that you and dear Mary were well, and taking pains with your education. The greatest pleasure I have amidst my toils and troubles, is in the expectation which I entertain of finding you improved in knowledge, and that the understanding which it has pleased God to give you both has been cultivated with care and assiduity. Your future happiness and respectability in the world depend on the diligence with which you apply to the

attainment of knowledge at this period of your life, and I hope that no negligence of your own will be a bar to your progress. When I write to you, my beloved child, so much interested am I that you should be amiable, and worthy of the friendship and
VOL. II. X esteem of good and wise people, that I cannot forbear to second and enforce the instruction which you receive, by admonition of my own, pointing out to you the great advantages that will result from a temperate conduct and sweetness of manner to all people, on all occasions. It does not follow that you are to coincide and agree in opinion with every ill-judging person; but after shewing them your reason for dissenting from their opinion, your argument and opposition to it should not be tinctured by any thing offensive. Never forget for one moment that you are a gentlewoman; and all your words and all your actions should mark you gentle. I never knew your mother, your dear, your good mother, say a harsh or a hasty thing to any person in my life. Endeavour to imitate her. I am quick and hasty in my temper; my sensibility is touched sometimes with a trifle, and my expression of it sudden as gunpowder: but, my darling, it is a misfortune, which, not having been sufficiently restrained in my youth, has caused me much pain. It has, indeed, given me more trouble to subdue this natural impetuosity, than any thing I ever undertook. I believe that you are both mild; but if ever you feel in your little breasts that you inherit a particle of your father's infirmity, restrain it, and quit the subject that has caused it, until your serenity be recovered. So much for mind and manners; next for accomplishments. No sportsman ever hits a partridge without aiming at it; and skill is acquired by repeated attempts. It is the same thing in every art: unless you aim at perfection, you will never attain it; but frequent attempts will make it easy. Never, therefore, do any thing with indifference. Whether it be to mend a rent in your garment, or finish the most delicate piece of art, endeavour to do it as perfectly as it is possible. When you write a letter, give it your greatest care, that it may be as perfect in all its parts as you can make it. Let the subject be sense, expressed in the most plain, intelligible, and elegant manner that you are capable of. If in a familiar epistle you should be playful and jocular, guard carefully that your wit be not sharp, so as to give pain to any person; and before you write a sentence, examine it, even the words of which it is composed, that there be nothing vulgar or inelegant in them. Remember, my dear, that your letter is the picture of your brains; and those whose brains are a compound of folly, nonsense, and impertinence, are to blame to exhibit them to the contempt of the world, or the pity of their friends. To write a letter with negligence, without proper stops, with crooked lines and great flourishing dashes, is inelegant: it argues either great ignorance of what is proper, or great indifference towards the person to whom it is addressed, and is consequently disrespectful. It makes no amends to add an apology, for having scrawled a sheet of paper, of bad pens, for you should mend them; or want of time, for nothing is more important to you, or to which your time can more properly be devoted. I think I can know the character of a lady pretty nearly by her hand-writing. The dashers are all impudent, however they may conceal it from themselves or others; and the scribblers flatter themselves with the vain hope, that, as their letter cannot be read, it may be mistaken for sense. I am very anxious to come to England; for I have lately been unwell. The greatest happiness which I expect there, is to find that my dear girls have been assiduous in their learning.

May God Almighty bless you, my beloved little Sarah, and sweet Mary too.

Ocean, (it Sea, February 18, 1809.

1 am truly sorry to hear so bad an account of the health of your good brother, and the fears that were entertained for him. I would hope for him, but your letters give me little encouragement, and I already feel for the loss of a good and kind friend. Whenever I land, (if I ever do,) I shall come to a country of strangers, unknowing and unknown to all but my own family. What melancholy changes have taken place since I left home!

I beg of you to take care of late hours and hot rooms. I, who enter into no pleasures, go to no feasts, or festivals, or midnight gambols, have no complaints but those arising from sheer fatigue of spirit. My time is so occupied, that even the common visits of civility are very inconvenient to me; and Malta is the most gossiping, gormandizing place I ever heard of The merchants there, who two years since were very little men, from the extension of their trade, the exclusion of all other nations from participating in it, and the ample protection given to their speculations, are become suddenly exceedingly rich. I have heard that some of them have made a hundred thousand pounds, and several from ten to fifteen thousand a year. The ladies, who have so lately emerged from the humblest duties of domestic industry, now vie with each other in all the shining finery of tassel and tinsel, and pass their nights in routs and revels; their days go for nothing. I just saw enough of it to know that it would not do for me. Neither my health nor my occupations were suited to it, and I declined all invitations. On the 1st of January I wrote to you a short letter, to wish you much happiness and many returns of your birthday. I was then on my way to Malta, with my ship in a very ricketty and bad condition, from an ill-judged experiment which the Surveyors of the Navy were making, in the mode of securing the vessels. Had we met with another gale like that we experienced off Toulon in December, I do not think she would have kept together, but separated, and left every one to take the best care of himself upon a plank. I have written so harshly, but so truly, to the Admiralty and the Navy Board upon this subject, that they may perhaps be displeased with the freedom which I have taken with their plans; but if it be a means of correcting what to any scientific mind must be obviously wrong, I shall be satisfied, and bear any little resentment to me with patience. I gave my opinions in behalf of England, whose existence depends upon her Navy. Had the French devised a plan for its destruction, they could not have discovered a more effectual one. We have now replaced all the copper bolts with iron ones. Several of the ships have suffered from the same cause; but this being larger and higher, was injured more.

I never can care enough about Chirton to consider much about it. One thing only interests me, that no person should be removed from a house or farm, unless his conduct has made him very obnoxious. It is the interest of an old tenant to give a fair rent; and when he does, it is shameful to have him subjected to a higher bidder. I have lived now long enough without wealth to be very indifferent about it; and I hope I may always be comfortable without putting others to difficulty. That Mr. sent me a letter, about a book to be published, which I tucked under the sofa, and it is gone to the winds long since. I suppose he is one of those book-making gentlemen who write their own reveries, and call them histories or anecdotes. There was an account of my life in some Naval Magazine, which vexed me very much; for it related a heap of stuff, that had not the least foundation in truth, and was in many parts exceedingly offensive to me. Here is a Scotsman who has written to inform me that he is about to publish a Memoir of the House of Drummond; and as I am (he says) immediately descended from it, and closely allied by intermarriage, he requests the honour of my support. I shall answer him, that I apprehend his letter must have been intended for some other person, as I have not the honour of being connected, in the most distant degree, with any family or person north of Tweed.

I have lately been negotiating with the Dey of Algiers for a peace with Sicily, and hope that the Ministers will not disapprove of what I have done. The Court of Sicily knew nothing of it; but when I see an opportunity to do a good thing, I do not wait to consult until the season be past. I have brought the Dey to consent to peace on certain conditions; but the Sicilians are very poor things, and though it would be highly advantageous to them, they will not be able to accomplish it.

I was surprised to see Mr. come out again. They think, when they have served six years at sea, they should be made Lieutenants, and never deem it necessary to qualify themselves. He is a good, quiet young man, and walks about, doing no harm; but he has no activity in him. Such people become rather pensioners upon the Navy, than officers in it.

I hope they will send out somebody to relieve me. I wish very much to return to England; and I believe, when I go, every Admiral here will ask to go also.

TO LADY COLLINGWOOD.

Ocean, Februarj 25, 1809.

I so seldom hear from England now, that I scarcely know what is going on in the world. I conclude every body is so occupied with Spanish affairs, that they can think only of them. I have had my share of them, and but very little satisfaction. In Catalonia we have given them all possible assistance: they have not profited much by it. It has been said, that I thought coldly of the Spaniards, and did not give them the credit which is due to a brave and great people. I believe that the sentiment of national honour and devotion to the country is no where to be found in greater purity than in Spain. At the same time, among the people of rank and property, perhaps there are as many who ought not to be trusted; and when one considers how many years the Prince of the Peace was Minister, and how many people owe their rank and fortune to his favour, it is not to be wondered that many retain their attachment to him. I have done every thing for them in my power. I wished the General, Sir John Stuart, to send a detachment of his forces to assist them; but he does not find his army in a state to spare them from the service that may require them in Sicily. I went from Malta to Palermo, where I had long promised myself the pleasure of paying my compliments to the King and Queen, and I gratified a curiosity which had been excited by many strange stories which I had heard. I arrived the day before Ash-Wednesday, the last of the Carnival, when the Queen gave a grand ball and supper to the nobility. I received an invitation as soon as we anchored, and was glad of an opportunity to see all the Court and those far-famed Princesses at once. The King and the Queen received me most graciously. The King has much the appearance and manner of a worthy honest country gentleman. Nature certainly intended him for that state; but blundering Chance has cast his lot awry. The Queen would appear to be penetrating into the soul and mind of every body that comes near her. She would be thought a deep politician; yet all her schemes miscarry. She broods over what is impracticable with her little means, and frets herself continually that others are not as dim-sighted as herself. Her lot also has been cast awry, or, in the distribution of stations for this world, so loose a morality and such depravity of manners would never have been found perched upon a throne, from whence should issue the bright example of all that is good and great. The King lives generally in the country, about four miles from the city, where he amuses himself in planting trees and shooting. We dined with him on Sunday at his country-house, and he carried us all over it. It is the prettiest thing that can be; the rooms not larger than ours at Morpeth, and the house not much bigger. We went over his grounds; and

His Majesty seemed particularly desirous that I should see all his improvements, when I told him that I was a great planter myself. I have also seen a great deal of the Princesses and Duchesses of Sicily; and all I shall say of them at present is, that the more I see of them, the more I bless my stars that I was born in England, and have got a darling wife who is not a Princess. They were very polite and attentive to me. I believe the Queen was relieved when I took leave of her. They had been told of the opposition which I gave to their son going to Spain, and of many other things also which were not true; and I believe suspected that I had been the cause of Saint Clair being ordered to leave Gibraltar so suddenly, which I was not. I do not know what possessed them on my arrival, but the consternation seemed to be general; and Sir John Stuart having come there to meet me, made an appearance of business of consequence. There was a great alarm and suspicion that we were come to insist on all the French leaving the island; and as most of her favourites are of that nation, I do not wonder at the concern that was very visible. They never desire, I am sure, to see my face again.

Ocean, off" Cape Sebastian, March 7, 1809.

The letters vvliicli I have written to the Admiralty from Malta, and since, will inform your Lordship of the communication made to me by General Sir John Stuart, that he was instructed to send such a detachment as could be spared from the defence of Sicily to the assistance of the Spaniards in Catalonia, on which I appointed the Alceste and a sloop to convey them. From Malta I went to Palermo, to confer with him on the subject of this aid to be sent to Spain. On that occasion I described as fully as was in my power what I believed to be the state of the Spanish army in Catalonia; that they were more numerous than that of the enemy, who have less than 20,000 men, most of them disaffected Italians; and gave him my opinion, that a small British force, sufficient to give a proper importance to three or four skilful and judicious officers, who should command them, men who could propose measures to our allies without seeming to dictate or control them, of which they are exceedingly jealous, and who could give to their own plans the semblance of their having originated with the Spaniards, would by their counsel and example materially aid in the arrangement of the Spanish force, which is already superior in number.

The General, on the other hand, stated the very numerous army which the enemy had in the kingdom of Naples, said to amount to 45,000 men; that any reduction of his force at this time would have the effect of inviting them to invade the island; that the native army was little proportioned to the service that would be required of them, a great part of it, I mean the Prince of Butera's volunteers, being merely nominal; and that he had, moreover, authorised the Sicilian Government to assure that of Vienna, that whenever the Austrian army takes the field, he will make a powerful diversion in the south of Italy. For those considerations, the General determined that it was not expedient to make any detachment from the forces in Sicily. The Court appear to confine all their views to the re-possession of Naples. It is their constant theme; whatever has not that for its immediate object would not be approved; for they do not consider that both the re-possession of Naples, and the maintaining themselves in Sicily, must ultimately depend on putting a stop to the progress of the French power, which can only be done by opposing them where they are in activity and force, and not by waiting until they come to them.

After the taking of Capri they complained that they had not naval protection. I assure your Lordship, that in the distribution of the ships I do every thing in my power, that no important point shall be left unguarded. All the coast and approaches to Sicily have constantly had ships stationed on them: but when they are out of sight, they consider themselves as abandoned: and when they are in port, the enemy is doing what he pleases, unmolested. It would require a squadron in every port to remove all their apprehensions. The ships have suffered much by the violence of the winter, and more of them are at Malta refitting than usual, where every exertion is making to prepare them for sea again. Four frigates, with active and intelligent officers, are employed on the coast of Catalonia, the only place where operations are going on, and their assistance animates the Spaniards.

320 corrkspondencp: and memoir of TO THE SAME.

Ocean, of Minorca, March 16, 1809.

On the 10th we were close in with Toulon, where were thirteen ships of the line (including two Russians), and five frigates in the outer road. The Admiral was bending his sails when we approached, obviously for the show of preparation. I considered this as an indication that they were not in a state to proceed immediately to sea; and leaving two ships to watch them, came here with the squadron to complete it.

The Spanish ships have been the object of my constant solicitude. Your Lordship will have been informed by Admiral Purvis that those at Cadiz are rigged and armed before this time. I have more anxiety for those at Carthagena. In reply to a letter which Admiral Thornborough wrote to the Spanish Commander when I was absent, he said that the preparing and mooring the ships depended on orders which the Supreme Junta must give. I have written to Mr. Frere, at Seville, submitting to him the necessity of urging this point with the Government, and that they will order those ships to be removed without delay to Cadiz or

Algeziras. They would be better in any port than Carthagena, as, from information I got last summer of the disposition of the higher orders of people in that part of Spain, I have entertained an opinion not favourable to them; and from this suspicion the officers of the Navy are not exempt.

On my arrival off this island, the Elvin brig joined the squadron, and brought me the intelligence of the French ships having sailed from Brest. If they come into this sea, they may, on the supposition that the English fleet is off Toulon, proceed directly to Sicily, which is the great object of the French in the Mediterranean. But until I have some intelligence, I must not leave this quarter; for these Islands are defenceless, and would be reduced by a small force. Most of the Spanish troops are withdrawn from them, and they are left to the protection of an ill-appointed militia, of which the portion allotted to the defence of Minorca is 84 men. The Junta have applied for a British military force, which cannot be given to them: they have no confidence in their chiefs, and state that a number of disaffected and ill-disposed persons are amongst them. The Captain-General Cuesta is little re-

VOL. II. Y spected amongst the people; and if he be faithful to his Country's cause, he has no energy. The Governor at Minorca is considered as completely attached to the French interest. It seems very extraordinary that the Spanish Government should continue in important situations men whose character and attachment to the enemy seem to be generally known.

TO THE EARL OF MULGRAVE.

Ocean, March 22, 1809.

I have received the medal for Captain Stewart, of the Sea-horse, and shall have great pleasure in presenting to that gallant and meritorious officer this distinguished mark of His Majesty's approbation of his conduct. Last week I sent the Halcyon to Algiers, to propose to the Dey a cessation of hostilities with Sicily, and that Ministers should be appointed to treat of the terms on which peace and friendship should be established. She is returned, and brought me the account of another revolution in that Government; the Dey, who had ruled about four months, with his Ministers and adherents, being put to death on the 4th instant. The newly-created Dey received my proposal favourably, and expressed his desire to be at peace with the friends and allies of the King; and has sent me a passport for a Sicilian Minister to go to Algiers to treat of the conditions. I shall send it to Sicily, but I doubt whether it will ever be used.

25th. Mr. Mellish has informed me, in a letter which I received to-day, of the proposals which have been lately made, on one side and the other, by the Courts of Vienna and London. I have stated, in my letter to the Admiralty of the 22d, what my apprehensions on this subject are, that the preparation of Austria has been enough to ensure to them the hostility of the French, but too late to make any useful diversion for the Spaniards, who are tardy and languid every where in the greatest degree. The burst of enthusiasm which inspired the common people at first, seems greatly to have evaporated, and I doubt whether there is any other power in Spain. Nothing could be so ill-advised as sending the French prisoners to these islands. They were in imminent danger before; this measure will ensure their loss. In Catalonia, the application for supplies are unlimited, they want money, arms, and ammunition, of which no use appears to be made when they get them. The works at Tarragona are in bad repair, and they remain so; the guns on the ramparts, old and ill mounted, while in the town they have abundance of cannon in no situation for use; their army is numerous, above twenty thousand, while the French, in their neighbourhood, do not amount to ten. In the English papers I see accounts of successes, and convoys cut off and waggons destroyed, which are not true. What has been done in that way has been by the boats of our frigates, which have, in two or three instances, landed men, and attacked the enemy with great gallantry. The Simotines range the hills in a disorderly way, and fire at a distance, but retire on being approached. This state of things made me anxious that a body of English, however small, conducted by intelligent and temperate officers, should have been sent, in hopes that their presence and example might have animated the Country. It was an experiment, in my own view of it, for even of the success of that I was not sanguine. They have sent to Sicily and Malta to crave supplies; at both places they have received arms, while they make little use of those they have, and I fear they will all fall into the hands of the enemy very soon. The want of money is their constant complaint; while at Cadiz, I am told, they have more than twenty-five millions of dollars. There is little communication, and no concert, between the provinces, nor even between towns that are twenty miles apart. Your Lordship may judge what my feelings are at a prospect at present so dreary. What change may be effected by the part Austria is taking, will depend on their success, and even that will be vain if it be not soon.

TO J. E. BLACKETT, ESQ.

Ocean, Port Mahon, March 25, 1809.

I have had nothing but distresses and disappointments; misfortunes proceeding from the very violent weather which we have experienced, and disappointments in the languor and want of energy that appear amongst the Spaniards. Unless a great revolution take place in that Country, which I do not expect, it is lost, and the liberal aid which we have given them will not save it from falling under the domination of France. I am sure I have exerted myself truly; but I do not possess power of mind to conduct so arduous a machine as the public service is now become. I give all my time and all my strength to it, from daylight until midnight, often borrowing an hour or two of the next day, and have scarce time to eat my scanty dinner. I am worn out, and wish to retire from it; but it seems that I must not; and my greatest fear is, that my unfitness will grow upon me. His Majesty is kind to me, and rewards me beyond my desert. It is only my desire to do what is best, that gives me any claim to his royal regard. The appointment to the Marines is very flattering to me, because, of many candidates, he gave it to me who was not a candidate, and never have asked for any thing pecuniary or for myself. The Ville de Paris is coming out to me, when I shall send this ship to England, as she has suffered greatly in the severe gales that we have had in the winter; on which subject I have said so much, that I am afraid I shall be out of the good books of the Surveyors of the Navy.

Ocean, Minorca, March 26, 1809.

I have just received the honour of your Lordship's letter of the 3d January, by the Minstrel, and beg to express to your Lordship the extreme gratification I feel at the manner in which you are pleased to express your estimation of my service. My cares and best judgment have ever been given to my duty, and while I have health they ever will. I have no object in life that I put in competition with it; but the failure of my strength made me apprehensive that I could not long continue the exertions which are necessary. I lament the death of Lord Gardner exceedingly. His worth, both in his public station and in private life, obtained for him the high respect and esteem of the Country and his friends. His Majesty's goodness, in having been graciously pleased to appoint me his Lordship's successor, as Major-General of the Marines, awakens in me the warmest gratitude to the King for this highly honourable distinction, and to your Lordship for the very flattering terms in which you have been pleased to notify it to me.

Admiral Martin has informed me that he has applied to the Admiralty for leave to return to England. He will be a great loss to me; for he is a most intelligent officer, temperate and conciliating, qualities that are always necessary, and for which the present state of our affairs particularly call. As your Lordship has given me permission to name to you the officers whom I would prefer, I will beg to say, if Sir Samuel Hood could be spared from other service, and he himself liked it, I should think myself very fortunate.

I have written to your Lordship pretty fully on the affairs of Spain; but I must repeat my apprehensions that His Majesty's Ministers think better of them than their real state deserves. All exertion in the eastern part of Spain has disappeared, though they still crave for stores and money, which would only fall into the enemy's hands.

TO REAR-ADMIRAL PURVIS.

Ocean, Minorca, March 26, 1809.

You observe the anxiety which Ministers have that the Spanish ships should not, in any event, fall into the hands of the enemy; and to prevent this, in case of affairs going to extremity in Spain, will require much delicacy of conduct and skill: but it cannot be in better hands than yours. Repeated demands and requests to them to move the ships into the Bay, (where, indeed, they ought to be, for the defence of the town,) tend to create a jealousy of us, and a suspicion that we have sinister views. The enemy has emissaries every where to fabricate stories which are not true, and draw conclusions from them which will tend to increase their apprehensions; and I am afraid that they have been much assisted in making this impression by the appearance of our troops at Cadiz, and the proposal for their landing. We knew before how averse they were to this measure, and I am rather sorry that it was pressed upon them.

Every thing should be done to give the Spaniards that perfect confidence in us which the honourable part we have taken in their affairs deserves: and the manner of doing it should afford as little argument as possible for the advocates of the enemy. They are present every where, and in the Spanish Navy more numerous than in any other department. I think Mr. Frere should know, or demand, from the Supreme Junta, what is their ultimate plan in the event of complete subjugation. Do they mean to embark in their fleet, and go to America, taking all the loyal Spaniards and their property to a new establishment? or do they mean, when resistance is no longer possible, to make the best terms they can? In the first case, the town of Cadiz would be the rendezvous of all who fled from the tyranny of the usurper. Cadiz should be made impregnable, and the ships placed so as to defend and be defended by it. Whatever will inspire them with perfect confidence in us should be done. It is their cause, in which we have no interest but their success. If, on the contrary, they have not determined to seek an asylum in America, but, in the case of Spain lost (which God forbid), prepare to make those evils as little ruinous to them as they can, and save from the wreck their unhappy lives, to swell the triumph of the tyrant, and be the reproach of the world, they will keep their fleet out of reach in the Carracas, in order to appease the violence to which they will have to submit. The officers of the Navy will, I believe, join most cordially in the latter scheme.

By what they do at present we may understand what is their intention for the future. If they adopt the plan of securing the fleet, by bringing them down to the town, it may be concluded that they intend to preserve them from the enemy, for their own use in defence or for emigration. If they pertinaciously keep them at the Car-racas or Puntal, it can only be with a view of making better terms for themselves.

This view of their conduct should direct us in ours. If they bring their ships to the Bay, we should do all for them we can, if they keep them up the Puntal, it is not for Spanish purposes, and we should do as little for them as can be, without betraying suspicion. We may find that, at last, all our cares and expenseall your zeal and anxiety, have been to fit a fleet to fall into the hands of the enemy.

I am very desirous that the Junta should give orders for the ships at Carthagena to be removed from thence. To Algeziras is best, but Cadiz better than Carthagena; and that you send two ships to assist this work. Captain Donnelly is an active, able officer; but, above all things, what is required in our intercourse with the Spaniards is temper and forbearance. As our eiforts are purely to assist them in maintaining the independence of their Country, they should have no reason to suspect that any other object existed; and if Captain Donnelly be patient, as he is qualified in every other respect, I think he would be a proper officer to go there.

The Junta must send their directions, or nothing will be done. Our officers should manage to make the tenor of those orders known among the sailors, who abhor the French, and they will oblige their officers to act. I hope I shall see the Ville de Paris soon, and such other ships as can be spared from your service. I do not know how much I shall have to do soon. I hope a great deal.

TO LADY COLLINGWOOD.

Ville de Paris, Minorca, April 10, 1809.

It is not long since I wrote to you; since which a continuation of bad weather has brought the Ocean back almost to the state in which she was before her repair. I got near this island for shelter, and the Ville de Paris came to me. My habitation is soon changed. I have been in this ship four or five days, and like her very much; but all ships that sail well and are strong are alike to me; I see little of them, seldom moving from my desk. The Admiralty have been exceedingly kind and attentive to me; they have sent me the best ship in the Navy, and have reinforced my squadron; but what I most want is a new pair of legs and a new pair of eyes. My eyes are very feeble; my legs and feet swell so much every day, that it is pretty clear they will not last long. I am only afraid my Fleet, too, will drop off suddenly, for we have many here who are much worn.

was sent out again, poor thing, with all his infirmities. It makes my heart ache. The object, I suppose, is, that I should make him a Lieutenant, which I never will do, and that he may have an annuity and a livelihood on the naval establishment: but my duty is to seek officers capable of doing the service of the Country, and none others must expect advancement from me.

TO HIS DAUGHTERS.

Ville de Paris, Minorca, April 17, 1809.

I received both your kind letters, and am much obliged for your congratula- ti-ons on my being appointed Major-General of Marines. The King is ever good and gracious to me; and I dare say you both feel that gratitude to His Majesty which is due from us all, for the many instances of his favour which he has bestowed on me, and, through me, on you. Endeavour, my beloved girls, to make yourselves worthy of them, by cultivating your natural understandings with care. Seek knowledge with assiduity, and regard the instruction of Mrs. Moss, when she explains to you what those qualities are which constitute an amiable and honourable woman. God Almighty has impressed on every breast a certain knowledge of right and wrong, which we call conscience. No person ever did a kind, a benevolent, a humane, or charitable action, without feeling a consciousness that it was good: it creates a pleasure in the mind that nothing else can produce; and this pleasure is the greater, from the act which causes it being veiled from the eye of the world. It is the delight such as angels feel when they wipe away the tear from affliction, or warm the heart with joy. On the other hand, no person ever did or said an ill-natured, an unkind, or mischievous thing.

who did not, in the very instant, feel that he had done wrong. This kind of feeling is a natural monitor, and never will deceive if due regard be paid to it; and one good rule, which you should ever bear in mind, and act up to as much as possible, is, never to say any thing which you may afterwards wish unsaid, or do what you may afterwards wish undone.

The education of a lady, and, indeed, of a gentleman too, may be divided into three parts; all of great importance to their happiness, but in different degrees. The first part is the cultivation of the mind, that they may have a knowledge of right and wrong, and acquire a habit of doing acts of virtue and honour. By reading history you will perceive the high estimation in which the memories of good and virtuous people are held; the contempt and disgust which are affixed to the base, whatever may have been their rank in life. The second part of education is to acquire a competent knowledge how to manage your affairs, whatever they may happen to be; to know how to direct the economy of your house; and to keep exact accounts of every thing which concerns you. Whoever cannot do this must be dependent on somebody else, and those who are dependent on another cannot be perfectly at their ease. I hope you are both very skilful in arithmetic, which, independently of its great use to every body in every condition of life, is one of the most curious and entertaining sciences that can be conceived. The characters which are used, the 1, 2, 3, are of Arabic origin; and that by the help of these, by adding them, by subtracting or dividing them, we should come at last to results so far beyond the comprehension of the human mind without them, is so wonderful, that I am persuaded that if they were of no real use, they would be exercised for mere entertainment; and it would be a fashion for accomplished people, instead of cakes and cards at their routs, to take coffee and a difficult question in the rule of three, or extracting the square root. The third part is, perhaps, not less in value than the others. It is how to practise those manners and that address which will recommend you to the respect of strangers. Boldness and forwardness are exceedingly disgusting, and such people are generally more disliked the more they are known; but, at the same time, shyness and bashful- ness, and the shrinking from conversation with those with whom you ought to associate, are repulsive and unbecoming.

There are many hours in every person's life which are not spent in any thing important; but it is necessary that they should not be passed idly. Those little accomplishments, as music and dancing, are intended to fill up the hours of leisure, which would otherwise be heavy on you. Nothing wearies me more than to see a young lady at home, sitting with her arms across, or twirling her thumbs, for want of something to do. Poor thing! I always pity her, for I am sure her head is empty, and that she has not the sense even to devise the means of pleasing herself. By a strict regard to Mrs. Moss's instruction you will be perfected in all I recommend to you, and then how dearly shall I love you! May God bless you both, my dearest children.

TO THE EARL OF MULGRAVE.

Ville de Paris, Minorca, April 21, 1809.

The transports having the French prisoners on board are arrived off the port from Cadiz, which has caused the greatest consternation among the inhabitants, who

VOL. IL z consider their introduction as the prelude to their subjugation. They have no means of securing them; the only place they could confine them in being the Lazaretto, and that is already occupied by the sick from Tarragona. They have not a soldier on the island, and the only guard is about 80 of the Majorca militia, mere peasants.

The Governor has received about 400, whom he has put on the Hospital Island, and I propose leaving the Grasshopper to guard them, until the Spanish Government finds some place of safety to put them in.

It was certainly inconsiderate in the Junta at Seville to send them to those islands where they knew there were no troops; but the eastern provinces do not profit by their regard. Catalonia and Valencia are exceedingly destitute of every necessary for war; the troops are without clothes, with little pay, and the Generals complain of want of money or means to better their condition. I have written to the Junta of Majorca and to the Captain-General Cuesta, to afford relief and security to this island; but it has much the appearance of a determination to turn the islands over to the French, for the prisoners seem to be of every rank and class necessary to form an army. There are two Generals among them, and about 500 officers of every description.

I have just received a letter from Captain Mundy, who is off Barcelona: he informs me, that on the first of this month the army of General St. Cyr, consisting of 8000 men, mostly Italians, left Barcelona, and took the route to Granolles, leaving about 3000 in Barcelona; so that the whole French army in that part of Catalonia does not appear to have exceeded 12 or 14,000, while the Spaniards have always been stated at between 20 and 30,000, yet were constantly retiring before the French. I mention this to your Lordship as a proof how much the Spaniards want direction. The multitudes of men which appear in their accounts do not make a force.

As soon as the wind will admit of the squadron getting out of this port, I shall proceed off Toulon, where the weather still continues very boisterous. It has been an unusual season. The Sultan returned from thence yesterday, having suffered much from the severity of the winds, which are still like January.

HIS EXCELLENCY ROBERT ADAIR, ESQ.

Ville de Paris, Mahon, April 2b, 1809.

The steps which your Excellency has taken to promote the establishment of peace between the Sublime Porte and Russia were certainly an indication of the desire which the British Government entertained to diminish the misfortunes of war, and, as far as circumstances allowed, tended to introduce a correspondence of which the tone was friendly, and from which might have arisen the most beneficial results. The Russian Government seems to have considered otherwise, and rather angrily resented it, as the interference of their enemy with a negotiation in which they were engaged; and the demand which they made of the Porte, that your Excellency should depart from the Capital, was rather an intemperate expression of that resentment. I think they did not expect it to be regarded, and perhaps did not wish it; for I suspect that the connexion of Russia with France is on the wane. I think this probable, because it was not founded on the mutual interests of the respective Countries, but on the display of power, which could effect much mischief on the one hand, and of fear and the apprehension of that mischief on the other. Connexions so formed never can endure longer than the cause exists; and it is to be hoped, that in the change which has taken place in the States of Europe, the cause of Russia's fears has already diminished, and will soon totally expire; when she will naturally fall again into the arms of her ancient friends, and the Emperor pursue the obvious interests of his Country, if he be not prevented by new causes of fear, prepared for him on our part. In that case, he will only have the choice between two evils, instead of abandoning an oppressive ill, to adopt a supreme good. The sending a Minister to treat with the Porte, without the concurrence of the French Government, the part the Emperor is said to have taken in the affairs of the King of Prussia, in defiance of France, and the whole conduct that is attributed to him, tend to encourage the expectation that the connexion, for I would not call it friendship, will last no longer than the necessity of his affairs required.

With this view of the present circum- stances of Russia, I should, with great submission to your judgment and experience in this subject, and diffidence of my opinion, upon it, be led to doubt the expediency of any measure which might irritate and gall Russia at this moment; and leaving the path of reconciliation and peace open to her, I would lay no obstacle in her way to approach us.

I cannot form the smallest idea of the utility that could be derived from the occupation of Cerigo, or any of the little islands in the Archipelago. It would require a certain number of troops, who must be fed by provisions brought to them. The few French who are there have been in a starving condition ever since they went, and clamorous to be saved by being withdrawn. The garrison would require a squadron to protect them, and the services of squadron and garrison would be limited to the taking care of each other. There is not a port at Cerigo, and a very indifferent anchorage. It could have no control over what is done in the other islands: the ships must do that service, and they can better attend to it when not embarrassed by a settlement, which, of itself, must be totally helpless.

Ville de Paris, off Toulon, May 4, 1809.

I am writing this letter in a very severe storm, which shakes the ship to her keel, and am just recovering from a very great disappointment. I was at Port Mahon, driven there by the extreme bad weather, which reduced the poor Ocean to almost as bad a state as she was in last winter. This ship came to me, and I changed. The frigates were watching the enemy. When the ships were complete, and we were under sail from the harbour, I received a message from the Spanish Governor, to inform me that a squadron of the enemy's ships had appeared before Barcelona four days before. I was confident I should have them, and steered a course to meet them on their return. The day following we took two French ships, with invalid soldiers brought from Barcelona, and from them we heard that their ships of war had returned to Toulon. We had crossed their route about ten hours after they had passed; and on going to Toulon, the day following, I found they had arrived. I have an artful, deceptions, and timid foe to deal with. They are as secret as the night, and ingenious in devices; yet my perseverance may at last avail me. My constant study is how to counteract them, and I hope that my good fortune will one day be predominant. I would rather die any how than with grief and disappointment.

The Spanish Patriots (as they are called in England) are gone to ruin. In my prospect of Spanish affairs, from the beginning, I have not been mistaken. Their country is without government, their armies without Generals; the only classes who are and have been true to the cause which all talked of, were the priests and the people, they are brave, love their country, and detest the French. They would defend it; but, wanting a government, (for the Junta is nothing) and leaders to organise their force, what can they do? Nothing but a popular insurrection, general through the country, can give them a chance, and that I fear would be small. The people of property are generally wanting in integrity; and when we consider how little of public virtue is to be found any where, why should we expect it in Spain? From Sicily, and indeed from every quarter, I have demands for assistance; and were I to comply with them, I should divide my squadron till none of its parts would be equal to the contest when it arrives. We should have ships every where, but a force no where.

TO THE EARL OF MULGRAVE.

Ville de Paris, of Minorca, May 5, 1809.

The success of the French in getting a supply of provisions into Barcelona, and the escape of their squadron afterwards, have given me very great concern: but the catching them in those short expeditions must ever be a thing of chance, as they will always take opportunities most favourable to them, and which it is not possible to prevent from occurring. They eluded the watch of two very vigilant ships, the Unite and Cambrian; and the first intelligence I had of them was from Tarragona, and in so short a time after their appearance off Barcelona, that I had the greatest expectation of meeting them on their return; but they were fortunate in winds, and got in before we arrived on the route they took.

I enclose to your Lordship the proposals and demands of Ali Pacha of Albania. I have, on a former occasion, stated to your Lordship what I had been able to collect of the character of that Vizier. Before he got the cannon, c. which were necessary for the attack of Parga, nothing else was represented to be wanting, his army was numerous, his power great; he waited only for our concluding peace with the Porte, to declare his alliance with England; and for the arrival of the cannon from Malta, to begin his operations against the French. The peace is concluded, and he has got his cannon, and now he reveals overtures which have been made to him by the French, which he doubtless means should be considered as the cause why he suspends hostilities against them. But he makes amends for that, by proposing to extend the scale of the war. This will require an increase of aid in money, cannon, and stores; and he has now the advantage of a British Agent at his Capital, which greatly facilitates the transmission of his requests. Your Lordship, who can better judge of Ali Pacha's political character and importance, and the dependence that may be placed in his integrity to us, will estimate these observations truly.

The affairs of the Spaniards in this quarter are such as can only excite grief and sorrow. There does not appear to be any government in the country that extends to Catalonia, and the people complain of the little assistance which they receive from the Supreme Junta. The Generals who have commanded their army in Catalonia at different periods, seem to have been selected so as to ensure the failure of the cause. Vives was a dependent of the Prince of the Peace; Reding, who succeeded him, was brave and active; but his talents, I am told, were limited. He could not direct combined operations, and was totally ignorant of what was not in his view. He wore himself with fatigue, and died lately of a fever. The command has devolved on General Coupigny, who is old and infirm, and with a mind partaking of the inactivity of his body. The French are at present at Vich, plundering that town; and the Spaniards, at or near Tarragona, lamenting it. The Samotines are the only people who give constant opposition to the enemy; but they are few in number, and irregular in their attacks. The vigour of the people, and their attachment to the cause, are perhaps undiminished; but every attempt to organise them fails, probably because it is undertaken by those who are incompetent to the task. The priests and their dependents, at Mont-serrat, have repulsed every attack of the enemy. It is their property they fight for; but most of the people of Spain are endeavouring to save theirs by not fighting. Such, my Lord, is represented to me to be the state of the eastern provinces, and truly sorry I am that I cannot give a more favourable account of them. '

TO LORD AMHERST.

Ville de Paris, of Toulon, May 25, 1809.

I have received the honour of your Lordship's letter by the Porcupine, and congratulate you on your arrival at Palermo, at a period which appears to me particularly important, as the Austrians have taken the field, the war against France has commenced, and the fate of Sicily and of Europe depends on the success of their arms. The great object, then, of all who hope for emancipation from the French power, will be to give every aid, and make such diversion with their forces, as will favour the enterprises of the Austrian armies.

I have sent a powerful squadron into the Adriatic, to act in co-operation with them, to prevent the army of Dalmatia from passing into Italy by sea, and to protect the transport of our allies to points where their force is most wanted. A division of that squadron is acting in aid of the Pacha of Albania, if he has undertaken, or will proceed in, any attack against the French possessions. Two ships of war are upon the coast of the Papal territory, where, on the supposition that the small garrisons which the French had upon that coast will be withdrawn to join the army, the Commanders are ordered to land, alarm the country, and destroy the cannon which defend the coast. This I meant to draw the attention of the enemy to points distant from where I supposed the British forces from Sicily would make a descent. Two other ships are on the Tuscan coast for the same purpose, and, by opening a communication with the inhabitants, to endeavour to discover their disposition, and what part they will take, if the success of the Austrians open to them an opportunity of expelling the French. I do not expect that they will take any measures, however well disposed they may be, until an army shall enter their country. What the dispositions of the Neapolitans are, is yet to be proved by experience: your Lordship will obtain much information of them at Palermo. The Queen has always maintained a sort of correspondence with a party there. Of their integrity, or importance in the state, I am uninformed; but nothing has come to my knowledge that gives me any confidence in them.

On the Spanish affairs in this quarter I can make no favourable communication to your Lordship. The most destructive languor seems to prevail amongst them. They have no leader to conduct the war; and General St. Cyr is marching over the country, with a small body of troops, laying it under contribution, and plundering it without opposition. There are not more than 3000 men at Barcelona and the fortresses. Twice have plans been concerted with our Commanders on the coast for seizing the garrison of the town and citadel by night; the ships went in, performed their part by making the attack upon the batteries, but no Spaniard moved. They are loud in their complaints of the neglect of the Supreme Junta in not giving tliem support, and sending them supplies of arms: at the same time, I am informed that arms, which were sent to them from England, are sold at Tarragona. Several, which had heen bought there, were lately found in a vessel at Gibraltar. The destruction of the enemy's fleet at Rochefort will enable them soon to send a great number of seamen to their fleet in Toulon, of whom they are at present much in want.

TO F. PETRUCCI, ESQ.

Ville de Paris, of Tonlon, Mai 26, 1809.

I have only at this time received your letter of the 30th of September last, enclosing to me those which were addressed to Lord Hawkesbury from the Pacha of Egypt and Mahomed Elfi Bey, with the proposals and alliances which those Chieftains offer to the consideration of His Majesty's Ministers; and your opinion of the great advantage which would result to England from the acceptance of them.

Having transmitted those papers to Government, I shall forbear to make any comment on the subject of them, further than this, that it has ever been his Ma- jesty's most anxious desire to maintain peace and friendship with all nations; and that from the time of the rupture of the long-existing harmony between England and the Sublime Porte, he has sought to restore the former good understanding and the relations of friendship by all honourable means. As the proposals contained in the letters of the Pacha and of Elfi Bey, although diametrically contrary in their tenor, both have for their object the establishment of a power which shall be independent of the Sublime Porte, now our friend and ally, I can say nothing more on this subject than that I am confident that the good faith and integrity of the British Government will never be swayed by supposed motives of interest; and that when Sovereigns seek and obtain the friendship of His Majesty, every subject of their States is included within the contract and duties of peace. I must, therefore, desire that you will not speak in the name of England one language to His Highness the Pacha, and another and different one to Mahomed Elfi Bey.

SCIAHxn BEY, EMIR ELLOCK, MAHOMED ELFI,

Valorous and bold, faithful to his Friends, and terrible to his Enemies, health and prosperity.

MOST ILLUSTRIOUS PRINCE, I have received the letter which your Excellency sent to me by the means of your trusty friend, Mr. F. Petrucci, together vvith the proposals which you have made to the British Government. From the treaty of peace which His Majesty concluded with the Sublime Porte, your Excellency will perceive that there exists a new state of affairs since your letter was written; and His Majesty having re-established that alliance with the Ottoman Government, which had been suspended for a time by the intrigues of France, can now only consider how best the relations of sincere friendship are to be maintained, and the happiness and interests of the faithful subjects of the Sublime Porte advanced, as they are connected with their due dependence on the Supreme Government.

The Beys of Egypt, and particularly your great predecessor, Elfi Bey, have at

VOL. II. A A all times enjoyed the friendly regard of the British nation, and it was with high satisfaction that it saw them in enjoyment of that dignity and splendour which attach to illustrious characters, and at once strengthen and adorn the Government of which they are members. The only danger to which the integrity of the Sublime Porte and its dependencies were exposed, arose from the ambitious projects of France; and it was to oppose those projects, and the artful intrigues of her agents, that the British council and arms were engaged, even at a period when the French had got such an influence at Constantinople as to suspend the friendly intercourse between our countries. In the present case, your Excellency will not think it necessary that the supplies which you requested should be sent to you, as there does not appear any immediate danger from your greatest enemies, the French, who have now full occupation in the war with Austria.

TO THE EARL OF MULGRAVE.

Ville de Paris, off" Toulon, June 16, 1809.

Your Lordship will be informed by the despatches to the Admiralty, that in the Adriatic the frigates have been very actively employed, and have destroyed a great number of the enemy's vessels. If the Russian ships sail from Trieste, I do not think they can escape from our squadron; but unless that nation takes a part against Austria, the ships will probably remain where they are. Their officers profess to be averse to any co-operation with the French. The Russian Commodore told the Governor of Trieste, that while he received orders from Paris, he did not think his ships sea worthy; but were they to come from Russia, and direct him to join the English, he would be ready the next day.

1 have not heard from Captain Hargood since he arrived in the Adriatic, but am well assured he will make no delay. At Corfu the French are distressed for want of provisions, as five vessels have lately been taken or destroyed, laden with grain, c. for that island. The people there are impatient of the government of the French; but I do not believe that any amelioration of their condition can be obtained for them without a military force, not only to expel the French, but to control the parties among themselves while they are fixing a government. They have an English party, many of whom are at Malta, and promise much; and a French party, which remains in the islands; so that their number and power are less known. All are agreed that their former Government was in improper hands, ill administered, and required much reform; but none are agreed who should succeed to power, on the re-establishment

of the Republic. The French are so few in the smaller islands, that they might expel them, but for the existing parties; and they know that it would be but exchanging an oppressive Government for anarchy and, perhaps, civil commotion. Some of their people at Constantinople have struck the French colours in their ships, and hoisted those of the Republic. I cannot see how their cause is to be advanced by that measure: it is merely an expression of attachment to their former Government, which before was not doubted; but the real interests of their Country are rather embarrassed by it, inasmuch as they quit a situation in which they could have supported them, and probably will subject those who remain to more severe restrictions.

I beg to mention to your Lordship that many of the ships must necessarily return to England soon, being leaky and in ill condition; and having mentioned the ships, I am sorry to add, that the Commanders also suffer from the almost unremitted service at sea. Admiral Thornborough has for some time past been falling into an ill state of health, and I am much afraid must apply to your Lordship for relief The state of Captain Bennett and Captain Inglis alarms me very much. Lord Henry Paulett received material injury from a fall which he had in a gale of wind; he does not complain, but it is obvious that his general health has suffered greatly. I mention these circumstances because I am sure your Lordship vsill regard the condition of those officers as much as is consistent with the public service.

TO LADY COLLINGWOOD.

Ville de Paris, off Toulon, June 17, 1809.

I am writing you a letter, my love, because there is nothing I so much delight in as a little communication with her on whom my heart for ever dwells. How this letter is to go to you, I know not. I never hear from your world, and cannot tell whether any thing from ours ever reaches you; but I take the chance of sending you my blessing. I am pretty well in health, but have fatigue enough; nothing that is pleasurable ever happens to me. I have been lamenting our ill luck in not meeting the French ships the only time, perhaps, that they will shew themselves out of port for the summer; but it was not to be avoided; they never come out but with good assurance of being safe. Now that the French fleet is destroyed at Rochefort, they may surely select some officer to relieve me, for I am sadly worn. Tough as I have been, I cannot last much longer. I have seen all the ships and men out two or three times. Bounce and I seem to be the only personages who stand our ground. Many about me are yielding to the fatigue and confinement of a life which is certainly not natural to man, and which I have only borne thus far from a patient submission to my duty, and a natural desire to execute the duties of my profession as long as I was able, without regard to any personal satisfaction. The only comfort I have is to hear from you.

LIEUT.-GENERAL SIR JOHN STUART.

Ville de Paris, of Toulon, Jam 21, 1809.

I hope the time is now arrived when the operations of the army under your command will be attended with the most decisive benefits to the general cause of Europe. I believe I informed you, in a former letter, that I had sent ships, in small divisions, to annoy the coasts of Italy, and draw the attention of the enemy from the points where the British army were supposed to be intended to act. On the Roman. and Tuscan coasts, where they have landed, they have found the country without troops; and every information stated that most of the regular forces had marched to the north. The kingdom of Naples will naturally engage your first attention; but it is a subject for consideration, whether that State will not be most surely subdued by giving, in the first instance, all possible support and countenance to the operations of the Aus-trians. On their success must depend the ultimate fate of Italy. If they be successful, Italy wdll certainly be restored and secured to its legitimate Sovereigns. If Austria fail, no temporary possession of Naples can be of use, and its only effect would be to increase the misfortunes of those who are loyally attached to their Sovereign. In this view of circumstances, the first consideration appears to be, how we may best ensure the success of Austria, and whether an undertaking nearer the field of the Archduke John's operations would not tend to establish it. The coasts of Tuscany are open; and from Trieste I was informed that the intended movements of the Austrians were to be to Romagna; and application was made to the squadron there for assistance in transporting a body of troops to Rimini and Pesaro. Your Excellency will doubtless have been informed whether that project was executed. If it were, the possession of Florence would loosen Tuscany from its bondage, and the few troops in Leghorn would have no means of supporting themselves. You mention the intention of possessing the island of Ischia. I cannot say that I perceive the advantage which would result from our having any of those islands. They are useful to the Power that possesses Naples, but not to any other. Whatever the movement of the army may be, I shall carefully attend to it, and use my utmost endeavours that no assistance shall be wanting which can be derived from naval co-operation.

TO HIS IMPERIAL HIGHNESS
THE ARCHDUKE JOHN OF AUSTRIA.
Ville de Paris, June 22, 1809.

The letter which your Imperial Highness did me the honour to write on the 20th April, is only at this time come to me. The perfect satisfaction which I have felt at the re-establishment of that friendly correspondence which the British nation has ever desired to maintain with Austria, and on which the most important interests of both nations so much depend, is much increased by the detail of the successes of the Austrian army under your Imperial Highness's command. Your Highness will have been informed of the arrival of a powerful squadron in the Adriatic. When advice was brought to me from Malta, that little doubt remained of Austria engaging in the war against France, to oppose the violation of the rights of nations, and to rescue Europe from the degradation under which she was suffering, I lost no time in sending a squadron of ships of the line, with a number of smaller vessels, and gave to their Commanders instructions to co-operate with the Austrians, protect the coasts of the Empire, and give all the assistance to the operations of His Imperial Majesty's arms that is due to the friend and ally of my Sovereign. Your Imperial Highness may depend upon the vigilance of the officers whom I have sent on that service; and I entreat that you will be pleased to give instructions to the Governor of Trieste and the officers employed near the coast, that they will communicate with Captain Hargood, who commands the English squadron, and point out in what manner he can best assist the Austrian army in its operations.

TO REAR-ADMIRAL SOTHEBY.

Ville de Paris, off Toulon, June 30, 1809.

I was very glad to receive a letter from you, from whom I have not heard for a long time indeed. I hope you continue in good health, and are as happy as an amiable Lady and all the comforts of England can make you. It would be a great pleasure to me to serve your nephew, and to have an opportunity of obliging you; but the truth is, that I have no opportunity to promote any one, from year to year. The chances are as rare as the appearance of comets; and some of the same officers who were with me in the Sovereign, are still here, waiting in hope of promotion. All vacancies, but those made by death, are filled by the Admiralty; and people are loath to die, and manage to live on very comfortably; though I shall myself make a vacancy soon, for I am worn threadbare of constitution.

The French have a good squadron here; thirteen sail of them and seven frigates are quite ready, and appear to be deep in the water. I have from nine to eleven, and one frigate. It is all I can keep up, but it must do, and I shall bless the day when we may try what it can do. We are carrying on our operations in the Adriatic and on the coast of Italy with great eclat. All our frigate Captains are great Generals, and some in the brigs are good Brigadiers. They have taken seven forts, garrisons, or castles, within the two last months; and scaling towers at midnight, and storming redoubts at mid-day, are become familiar occurrences. The enemy cannot stand a galling fire from the launch's carronade, or a sharp fire of grape and musketry from the jolly boat. It is really astonishing; those youths think that nothing is beyond their enterprise, and they seldom fail of success.

The Spartan, Araphion, f and others, have taken and blown up three fortified places. Stewart in the Seahorse, and the Halcyon J brig, took two small islands, in which were fortified forts and towns; Al-ceste II and Cyane, three towers, by escalade, at midnight; and the Scout, not to be behindhand, divided his force, and making a brisk attack with his boats in front, stormed a French work in the rear, and brought seven vessels out of the port. This activity and zeal in those gallant young men keep up my spirits, and make me equal to bear the disagreeables that happen from the contentions of some other ships. I hope that they are over; but the exercise of power

Captain (now Sir Jahleel) Brenton.

f Captain (now Sir William) Hoste.

j Captain H. W. Pearse.

II Captain (now Sir Murray) Maxwell.

Captain (now Sir Thomas) Staines.

H Captain Raitt.

necessary to remedy them is very, very painful to me indeed. In such an extensive Navy as we have, there must be some bad. Those who do all the service give no trouble; those who give the trouble are good for nothing. I am glad to hear Clavell is well again. He is a valuable officer, has skill and temper, and I shall be very happy to serve him in any thing. It is a great mistake for an officer to come here with his wife and family. Who would think of bringing a poor woman from the society of her friends to live, where? at Malta. All his pay would not pay her house-rent. At Palermo, among the Princesses? That, in my opinion, whatever she might think of it, is worse: unless she can paint her face well, and intrigue by moonlight, she will be nobody there. She has no more chance of seeing her husband here than if she were in England, on which she will fret; and a teasing wife is the devil. I have been more than six years from home, and there is my good wife, who makes herself as contented as she can; but she is a sensible woman, and knows that the times require I should be abroad, and that it is proper she should be at home.

The brilliant exploits of the fleet, in the destruction of convoys, telegraphs, and towers, obliged the enemy to keep an army in movable columns in their batteries along the whole line of the French and Italian coasts: and so important did these unremitted attacks appear to Lord Collingwood, that he proposed to keep two or three battalions of marines afloat in ships, to be prepared for that purpose, and to extend this mode of warfare as far as Government would furnish the means. The difficulty of manning the fleet had increased with the length of the war, and was particularly felt on the Mediterranean station, where the fleet had few opportunities of recruiting its numbers from merchant vessels. Lord Collingwood had been ever adverse to impressment, and early after the mutiny at the Nore had been studious to discover some means of avoiding the too frequent recurrence to that system. He had found that Irish boys, from twelve to sixteen years of age, when mingled with the English sailors, acquired rapidly the order, activity, and seaman-like spirit of their comrades; and that in the climate of the Mediterranean they often, in less than two years, became expert topmen; while adults, who had been little habituated to the sea, but torn by impressment from other occupations, were generally ineffective and discontented. He accordingly proposed to the Admiralty to raise yearly five thousand Irish boys, and to send a large proportion of them to his command, where he would have them taught and prepared in ships of the line, before they were sent into smaller vessels. By these means, and by the extension throughout the Navy of that humane and temperate discipline for which he was ever distinguished, and by which he had gained the honourable title of the Sailor's Friend, he was convinced that a large and effective force might be maintained, by which he intended, in the succeeding year, to have made more frequent and formidable attacks upon the shores of France.

TO SIR JOHN STUART.

Ville de Paris, off Toulon, July 15, 1809.

I beg to offer you my congratulations on the success of your enterprise against Ischia. The expedition I have considered as having two objects, in one of which you have perfectly succeeded; in the other, I am afraid that greater difficulties will present themselves. The first was, to make a diversion to favour the Austrians in the north, and prevent those reinforcements being sent to the French army, which had, in fact, departed from Naples. They were recalled, and so much time is gained to the army of our ally. The second object was to try the disposition of the nation towards their Sovereign, and whether inclination or means were to be found in them to expel the usurper of his throne. I am sorry to find the prospect in this is not so flattering as the reports brought to Sicily would have led them to believe. The possession of the islands could only produce good in those two points. Any attempt to maintain them, I should apprehend, is not in your contemplation; because I cannot comprehend their smallest utility, but see many inconveniences and dangers in holding them. From their situation, they must be dependent on whoever possesses Naples. I understand that they do not produce food for the inhabitants, and must consequently be fed from other quarters. To garrison them with a few troops would be submitting them to a danger which is inevitable: to provide more largely for their defence would be to weaken that of Sicily, which is already scarce competent to the service which it may have to meet. To destroy the works, and remove the stores and cannon, is what I would recommend, and to harrass the enemy, by making demonstration and threatening other quarters.

I would propose, that, after returning to Sicily, there should be despatched 1000 men to Cephalonia and Zante, which are said to be ripe for insurrection. From the information which I have, the Islanders are all adverse to the French, and would heartily join in expelling them. In forming an administration for their government afterwards, there would possibly be more difficulty; but an officer of temper and judgment would have great influence in deciding them. Such a measure would exceedingly distract the French in their operations, and probably open the way to the reduction of Corfu. Many and great advantages would result from the liberation of those islands, and from attaching them to us, and to us alone. In the maintaining Procida and Ischia I see nothing but the imminent danger of exposing a part of the army to misfortune.

VOL. II. E B

They can have nothing to do with the ultimate fate of the kingdom of Naples, no more than Capri had; Capri was a little evil, and they will be a greater one.

I know that in this case you would have to contend with the politics of the Court of Palermo; but I believe that whenever those politics can decide upon the service of your army, it will meet more difficulties than it can encounter successfully, were it more powerful than it is.

I hope you will pardon me for the freedom of expressing my opinion: but I feel convinced that the fate of the kingdom of Naples does not depend on any conquest which the army can make, unsupported by the general sentiment of the nation, but on the ultimate success of the Austrian arms; and whatever diversion is made to favour them, operates in favour of the emancipation of Naples.

Having made these observations on your situation, I must now inform you what is my own. Ever since the movement of the army from Sicily, there appears to have been a particular degree of activity at Toulon. They have a fleet of twelve sail of the line, seven frigates, and many smaller vessels, lying at the outer part of the harbour, where they never laid before, as if ready for a start. A Vice-Admiral has lately joined their fleet, probably Allemande, from Rochefort, and he may have brought the seamen from thence. There is no destination so likely for them as to succour Murat, and counteract your measures. I do not think they would come out to fight the English squadron, which is ten sail of the line and a frigate; but they are strong enough not to require much caution to avoid it. In weather, when I can keep close off the port, I do not think they will move; but ten days since, we had a gale from the N. W. which drove the fleet almost half way to Minorca; and had they been ready then, they might have sailed, and probably have

On one occasion, during the summer of 1809, the English squadron was reduced to nine sail of the line, while the enemy had fourteen completely manned by the arrival of their seamen from Rochefort, where many of their ships had been disabled or destroyed. One day the enemy got under weigh, and prepared to come out; but on the immediate approach of the English squadron before the port, they again anchored, and the next morning Lord Collingwood was joined by another ship. In consequence of this affair, the two French Admirals quarrelled, and one was superseded.

been near Naples before I could have known that they were out of port. This may happen again, and most likely will. It is a circumstance over which we can have no control; but it is for consideration, whether the ships and transports are so secured at their anchorage at Ischia as not to be endangered by such a fleet, if enabled to make a sudden attack.

But there are other objects for the enemy, not of less consideration. Why, in such a case, may they not go to Palermo? and if they did, what is there to resist them? I am afraid from the people of Sicily they would meet little opposition. They have near 5000 men, of Dupont's army, in the island of Cabrera, whom the Spaniards would not trust in Majorca. These men want only arms to be an army; and while a part of their fleet may be leading me a chase, a detachment might embark them, and transport them to Palermo for a garrison.

Wherever Sir Arthur Wellesley has been engaged with the French he has been successful: of other operations in Spain I know little. In Catalonia the French are doing what they please, without opposition, except from about 180 Samotines.

I believe I informed you of the success of General Blake at Alcaniz, where he would have obtained a complete victory if his cavalry had not deserted him. He afterwards advanced to the neighbourhood of Saragossa, with an army of between 20 and 30,000, who, on being attacked by the French, deserted him, both horse and foot. An Officer from Valencia informed me that the General was on his return to Tarragona, to endeavour to collect them again; but if he finds them they will probably be without arms.

TO REAR-ADMIRAL MARTIN.

Ville de Paris, off Toulon, July 15, 1809.

1 have to acknowledge the receipt of your letters on the surrender of the islands of Ischia and Procida, and beg to express to you the great satisfaction I have derived from the success of the enterprise which you are engaged in. By the letter I have received from Sir John Stuart, he appears to have found nothing in tlie conduct of the superior orders of the Neapolitans which indicates any disposition to take an active part in the restoration of King Ferdinand; but the fair opportunity to shew their attachment has not presented itself. No power has yet appeared which can give them permanent protection, nor is such a power likely to be found but in the success of the Austrian arms. A temporary possession of any place cannot be productive of good. I have explained to the General what are my sentiments on this subject, and sincerely hope that he will not think of making any establishment on those islands. With all the feeding and nurturing that Sicily can give them, they will not be preserved from falling, whenever the enemy shall please: but they have an interest in our holding them, as they divide the force of our army, and will always require the assistance of ships, which in winter cannot protect them. I should suppose that threatening descent at different places, harassing their troops, and making it necessary to retain them in Italy, is as much as could be done; but I have proposed to the General a measure of real operation, which, if he sees it in the same view that I do, I think he will undertake.

It is to make a detachment of 1000 men, to take possession of Cephalonia and Zante, which, from the accounts I have received of the state of those islands, I think is very practicable. The advantages to us in restoring the Republic in those islands would be great, diminish the value of Corfu to the French, and probably lead the way to its being rescued from them. I beg you will consult with the General pjnvately on this subject, for if it were known at Messina it will pass to Calabria, and a resistance be prepared in the islands, which will defeat the undertaking.

If the General should make a detachment, I have suggested that a public order should be given to the Commander of it to proceed to Syracuse, and that the orders directing the particular service should not be opened until they shall be at sea. The Naval Commander should be directed to steer towards Syracuse, and being so far from land as not to be discerned from the shore, open his orders; after which, never to come in sight of the coast of Calabria, but proceed to Cephalonia first (not Zante), where he will find the ships stationed off Paxos, and receive pilots from them.

I beg you will take every means of keeping up the correspondence with me. Malta absorbs all the sloops; I cannot get them from thence, and am considering of some means to correct what will be ruinous to the naval affairs if it not be corrected. Having given you my opinion of establishing a garrison at Ischia, c. and how I think a detachment of the army could be advantageously employed, I come to that which, although put last in order, is first in importance, the state of the enemy's fleet here. They lie at the outer part of the harbour, ready for an opportunity to sail. The first service they may have in view, I suppose, may be Naples, suddenly to come upon the islands where you are, and attack you with such a force as you cannot resist. The other is to go to Palermo, where there is nothing to resist them, and where they would probably be hailed by the majority of the people.

You may depend upon it that I shall keep the best look-out I can on them; but the course of natural events will, notwithstanding, give them opportunities which I cannot control. Are the islands of any use? I cannot comprehend it. The risk of being surprised on them is total ruin. When I wrote to the General this morning, I mentioned the probability of their using the prisoner troops upon Cabrera, since which the Apollo has joined me with information that the French were about to send arms and ammunition to those people. There is a Spanish frigate watching them, but the ships that can receive those 5000 men will not be prevented by a frigate. In service, such as our army is now employed on, it will not do to be long in a position; while their operations are quick, and their movements sudden, they will be successful. Your account of the good services of the Cyane, and the gallant conduct of the Commander, gave me great pleasure, which was damped by my sorrow for the misfortune which befell Captain Staines. He has, on every occasion, distinguished himself as an officer of consummate skill, and of a daring, which shewed that His Majesty's service was the object nearest his heart. It is to be lamented that he must necessarily be withdrawn from it for some time, as he will probably recover better in a cooler climate; and as his ship wants repair, which will sooner be done in England than here, I enclose an order for her to return thither.

Ville de Paris, off Toulon, July 17, 1809.

I do not know that it was ever the intention of the General to make an establishment on the islands of Ischia and Procida; but I have no doubt that it is what the Court of Sicily looked to. It was proposed to Sir John Stuart, at Palermo, that Prince Leopold should embark, and serve as a Volunteer in the British army, an honour which the General declined; and the Prince went with the Sicilian army. On the surrender of the islands, the Prince produced his commission from the King his father, appointing His Royal Highness Viceroy of them, and any other parts of the King's dominions which might be wrested from the enemy. The Prince is attended by a person who was formerly Minister of Police at Naples, and some others, who are said to be equally obnoxious to the people, and of whom they are much more afraid than they are of the French. In the military department is Lieutenant-General Bouchard, who is said to be respectable as an officer, and in every view. He is the nominal Commander of the Sicilian forces; but the Marquess St. Clair is the chief Counsellor of the Prince, and your Lordship knows that his influence pervades all departments.

As there is no hope of advantage from the insurrection of the people of Naples, there are good reasons why the troops should not be long from Sicily. Admiral Martin tells me that it is impossible to describe the unsettled state of people's minds in Sicily on the British troops embarking, as if it seemed to be an event from which something was to be derived. At Messina it was near breaking out before their departure. Several persons, it seems, had been imprisoned on suspicion of disaffection, and a Judge had been commissioned to try and execute them. It happened that one of them died in prison, and suspicion went abroad that he had been put privately to death or tortured. Every thing bore the appearance of immediate revolt against the Government; but they were at last appeased by Sir John Stuart ordering the body to be examined by surgeons; and their report was, that no marks of violence appeared upon it.

Ville de Paris, of Toulon, July 17, 1809.

It gave me great pleasure to find you were enjoying good health, and every happiness that the society of your amiable daughters can give. It is a great blessing; but I am afraid one of those which I have little chance of enjoying. I am pretty well pleased and thankful when I am not in pain, which, between the headach by day, and cramps by night, is not often the case. This mortal body of ours is but a crazy sort of machine at the best of times; and when old, it is always wanting repair: but I must keep it going as long as I can. From England they tell me of my being relieved at the end of the war. I wish to heaven that the day were come.

TO SIR JOHN STUART.

Ville de Paris, off Toulon, September 1, 1809.

I have received a letter from Admiral Martin by the Topaze, in which, after informing me of his arrival at Palermo, and of the armistice which had been agreed to by the Commanders of the Austrian and French armies, he mentions his having received a letter from your Excellency, in which you seem to intimate an opinion that those events offer a reason for deferring the expedition to Cephalonia and Zante, which I had proposed to you, and that he thought you would wait in this new state of affairs until you heard my sentiments further on the subject. I cannot say that I can perceive any thing in the events that are passing in the armies which can at all interrupt the project against the French in the islands. I always considered it as an experiment to try the power of the inhabitants to maintain an independent state, and of their disposition to exert it, both of which they are represented to possess. By the acquisitions which the French are likely to make in the Adriatic, the importance of holding a port, or of establishing an independent power at the entrance of it, is very much increased. They have stated that they have means and men for their defence, if they were once liberated: whether they have or not, will never be distinctly known until they are in a situation to use them; and in any event, the appearance of a force there will occupy the French troops. They will probably think it necessary to reinforce Corfu, which will expose them to risk of capture: and whatever their intentions may be in future with respect to the Morea, their difficulties, by our having a friendly intercourse in those islands, would be increased.

I would propose to your Excellency to extend the plan of operation for that detachment; and whether they succeeded at the first places or not, to go on to the island of Cerigo, where a few Frenchmen (I am told not exceeding forty or fifty), with some Russians, who have never been withdrawn since the island was given up, make a sort of garrison, which gives protection to the privateers. The island itself is a miserable, unproductive place, and any people left there must depend on supplies being sent to them for support. It will be for the officers who are there to determine whether any advantage could be derived from keeping it, or whether it would not be advisable to destroy all its defences, bring off the cannon, and leave its inhabitants to possess only what can be useful to them in peace.

Ville de Paris, off Minorca, October 2, 1809.

I learn that the French are about to sail from port; but what their destination is, must remain unknown until they proceed. The current reports which have come to me have stated Barcelona only to be their object; but their equipment seems to be more studiously finished than would be necessary for so short a voyage. If the war with Austria ceases, I have no doubt that the possession of the Morea is in the contemplation of Buonaparte. A great body of troops may not be necessary for the purpose; for the probability is, that he has already settled, by his emissaries and his intrigues, the condition of its being submitted to him. I have written to Sir A. Ball to have pilots for the Morea ready for the fleet, and particularly for the Gulf of Le-panto. Whatever direction the enemy may take, I will leave nothing in my power undone for the service of our Country. The uncertainty as to that direction induced me to send orders to Captain Hargood to leave the Adriatic with the ships of the line. Several reasons led to this resolve.

The advanced season makes it improper to leave the large ships in that sea, where they will not have a port. If the enemy here should make an escape, and go to that quarter, our squadron might be put in a very critical situation; but the reason which weighs strongest wdth me is, that (except a few troops joining Captain Brenton in his gallant and spirited attack of Lusin Piccolo) the Austrians have undertaken nothing on the coast in which the fleet could render them any assistance, nor are likely to do it. All the acts of General l'Espine shew that he had no plan. Every thing seemed practicable when it was distant, nothing when he approached it; so that the summer has passed in marching from Trieste to Fiume, from Fiume to Zara, and from Zara to Trieste again. If he had an anxiety about any thing, it was that the Russians should not be attacked. Captain Hargood is an active and a zealous officer; and, I believe, if he had found the Russian ships in a situation where they were assailable, he would not have been influenced by any opinion of the Austrian General.

The Sicilian Government is exceedingly tenacious of every rock that was pertaining to the kingdom of Naples. There can be no other reason for their keeping possession of the little Island of Penza. It produces nothing, and its inhabitants are dependent on Sicily for food; yet a garrison is kept there, which might be usefully employed in Sicily; and to protect that garrison all the marine force which they have is stationed.

TO MRS. HALL.

Ville de Paris, October 7, 1809.

I had great pleasure in the receipt of your very kind letter a few days since, and give you joy, my dear Maria, on the increase of your family. You have now three boys, and I hope they will live to make you very happy when you are an old woman. I am truly sensible of the kind regard which you have shewn to me in giving my name to your infant: he will bring me to your remembrance often; and then you will think of a friend who loves you and all your family very much. With a kind and affectionate husband and three children, all boys, you are happy, and I hope will ever be so. But three boys, let me tell you, the chance is

The daughter of his uncle and early friend, Admiral Brathvvaite.

VOL. II. C C very much against you, unless you are for ever on your guard. The temper and disposition of most people are formed before they are seven years old; and the common cause of bad ones is the too great indulgence and mistaken fondness which the affection of a parent finds it difficult to veil, though the happiness of the child depends upon it. Your measures must be systematic: whenever they do wrong never omit to reprove them firmly, but with gentleness. Always speak to them in a style and language rather superior to their years. Proper words are as easily learned as improper ones. And when they do well when they deserve commendation, bestow it lavishly. Let the feelings of your heart flow from your eyes and tongue; and they will never forget the effect which their good behaviour has upon their mother, and this at an earlier time of life than is generally thought. I am very much interested in their prosperity, and that they may become good and virtuous men.

I am glad that you think my daughters are well-behaved girls. I took much pains with them the little time I was at home. I endeavoured to give them a contempt for the nonsense and frivolity of fashion, and to establish in its stead a conduct founded on reason. They could admire thunder and lightning as any other of God's stupendous works, and walk through a churchyard at midnight without apprehension of meeting any thing worse than themselves. I brought them up not to make griefs of trifles, nor suffer any but what were inevitable.

I am an unhappy creature, old and worn out. I wish to come to England, but some objection is ever made to it.

TO CAPTAIN CLAVELL.

Ville de Paris, October 20, 1809.

I am very sorry that you have so little prospect of getting employed at sea; because I am sure that there is no officer who takes the service more to heart, or would do it more justice than you would. I have so little influence at the Admiralty, that I have no reason to suppose any thing which I could say would avail you. Lord Mulgrave knows my opinion of you, and the confidence I have in you; but the truth is, that he is so pressed by persons having parliamentary influence, that he cannot find himself at liberty to select those whose nautical skill and gallantry would otherwise present them as proper men for the service. A hole or two in the skin will not weigh against a vote in Parliament, and my influence is very light at present. But the French fleet is ready for sea; and if God should bless me with a happy meeting with them, I shall hope that I may afterwards venture to ask a favour, and there is not one for whom I would rather ask it than for you. In the meantime, occupy yourself in all sorts of naval studies. Whenever you come forward to service, come with more knowledge than when you left it. It was a misfortune that your health obliged you to go to England; but that was a circumstance not to be avoided. Officers who take the service to heart, as you have always done, will be borne down by the weight of it when it is arduous; and a little relaxation was necessary to you. Except the short time the Ocean was under repair at Malta, I have been at sea ever since you left this country. My health and strength are wearing fast away, and I am become an infirm old man; but I am content to be so, and satisfied that my life could be no where so well spent. I am much obliged to you for inquiring about my daughters. I wish you had seen them; for it gives me much pleasure, indeed, it is the only pleasure I have, to hear of them from every body. It grieves me that Sir Peter Parker is so ill. He is a good man, and has had a parental regard for me. Would that I could rejoice his heart once more with the success of this fleet.

TO LADY COLLINGWOOD.

Ville de Paris, October 30, 1809.

You will have great pleasure in hearing of my success, and particularly of its having been effected without a hair in any body's head being hurt, and almost without a shot being fired. I told the Admiralty what my plan was in September, and it has succeeded to a marvel. I knew, from the intelligence which I had received, that the French were impatient to supply Barcelona with provisions, and that while I was off Toulon, they would not attempt it until the squadron was blown off; and, in that case, I should not be able to prevent them. After one of those strong gales, I retired to Minorca, sent several of my ships into the harbour, where they just remained long enough to seem settled and for the intelligence to go to Toulon that we were there, when I called them out and proceeded to Cape Sebastian, to which place the frigates, stationed at Toulon, were to bring me intelligence. On Sunday night, the 22d, one of them came with the signal that the enemy was approaching. Every soul was in raptures; I expected their whole fleet, and that we should have had a dashing business. The next morning, between eight and nine o'clock, they came in sight; but they were few, only one Rear-Admiral, with three sail of the line, two frigates, some other armed things, and a convoy of about twenty vessels. As soon as they discovered us, they made off. Night came on, and I thought that we had lost them; but as the fleet separated in different parties, by good luck, Admiral Martin's division fell in with them, near their own shore, in the Gulf of Lyons, where he chased them on shore on the 25th; and on the 26th, the French Admiral set fire to his own ship, the Robuste of 80 guns, and the Lion of 74. The Boree of 74 guns, and one of the frigates, run on shore at Cette. It blew almost a gale of wind, and our own ships were in a very dangerous situation. The first day of the chase the Pomona burnt five vessels of the convoy, and one has since been taken; the rest are in a port near to which I have sent a good squadron to endeavour to destroy them or bring them off; and if they are to be come at, I know that it will be done. So much for ships: next for our land operations. As soon as it was found that the army could do nothing at Naples, I sent to the General, requesting that a detachment of the army might join a squadron which I had ordered to reduce the Islands of Zante, Cephalonia, c., and to restore the Ionian Republic. This expedition was undertaken with such secrecy, that none of the people knew in the least where they were going; and at Malta and Sicily I do not believe that there was the smallest suspicion of such a thing being in contemplation until it was all finished. This day I have received the despatches which inform me that Zante, Cephalonia, Ithaca, and Cerigo, are wrested from the French, and the Republican Government established under the protection of England. This business has been accomplished with great skill: the people are delighted at their emancipation, and I trust that they will exert themselves in defence of the liberty which we have restored to them. I hope this last expedition will be approved in England by His Majesty; but I have undertaken it without instructions, and on my own responsibility. The General seemed rather adverse to it, and doubtful whether he could safely spare the troops from Sicily. It is done well done, and I hope that there will never be cause to repent it. Those things, and preserving the peace with Algiers and yet maintaining our right which caused the discussion, will, I hope, be satisfactory to the King. His Majesty will, I am sure, in any event, receive them as proofs of my zealous perseverance in the public service. To you, my dear Sarah, I am sure it will be a gratification that I am usefully employed, and that, although we cannot always command success, I spare no pains to deserve it. I am in great distress just now: Admiral Thornborough has been out of health some time; he is impatient to get home to Bath, and is urging me very much to allow him to go. I do not like to part with so firm a man. He would be a host to me in battle. Sir Alexander Ball, too, I hear is very ill. There is hardly in England another person fit for Governor of Malta. He has all the knowledge and qualities for it, which few men have. These are great drawbacks on me.

TO LORD RADSTOCK.

Viue (k Paris, November 3, 1809.

I am sure, if you knew the kind of life I lead, you would excuse my not writing very often; the truth is, that I have much more to do than comes to the share of any one person. The time that I am eating my miserable dinner seems to be lost to me; and but for the demands of nature, I could ill spare it. Would it were peace. The taking of the Islands of Zante and Cephalonia was well done. They may turn out to be very great acquisitions; but it will depend on the exertions of the people to defend their Country. It is not possible that England can uphold all the broken-down States that have neither virtue nor energy enough to help themselves. I am one of the few who have never changed my opinion of the Spanish affairs. I never thought them otherwise than as they now appear. They have defended the Cities of Saragossa and Gerona well: I believe the women have more to do than the men, and the priests a great deal more than the laity; for whenever they are separated, they have done and do nothing.

Dupont surrendered, nobody knew why. Without the ladies, who used to drive about his camp in coaches, he grew tired of the disagreeable noise of guns, and that raised a name for the Spaniards; but the higher orders never shewed any patriotism, and the ignorant commons could not conduct the affairs of the Country. As they became more removed from the clergy who directed them, they lost their energy, and now I do not think that there is such a thing in Spain.

By the last accounts I heard from Malta, Ball was very ill, almost hopeless. I love him, and am in despair for him. He cannot be replaced in Malta, nor is there a man in England qualified to govern the Maltese but himself They are all too little or too great.

TO THE EARL OF MULGRAVE.

November 3, 1809.

Your Lordship would be prepared by my former letters to hear of the reduction of the Islands of Zante, c. That Island, Cephalonia, Cerigo, and the small Island of Ithaca, were taken by Captain

Sprainger and Brigadier-General Oswald without any loss. The whole affair was conducted by those two officers with ability; and I cannot say too much to your Lordship of the zeal and talent of Captain Brenton: of these he gives proof whenever he is employed; and he seems to be every where. At Lusin he undertook and accomplished a service which would have established a reputation, had he never had other opportunity; and now at Cerigo his conduct has not been less distinguished.

TO J. E. BLACKETT, ESQ.

Ville de Paris, November 24, 1809.

I have been ill and confined ever since I came into port; yet I cannot tell what to say on the subject of my coming on shore. My declining health will make it necessary soon; my weakness unfits me for the arduous situation which I hold.

The accounts I receive of my children are my greatest comfort. God has given them good understandings; and if they have imbibed from Mrs. Moss a proper contempt for vanities, and a taste for useful knowledge, she will have done the duty of a friend for them, and laid a sure foundation for their happiness. Their respectability in life, next to their own suavity of manners to all people, will depend upon a proper selection of their company; such as the flock is, such is the lamb.

The morning of the 1st November we burnt the convoy which had escaped into Rosas Bay. The attack was highly spirited; there were five armed ships and vessels amongst them, moored under the protection of the castle and strong batteries. They were boarded by the boats, carried in a short time, sword in hand, and all on fire. We lost sixteen men, and had between fifty and sixty wounded. The loss of the enemy was great, most of the crews being blown up in their ships, which had powder on board.

The defence which our army made at Talavera was highly honourable to the British name. There could not be a finer exhibition of bravery and skilful conduct: but such victories, under such circumstances, exhaust our strength, and do not advance our cause. I am afraid that of Spain is languishing. I have never thought better of it, because from the beginning I saw and represented the Spaniards as they were and are. The people of England proclaimed them what they wished them to he.

FROM

H. R. H. THE DUKE OF CLARENCE.

MY DEAR LORD, Bushy House, Dec. 9, 1809.

Your Lordship's agreeable letter of November 3, from off Cape Sebastian, has reached me, and I congratulate you sincerely on the event of Admiral Martin having destroyed the ships of the line, and Captain Hallowell having made an end of the convoy. I am only to lament that the enemy did not give your Lordship and the British fleet an opportunity of doing more; and trust, from the bottom of my heart, that the next letter which you will have occasion to write will bring the news of the Toulon squadron being in your Lordship's power.

It is odd that the enemy should have selected the 21st October for sailing; and extraordinary also that the French should build such fine ships, and handle them so ill. I am glad that your Lordship is satisfied with the conduct of our officers and men on this occasion; and am clearly of opinion that the Lieutenants deserve and ought to be promoted. I am for liberal rewards: the gallant Raitt, of course, comes within my ideas of promotion and gratuities. I have ever been and ever shall be of opinion that zeal and bravery ought to be the great and sole causes of promotion. Your former favourite, the Empress Catherine, knew well this secret of state; and your Lordship's observation is quite correct, that her Imperial Majesty carried the same notions even into her private amusements: " None but " the brave," my dear Lord!

I am glad that Sprainger has done his duty in taking four, out of the seven islands, and hope the remainder will soon fall. The enemy must feel very awkward without them, and cannot fail to be interrupted in attempting the Morea.

My best wishes attend your Lordship, publicly and privately; and believe me ever, my dear Lord,

Yours most sincerely,

WILLIAM.

Ville de Paris, Minorca, J an. 1, 1810.

Thus the years roll on; and as the season comes round, I congratulate you, at the same time, on entering a new year of the world and of your life, which, I hope, you will enjoy in health, and pass in happiness and comfort. I have been in port longer than I ever was since leaving England, and have saved my ships very much from a great deal of extreme bad weather. This I have been enabled to do by having luckily reduced the enemy's fleet, as you will have heard, in October, and given them a check which will make them very cautious. I am not without hope that they will make another attempt to victual Barcelona, which is straitened for provisions, and that we may have another meeting with them. It would have been a happy day if they had all come last time. I expected them, and was well prepared for them. In Sicily they are delighted; for as they are always in danger, whatever reduces the enemy's force diminishes their fears. I have a very handsome letter from the Prime Minister, who writes, in the King's name, to congratulate me. The Court there is very-gay at present, the Duke of Orleans being lately married to the Princess Amelia, who appeared to me to be a mild and pleasing woman. The old Duchess, who is a delightful old woman, seems to have forgotten her misfortunes, and they have been great; and is very happy in the choice which her son has made of a wife. I have been very unwell lately. The physician tells me that it is the effect of constant confinement, which is not very comfortable, as there is little chance of its being otherwise. Old age and infirmities are coming on me very fast, and I am weak, and tottering on my legs.

I had a great loss in the death of Sir Alexander Ball. He was an able and industrious man; and I fear Malta will never be so well governed again. We were Midshipmen together, and have always been on terms of the greatest friendship. The islands which we took will very much add to the commerce of Malta. That business was done particularly neatly. In a letter from a French Governor at Cerigo, he informs his Chief, that some Albanians, about 600, had come to that island, and that he was determined to get clear of them l)y some means. In the next letter he tells him that he found himself under the necessity of poisoning the waters, by which many died, and the rest, alarmed, went awaya deed worthy of the Devil.

TO CAPTAIN CLAVELL.

Villede Paris, Fehruan 10, 1810.

I have received your very kind letter of November, and am much obliged to you for the interest you take in our successes here. I should be very glad if you had a good ship to partake in the toils, for indeed it is all toil; we have little respite. Our falling in with that convoy, though it was but a small one, was fortunate. All that was possible was done for its destruction, and as little escaped as could reasonably be expected; but I am sorry to find that the ships which ran into Cette were not a bit hurt. When the weather was fine, they hauled them out of the mud, and they got back to Toulon in the first north-west wind. I dare say that you are very desirous of being employed again. If I had any influence with Lord Mulgrave, there is nobody in whose behalf I would u. e it in preference

VOL. II. I) D to you; and you may believe, that whenever I feel that I have any interest, I will exert it for you. I have been failing in my health very much for more than a year, and it is my constant occupation alone that keeps me alive. Lately I have had a very severe complaint in my stomach, which has almost prevented my eating. It is high time I should return to England, and I hope that I shall be allowed to do so before long. It will, otherwise, be soon too late. I am, my dear Clavell, with very great esteem, your most faithful friend and servant.

TO THE EARL OF MULGRAVE.

Vilk de Paris, February 22, 1810.

It has given me much concern that I have been under the necessity of writing to the Secretary of the Admiralty, stating the ill condition of my health, and requesting their Lordships' permission to return to England; and this, I can assure your Lordship, I have not done until I am past service, being at present totally incapable of applying to the duties of my office. My complaint is of a nature to which I apprehend it is difficult to apply a remedy, for I have hitherto received no benefit from medical advice. Since November it has been daily increasing, so that I am now almost past walking across my cabin; and as it is attributed to my long service in a ship, I have little hope of amendment until I can land.

Your Lordship on a former occasion was so good as to say that you would regard those Officers whom I mentioned as having served long with me. There are three Lieutenants who have served with me on this station more than four years, and are men of character. Lieutenant Joseph Simmonds was an Officer of the Royal Sovereign in the action: all his life has been service. Lieutenant George Brown was an Officer in the Victory at the same time, and is a well-qualified Officer, as is Lieutenant Richard Coote. I beg to present these gentlemen to your Lordship, as Officers whose services under my command have greatly interested me in their advancement.

THE GOVERNOR, CLERGY, JURATS, INHABITANTS OF MAHON.

Villede Paris, March 2, 1810.

I have received the honour of your letter of this day, and am extremely sorry to hear of the commotion which at present exists among the people of Mahon.

His Majesty has engaged to assist the Spanish nation in repelling the aggressions of a rapacious enemy, and in recovering those just and indefeasible rights which the French had attempted to usurp; but the British Government have never intended to interfere in any manner with the internal regulations and police of Spain. To defend this island from any attempt of our common enemy is my duty, and shall be the care of the British fleet; but the liberation or removal of the prisoners who are in your power, are, as I conceive, so exclusively subjects for the decision and direction of His Most Catholic Majesty and the Government of Spain, that I must refrain from further remarks upon them.

I have been obliged to leave the squadron from extreme ill health, and am so reduced, that it is impossible for me to apply to busi- ness. It is with the utmost difficulty that I can dictate this letter.

Lord Collingvvood had been repeatedly urged by his friends to surrender his command, and to seek in England that repose which had become so necessary in his declining health; but his feelings on the subject of discipline were peculiarly strong, and he had ever exacted the most implicit obedience from others. He thought it therefore his duty not to quit the post which had been assigned to him, until he should be duly relieved, and replied, that his life was his Country's, in whatever way it might be required of him. When he moored in the harbour of Port Mahon, on the 25th of February, he was in a state of great suffering and debility; and having been strongly recommended by his medical attendants to try the effect of gentle exercise on horseback, he went immediately on shore, accompanied by his friend Captain Hallowell, who left his ship to attend him in his illness: but it was then too late. He became incapable of bearing the slightest fatigue; and as it was represented to him that his return to England was indispensably necessary for the preservation of his life, he, on the 3d of March, surrendered his command to Rear-Admiral Martin. The two following days were spent in unsuccessful attempts to warp the Ville de Paris out of Port Mahon; but on the 6th the wind came round to the westward, and at sunset the ship succeeded in clearing the harbour, and made sail for England. When Lord Collingwood was informed that he was again at sea, he rallied for a time his exhausted strength, and said to those around him, "Then I may yet " live to meet the French once more." On the morning of the 7th there was a considerable swell, and his friend Captain Thomas, on entering his cabin, observed, that he feared the motion of the vessel disturbed him. " No, Thomas," he replied, "I am " now in a state in which nothing in this " world can disturb me more. I am dying; " and I am sure it must be consolatory to " you, and all who love me, to see how com-" fortably I am coming to my end." He told one of his attendants that he had endeavoured to review, as far as was possible, all the actions of his past life, and that he had the happiness to say that nothing gave him a moment's uneasiness. He spoke at times of his absent family, and of the doubtful contest in which he was about to leave his Country involved, but ever with calmness and)eyfect resignation to the will of God; and in this blessed state of mind, after taking an affectionate farewell of his attendants, he expired without a struggle at six o'clock in the evening of that day, having attained the age of fifty-nine years and six months.

"Those who were about his Lordship's " person," observes Mr. Macanst, the Surgeon of the Ville de Paris, in the report which he made on the occasion, " and who wit-" nessed the composure and resignation with " which he met his fate, will long remem-" ber the scene with wonder and admiration. " In no part of his Lordship's brilliant life " did his character appear with greater lustre " than when he was approaching his end. It " was dignified in the extreme. If it be " on the bed of sickness and at the approach " of death, when ambition, the love of " glory, and the interests of the world, are " over, that the true character is to be " discovered, surely never did any man's " appear to greater advantage than did that " of my Lord Collingwood. For my own " part, I did not believe it possible that any " one, on such an occasion, could have be-" haved so nobly. Cruelly harassed by a

"most afflicting disease, obtaining no relief " from the means employed, and perceiving " his death to be inevitable, he suifered no " sigh of regret to escape, no murmuring " at his past life, no apprehension of the " future. He met death as became him, " with a composure and fortitude which ' have seldom been equalled, and never " surpassed."

After Lord Collingwood's decease, it wa found that, vsith the exception of the stomach, all the other organs of life were peculiarly vigorous and unimpaired; and from this inspection, and the age which the surviving members of his family have attained, there is every reason to conclude that if he had been earlier relieved from his command, he would still have been in the enjoyment of the honours and rewards which would doubtless have awaited him on his return to England. His death was occasioned by a contraction of the pylorus, brought on by confinement on board of ship, and by his continually bending over a desk, while engaged in his Correspondence; of the extent of which, these Volumes can convey but an imperfect idea. So high was the opinion which was generally entertained of his judgment, that he was consulted from all quarters, and on all occasions, on questions of general policy, of regulation, and even of trade. Some of these letters would have been inserted here, to shew with what facility and power he treated matters the most foreign from the habits of his life, if this collection had not already grown far beyond the extent which the Editor had originally contemplated. On the merits of that Correspondence it is unnecessary for him to expatiate. All who have read these pages must have observed the talent with which Lord Collingwood adapted his style to the various habits of the Countries with which he was in communication, the sagacity with which he penetrated into the secret projects of France, and foretold the successive changes of the policy of Russia, his wise forbearance towards neutral States, and the vigour with which he endeavoured, when they had entered into the contest, to inspire into their councils his own activity and resolution. All must have admired the benevolent solicitude with which he sought not only to promote the happiness of his own sailors, but to mitigate to his enemies the horrors of war, and, as far as his influence extended, to call back contending Nations to the blessings of peace, manifest- ing, by another memorable example, how in every noble heart humanity and gentleness are the inseparable companions of true valour. And surely none can contemplate without emotion the picture which is here presented of a most affectionate husband and father, withheld from his family and home by a sense of public duty; yet still endeavouring to conduct the education of his daughters, and (while engaged, as he himself expressed it, in a perpetual contest with the elements, and with dispositions as boisterous and untractable) cultivating in their youthful minds benevolence, gentleness, and every female virtue.

Lord Collingwood was rather above the middle stature, and of a slender but well-proportioned person. He had a full dark eye; and, although in his latter years his fine countenance became faded with toil and care, it was ever strongly expressive of his character, for it was marked with thought-fulness, decision, and benevolence. He had an equanimity of mind, of which those persons were little aware who had only seen him amid the vexations arising from the minor details of his profession. He expected, perhaps, too frequently from others the same skill ajid unwearied attention by which he had himself been uniformly distinguished; and on such occasions betrayed impatience and displeasure, but ever in the guarded expressions that became a gentleman and an officer. On the first appearance, however, of difficulty or danger, he grew calm and composed, to a degree which excited the admiration of all around him. " The Ad-" miral spoke to me," observed Mr. Smith, his servant, " about the middle of the action " of Trafalgar, and again for five minutes " immediately after its close; and on neither " occasion could I observe the slightest " change from his ordinary manner. This, " at the moment, made an impression on me " which will never be effaced; for I won-" dered how a person whose mind was oc-" cupied by such a variety of most important " concerns, could, with the utmost ease and " equanimity, inquire kindly after my wel-" fare, and talk of common matters as if " nothing of any consequence were taking " place."

In his habits of life Lord Collingwood was abstemious, but fond of society, enliven-ing it often with many humorous remarks, and anecdotes derived from his extensive reading. His own table was plentiful and excellent of its kind; but there was about it a plainness and absence of display, which arose in part from the general simplicity of his character, and in part, perhaps, from the compulsory economy of his earlier life t but was by some erroneously attributed to a love of money. How far he was above any consideration of that kind, these Letters will have abundantly testified. Whenever he thought that he discovered the spirit of money-making among the higher Officers of the Navy, he never failed to speak of it with marked contempt, as a practice that degraded a most noble profession into a sordid trade. That in this instance, as in all others, he practised what he recommended, cannot be more satisfactorily proved than by the fact already recorded in this Work, of his having urged the Spanish Junta, at the commencement of their revolution, to despatch orders to the Canary Islands and their other colonies, to prohibit the sailing of their vessels, which, as he was informed, were preparing to run for Spain, and which, as no formal order for the cessation of hostilities had been issued, would have become the lawful prize-of the ships under his command. His acts of charity were frequent and bountiful; and in no instance, as was observed by one who knew him well, did he ever reject the peti- tion of real distress. The same spirit governed him in the final distribution of his property, for he made a most just and generous will, providing liberally for Lady Couingwood and different members of his family, and dividing the remainder between his two daughters: and having thus, as he observed in that instrument, disposed of the stuff which he left behind him, he prayed God to render the possessors of it contented and happy.

He was on every Sunday a regular and serious attendant at divine worship; and when the state of the weather did not permit the assembling of the crew for that purpose, he was used to retire to his cabin and read the service of the day and some devout book. His religion was cahn and rational, and devoid of all pretence. It raised his mind naturally upwards in devotion and gratitude towards God, and manifested itself in benevolence towards men. " I cannot," he once observed, "I cannot, for " the life of me, comprehend the religion " of an Officer who could pray all one day, " and flog his men all the next."

Lord Couingwood left a widow and two daughterssarah, afterwards married to tli Editor of these Volumes; and Mary Patience to Anthony Denny, Esq.

His body was conveyed to England, and deposited in St. Paul's Cathedral, by the side of Lord Nelson. The funeral was attended by his former patron. Sir Peter Parker, by several persons who had filled the highest situations in the Admiralty, and by many eminent members of his own profession. On that occasion. His Royal Highness the Duke of Clarence was pleased to address the following gracious Letter to Lady Colling-wood;

MADAM, Bushy House, Saturday Night.

I this mdrning received a mourning ring in memory of the deceased Lord Colling-wood, which, of course, I owe to your Ladyship's politeness and attention. No one can regret the melancholy event of the death of his Lordship more sincerely than I do; and I feel great concern in having been prevented from attending the funeral. I was informed that the interment was to be quite private, or else I should have made a point of attending the remains of my departed friend to the grave. No one could have had a more sincere regard for the public character and abilities of Lord Collingwood than myself: indeed, with me it is enough to have been the friend of Nelson, to possess my estimation. The Hero of the Nile, who fell at Trafalgar, was a man of a great mind, but self-taught: Lord Collingwood, the old companion in arms of the immortal Nelson, was equally great in judgment and abilities, and had also the advantage of an excellent education.

Pardon me, Madam, for having said so much on this melancholy occasion; but my feelings as a brother Officer, and my admiration of the late Lord Collingwood, have dictated this expression of my sentiments. I will now conclude, and shall place on the same finger the ring which your Ladyship has sent me, with a gold bust of Lord Nelson. Lord Collingwood's must ever be prized by me as coming from his Family: the bust of Lord Nelson I received from an unknown hand on the day the event of his death reached this Country. To me the two rings are invaluable; and the sight of them must ever give me sensations of grief and admi ration.

I remain ever,

Madam,

Your Ladyship's obedient and most humble Servant,

WILLIAM.

Without pursuing farther the comparison between these two distinguished Officers, which His Royal Highness has begun, it may be sufficient here to remark the difference of their end: the one falling gloriously in the moment of victory; the other exhausted with fatigue and care in the pursuit of an enemy, whom, with unexampled perseverance, he had sought in vain. Of both these eminent men, it may with equal truth be said, that their devotion to their Country was unbounded, and that in its service they sacrificed their lives. How Lord Couing-wood followed his illustrious friend in the earlier periods of their service has been already described: they may now be literally said to share the same grave.

A Monument was erected to Lord Col-lingwood, by a Vote of Parliament, in St. Paul's Cathedral. There is also a Cenotaph in his native town of Newcastle, which bears the following inscription.

acrtf to tje icmorn

VICE-ADMIRAL CUTHBERT BARON COLLINGWOOD,

Who was born in this Town, on the 26th September, 1750, OF AN ANCIENT FAMILY.

He served with great bravery in the Action of the 1st of June, 1704; and bore a distinguished part in

THE VICTORY OFF CAPE ST. VINCENT.

GREAT BATTLE OF TRAFALGAR

He led the British Squadrons into Action, and advanced with his single Ship into the midst of the Combined Fleets of France and Spain.

On that day, after the Death of his Illustrious Commander and Friend,

LORD NELSON,

He completed the most glorious and decisive Victory which is recorded in the Naval Annals of the World.

In the Command of the Mediterranean, to which he succeeded, he displayed unri-valled skill as a Seaman, and great talents and address in the conduct of many important Negotiations.

After five Years, during which he never quitted his Ship for a single night, he became anxious to revisit his Native Land; but being informed that his Services could ill be spared in those critical times, he replied, that

HIS LIFE WAS HIS COUNTRY'S, and persevered in the discharge of his arduous Duties, till, exhausted with fatigue, he expired, on board His Majesty's Ship the Ville de Paris, on the 7th 3Iarch, 1810, in the 60th year of his age.

In Private Life he was generous and aflfectionate a pious, just, and exemplary Man.

A Monument was erected to his liemory by Parliament, in the Cathedral Church of St. Paul, where he lies by the side of the Hero to whom he so worthily succeeded in

THE VICTORY OF TRAFALGAR.

His Widow, (daughter of John Erasmus Blackett, Esq. of this Town,) and his two Daughters, had caused this Cenotaph to be erected; and on Lady Couingwood's death, on the 17th September, IJilo, it was inscribed to both their revered and lamented Parents,

BY THEIR GRATEFUL CHILDREN.

VOL. II. E E

On Lord Collingwood's death, his title became extinct; but to his children, (or rather to the survivor of them, for Mrs. Denny was unhappily lost to her infant family, by her death in 1822,) and, as it may be hoped, to their children's children, he has bequeathed an inheritance of which they may be justly proud:, for of him it can with truth be said, that he did ' to his dear descendants leave

The first, best gift that man can claim; Better than pomp, by crowds adored. Or gold immeasurably stored, A PURE AND SPOTLESS NAME."

THE END.

LONDON:

J. MOVES, TOOK'S COURT, CHANf EIIY LANK.

Lightning Source UK Ltd.
Milton Keynes UK
UKOW01f0905100816

280362UK00001B/57/P